# Social Work and Social Perspectives

D0087438

# Social Work and Social Perspectives

Eileen Oak

*Consultant editor*:
**Jo Campling**

First published 2009 by
PALGRAVE MACMILLAN

Palgrave Macmillan in the UK is an imprint of Macmillan Publishers Limited, registered in England, company number 785998, of Houndmills, Basingstoke, Hampshire RG21 6XS.

Palgrave Macmillan in the US is a division of St Martin's Press LLC, 175 Fifth Avenue, New York, NY 10010.

Palgrave Macmillan is the global academic imprint of the above companies and has companies and representatives throughout the world.

Palgrave® and Macmillan® are registered trademarks in the United States, the United Kingdom, Europe and other countries.

ISBN-13: 978–0–230–00464–1
ISBN-10: 0–230–00464–4

This book is printed on paper suitable for recycling and made from fully managed and sustained forest sources. Logging, pulping and manufacturing processes are expected to conform to the environmental regulations of the country of origin.

A catalogue record for this book is available from the British Library.

A catalog record for this book is available from the Library of Congress.

10   9   8   7   6   5   4   3   2   1
18   17   16   15   14   13   12   11   10   09

Printed and bound in China

# Contents

# Introduction: Imagining Social Work, Sociologically

The aim of this book is to demonstrate the fundamental contribution of sociology to social work by examining three central themes. These are reflexivity, praxis (the integration of theory and practice), and critical reflexive practice. The interrelationship between these themes is explored using sociological theories and concepts. It is stressed that, in adopting this approach, the book is not seeking to make any claims for the exclusivity of sociology to inform social work practice but, rather, to identify the ways sociology can make a useful contribution to an understanding of the social work role.

This book seeks to use sociology to inform social work critical reflexive skills in several ways. Firstly, by the *way* it uses Wright-Mills' sociology (1959). Secondly, by the way it adopts sociological perspectives on the media to examine the global constructions of social work. Thirdly, through the way it identifies the practice relevance of sociological research methods. Fourthly, by showing how sociological theories underpin social work methods of assessment, intervention and evaluation. Fifthly, its approach to sociology is practice-orientated and this is reflected in its focus upon the major sociological theories and controversies, accompanied by easy and accessible definitions of sociological terms that enable students to unpack sociological jargon. Moreover, the work includes useful synopses of the main themes. Hopefully, this will promote critical analysis and the integration of theory and practice.

Highlighting the importance of sociology to social work is not new (Bosanquet 1902; Leonard 1966; Younghusband 1967; Jones 1996; Dominelli 1997; Horner 2006), nor is identifying the contribution of major sociological thinkers such as C. Wright-Mills (1959). However, I believe that this book adopts a slightly different approach to sociology as applied to social work practice. This is demonstrated in two ways: in the way it uses Wright-Mills' sociological analysis (1959) and the way it explores sociology's relationship to social work. For example:

- It locates the debate on the relationship between sociology and social work within the current focus on interdisciplinary practice to highlight how this will affect social work practice in the future.

- By the way it incorporates New Social Movement theory (NSM). This will enable students to understand how the Disabilities Rights Movement, Older People's Movement, and the Gay and Lesbian Movement, have sought to address issues of disablism, ageism, and homophobia.

- Through its focus upon the sociology of law that highlights the care control dimensions of social work, the legislative context and its implications for practice.

- The way it adapts C. Wright-Mills' 'sociological imagination' (1959) to highlight critical sociology's contribution to the development of holistic assessment models and to demonstrate how his critique of traditional sociology informs an understanding of the effectiveness of Evidence Based Practice (EBP) approaches in social work.

- Through the inclusion of both Eastern and Western sociological perspectives in the form of Muslim feminist approaches and Islamic Political Economy (IPE) and a focus on Sharia law to present alternative explanations of globalization and the reorganization of global welfare states.

- By the way it focuses on the development of cosmopolitanism and its impact on the global organization of welfare.

## The Structure of the Book

Chapter 1 presents an overview of the book by identifying the major sociological theories and debates and by highlighting their practice relevance. These are discussed in relation to the three main themes of the book, which are reflexivity, praxis and critical reflexive practice. It then demonstrates how they relate to social work. It defines these terms and shows how sociology has contributed to their development in social work practice. The rest of the book is divided into two parts. Part I is entitled 'Contexts of Social Work'. Chapter 2 ('The Changing Welfare Landscape') examines the contemporary global reorganization of welfare states. Chapter 3 ('Poverty, Social Exclusion and Citizenship') explores how these three interrelated issues impact on welfare and civil rights of citizens. Chapter 4 (entitled 'Sociology, the Law and Social Work Practice') reflects critically on issues of power and advocacy in social work within a legal context. In Part II, 'Arenas of Practice', the focus shifts to look at practice issues and the development of critical reflexive practice in three specific forms. Chapter 5 examines 'Work with Service Users', and Chapter 6 ('Valuing Diversity and Difference') explores issues of racism, sexism, sectarianism and homophobia, and how they affect social workers' capacity to challenge discrimination and oppression. The development of engagement skills is explored in Chapter 7 which focuses on sociological research methods and how they underpin the assessment, care planning and evaluation process. The final chapter, Chapter 8 ('Sociology and International Social Work') draws the major themes of the book together and re-examines sociology's contribution to social work by analysing the international social work context.

# What is Social Work?

The International Federation of Social Work (IFSW) defines social work as follows:

> The social work profession promotes social change, problem solving in human relationships and the empowerment and liberation of people to enhance well-being.
>
> Utilising theories of human behaviour and social systems, social work intervenes at the points where people interact with their environments. Principles of human rights and social justice are fundamental to social work.
>
> (IFSW 2000: 3)

Of course, *how* social workers 'intervene' and *how* they promote 'social change' or 'enhance well-being' will depend to a large extent on the socio-political and cultural context in which they practice. For this reason the nature of social work practice varies from one country to another. This does create diversity, and Mundy (1989) has sought to simplify this diversity by examining the commonalities in practice. He has identified that within the European Union, social workers tend to have a further or higher educational qualification and have to be registered to practise with their national professional registering body. In addition, social work is practised within a mixed economy of welfare (where state funded and private and voluntary organizations are involved in the provision of services). Moreover, social services are provided to specific client groups, such as older people, people with physical or learning disabilities, children and their families, people with mental health problems, and juvenile offenders.

There are also variations within these models. For example, in Germany there is a specialism in working with football hooligans (Price and Simpson, 2007) while in Tonga social workers provide services to a range of care groups although they are not accorded professional status. This is not so much due to hierarchical status battles between professions, but rather to the structure of Tongan society in which social responsibility and the value of reciprocity have led to strong informal welfare support networks.

Consequently, social work is seen as part of everyday life that everyone takes some responsibility for (Mafileo 2004). In Australasia, North America, Japan, South Asia, parts of Eastern Europe and South Africa, social work is conducted on similar lines to those in the EU. However, in some parts of Africa, the Middle East, Latin America and Eastern and Central Asia, due to the of lack public expenditure on welfare, social workers are more heavily involved in community development projects. There is also greater collaboration with voluntary and religious organizations and charities, in order to provide services (Dominelli 2005).

The difficulty of defining social work is also due to the fact that it is a source of international controversy regarding its role and function. For instance, Herscovitch (2001) dissents from the idea of an international social work profession, by highlighting social work's limited impact in addressing human need and suffering. She points out that social work has always been involved within those groups who are marginalized in society, such as the poor, older people, those with mental health problems, young offenders or teen mothers. It has had limited influence on social policy and, arguably, adopted a conservative (rather than transformative) role in society by controlling the aspirations and social protests of socially excluded groups.

In contrast, Healy (2001) argues that while there is controversy as to whether social work can be considered a global profession, it does have some global themes. For example, it addresses common social problems such as poverty, social exclusion, child and family problems as well as embodying shared values manifest in the growth of international social work organizations such as the International Federation of Social workers (IFSW) or the International Association of Social Workers (IASSWS), who have developed international codes of ethics and values. Dominelli (2002b) observes, however, that many of these international codes for social work tend to be dominated by Western and ethnocentric notions of equality, freedom and social justice and have to be adapted in Eastern countries to fit in with the more altruistic values of collective responsibility, communal spirit and social solidarity. However, their common elements are a respect for the worth and dignity of human beings, and the need to challenge discrimination and promote human rights. In addition, social work has some international theoretical underpinnings characterized by the disciplines of psychology, sociology, law, human growth and development, and social policy.

The difficulty in defining social work, therefore, is due in part to cultural differences and in part to the fact that it is the product of controversy. The contested nature of social work, the battle over its functions in contemporary society, is in part a reflection of this controversy. In its simplest terms this controversy can be understood as one between those who see social work as having a maintenance role, supporting the individual to make changes in their lives so he or she can become a responsible citizen (Davies

1985; Sibeon 1991; Smith 2004), and those who regard social work as having a political dimension addressing structural inequalities and promoting social change (Dominelli 1997; Jones 2000; Shaw and Gould 2001). Sociology informs an understanding of the contested nature of social work by unpacking these arguments.

# What is Sociology?

When thinking about definitions of sociology, several spring to mind that have social work practice relevance. Giddens (2001) refers to sociology's preoccupation with human interaction from the individual to global level. Cohen and Kennedy (2007) highlight its systematic nature and the way it seeks to locate behaviour in its historical or cultural context, whereas Price and Simpson (2007) relate sociology directly to social work by referring to sociology as 'the study of society' and argue this is why it should underpin any social work training course (p. 3). Hamilton and Thompson (2002) argue that sociology has the potential to raise our critical reflexive capacities by encouraging us to 'de-familiarize' ourselves from everyday routines, life experiences and using insights from sociology and feminism to start to question things we take for granted. Saraga (1998) argues that questioning common sense assumptions, or the 'taken-for granted' stocks of social knowledge, is a crucial element of critical sociology. This is because society is built on a stock of taken-for-granted knowledge (particularly with regard to issues such as poverty or homelessness), which also lays claim to the truth. She asserts that it is not just that these assumptions make society or human interaction understandable, but they do so in specific ways, creating issues of power and powerlessness. For these reason she argues that the sociologist should try to stand back from the taken-for-granted and try to identify which 'common sense knowledge' comes to dominate and why.

Healy (2001) and Cohen and Kennedy (2007) have identified a series of global transformations that both sociologists and social workers need to critically examine and respond to. These are globalization, the persistence of global poverty and social exclusion, increased ethnic conflict and the rise of New Social Movements (NSMs). We will look at these issues in further detail in the chapters that follow.

# Uses of Sociology

Hamilton and Thompson (2002) argue that sociology informs an understanding of a range of contexts. These include government and the public sphere, the organization of production and its impact on society, the rise of new social movements, the complex interrelationship between race and ethnicity, gender and class and the debate as to whether sociology can ever be value-free. For these reasons a number of social work academics have sought to identify the importance of sociology to an understanding of social work practice. Dominelli (1997) believes that sociology can enhance the social justice dimensions of practice by providing conceptual frameworks on issues such as family poverty, social exclusion and domestic violence. In addition, she points out that in order to be effective, social workers must understand the organizational context of social work within the wider social structures and how that relationship affects practice. Sociology provides theoretical frameworks to understand such relationships. Horner (2004) believes that in order to understand the complex nature of practice, social workers require a rigorous grounding and understanding of theory, and that sociology provides such a theoretical base. Moreover, he argues that sociological theory helps locate social work as a socially constructed activity in which certain groups become socially constructed as clients/service users.

Many of these uses of sociology have social work practice relevance. For this reason the book will focus specifically on key sociological themes and perspectives that relate to social work contexts and preoccupations. These include:

- Sociological perspectives on society, which provide explanations of the global organization of welfare states.
- Sociological perspectives on domestic violence and child sexual abuse.
- Sociological theories of dialectics, which provide insights into the relationship between human agency and structural constraints and the contradictions in the care and control dimensions of social work.
- Sociological theories, which examine the interconnections of ethnicity, gender, class and poverty.

Within these broad themes other sociological concepts will be evaluated for their ability to simplify what Coulshed (1991) termed the 'chaos' of practice. The purpose of these is to help students to theory build in order to enhance their critical reflexive skills. To assist this process various sociological concepts of power, ideology, discourse theory, praxis and reflexivity will be examined.

# The Development of Global Sociology

Like social work, sociology has always been a global phenomenon despite Western ethnocentric assumptions about its origins in the European

Enlightenment. The Enlightenment movement emerged in response to the socio-economic and political upheavals associated with the industrialization that occurred in Europe during the eighteenth and nineteenth centuries. This was a broad intellectual movement that sought to sweep away traditional ideas based on religious superstition and replace them with rationality and scientific ideas. These ideas were to influence Western (and in particular) European cultures over the next two hundred years. This influence extended to the discipline of sociology, which not only adopted the scientific method as part of its rationale but also Western Eurocentric assumptions about the nature and practice of sociology.

Due to the development of Western colonialism and imperialism there was a tendency of Western sociology to dominate in the nineteenth and early twentieth centuries. This dominance has not, however, continued unchallenged. The post-Second World War period witnessed the burgeoning of global sociology. In Latin America Chilean, Brazilian and Mexican sociologists have for decades been developing theories to account for the uneven development of capitalism in Latin America and to explain their countries' economic and cultural dependence on Europe and the USA. The Egyptian economist Samir Amir (1974), the Pakistani sociologist Hanza Alavi (1972) and the Jamaican sociologist Orlando Patterson (1982) have all developed sociological approaches to challenge Western sociological orthodoxy. Scott (1995) in his history of sociology makes reference to the Muslim social scientist Ibn Khabul (1322–1406) and his theory of conflict resolution between strong nation-states, as well the Japanese sociologist Noritake Koutaro's translation of Spencer's *Principles of Sociology* in 1882. Such Western ethnocentricism is also acknowledged by Ritzer (2003) who highlights the exclusion of black sociologists from the history of US sociology, and who notes the significance of W. E. B. du Bois's ethnographic studies of the experiences of African Americans for civil rights.

Reference to the ethnocentric dimensions of sociology is relevant here in order to prompt students' critical reflection on the value-laden nature of social scientific knowledge. The term 'ethnocentric' literally means to be culturally 'self-centred' and means to look at the world from the perspective of one's own culture and value system. At the same time, while exploring other cultures it is to assume that one's own culture and value-system is superior to anyone else's. Nineteenth- and twentieth-century Western sociology was steeped in this form of ethnocentric analysis, which also legitimized Western colonial expansion (Connell 1997; Said 1997).

The point is being made here to remind us that theoretical knowledge (whether within sociology or social work) develops in a specific cultural or historical context and will thus contain a series of value-laden assumptions. This is another reason why Wright-Mills' sociology (1959) has practice relevance. He emphasized the need to locate all human behaviour and knowledge within its historical and cultural context. This was to ascertain bias and also to obtain a holistic picture of the situation. These two things are what social workers seek to do when undertaking assessments.

# The 'Sociological Imagination' Revisited

Wright-Mills (1959) argued that any good, critical sociology was manifest in the ability of the sociologist to define his or her analytical concepts and to place them in the historical or cultural context. By doing this, the sociologist was then able to address the everyday milieu of human behaviour and locate it within its specific historical context. The 'sociological imagination' provides the most effective framework for good, critical sociological study. This is because it enables the sociologist to recognize that individual behaviour can only be understood in relation to its historical and cultural context. Above all, the 'sociological imagination' emphasizes that there is a contradictory and conflicting relationship between the structural context in which people live out their lives and the human agency they have (agency is a person's capacity for independent action and decision-making).

Wright-Mills (1959) uses his sociological imagination in his analysis of social policy by identifying how private troubles become public issues and, through locating public issues in America in their social and historical context, he demonstrated the power dynamics involved in social policy decision-making and by which interest groups get to set the agenda. Hamilton and Thompson (2002) argue that the 'sociological imagination' demonstrated the poverty of traditional sociology and its claim to value freedom – because Wright-Mills identified how US academic sociology had failed to deliver the vision of the 'founding fathers' to address social problems and instead had allowed itself to be used to perpetuate and promote government sponsored research. This in turn served the interests of the US establishment and the powerful interests groups within US liberal democracy. Consequently, under the guise of empirical study and the scientific method, sociology was used to legitimate the existing status quo in America.

# Personal Sociological Approach

My own sociological approach tends towards the neo-Marxist perspective of Rees (1998). Rees's work tries to explain the complex and contradictory relationship between structure and human agency, and the contradictory ways socio-economic, political and ideological factors all operate in people's experiences of exploitation and oppression. In this way his neo-Marxist analysis of human behaviour does not reduce everything to class conflict and thus can account for other forms of discrimination and oppression. However, due to the complexities of practice grand theories such as Rees's are insufficient on their own. Equally, therefore, I appreciate the need to incorporate micro-sociological theories which explain individual or small group interaction. In this respect labelling theory (Berger and Luckman 1967) or discourse theory (Foucault 1973) are particularly useful. (These will be explained in Chapter 1.)

At the same time, micro-perspectives such as these fail to consider the real material conditions of oppression and discrimination. It is this lack of awareness that undermines the postmodern perspectives of Lash (1994), Giddens (1992) and those of risk society theorists like Beck (1992, 2006). This weakness limits their analysis of the concept of reflexivity, which feminists like Gerhard (2004) criticize for their sexist bias and for the ways they render women's agency and reflexivity invisible.

# Conclusion

The book sets out to identify sociology's contribution to the development of effective critical reflexive practice skills. Interwoven in the ensuing chapters are the three main themes of reflexivity, praxis and critical reflexive practice. These are linked to sociological concepts of power, ideology, hegemony and discourse that appear repeatedly in the body of the text. These concepts are related to specific case illustrations so as to foster critical reflexivity and to demonstrate sociology's practice orientation. Thus, by the end of the book I hope the reader will be able to appreciate the diverse ways sociological analysis underpins social work.

# 1
# Social Theory and Social Work Practice

## Introduction: Theory, Reflectivity and Reflexivity

Chapter 1 addresses the main aim of the book, which is to demonstrate the importance of sociology to social work. It does this in two ways. First, it illustrates how sociology informs an understanding of the three interrelated themes of reflexivity, praxis and critical practice. Secondly, it identifies sociology's importance to an understanding of the *practice context* of social work, whether it is at the level of society, or of the individual, or at group level. By examining sociological perspectives on society and class, the chapter highlights key conceptual frameworks that can be used to deconstruct complex casework dynamics, such as power, marital conflict, sibling relationships, poverty, racism or the client–social worker relationship. This in turn enhances the development of critical reflexive practice skills. The perspectives on society and class will be explored in relation to the most common form of engagement with clients/service users: social casework. The chapter also examines the ethical dimensions of the client–social worker relationship.

## Key Words

theory, reflectivity, reflexivity, praxis, discourse

## The Problems of Theorizing

Before illustrating how sociology informs the casework relationship, it is first necessary to address the problems of theorizing, which cause so much consternation in the profession, and to consider the confusion over the concepts of 'reflectivity' and 'reflexivity'. Rosen's (1993) study of social workers found that few knew the difference between a social work theory, concept or method of intervention, while only 24 per cent of practice decisions were based upon theoretical rationales. The most common form of knowledge applied was agency policy and procedures, which served as justifications for intervention. Caney (1983) argues that knowledge of theory is essential in the creation of safe and competent practitioners because theory facilitates the capacity to recognize and act upon significant cues on a case:

> the failure to notice or appreciate the significance of relevant cues may lead to ineffective, inappropriate or dangerous treatment, which are the hallmarks of incompetence.   (Caney, 1983, p. 302)

Though reference here is being made to physiotherapy, I would argue that this is equally applicable to social work practice. Coulshed (1991) maintained that theory underpins social work by providing explanations of casework complexities in order that practitioners can identify regularities in behaviour. More importantly, Banks (2002) identifies several ways theory informs nearly every aspect of reflexive practice skills. First, theory provides models that describe what happens in practice in a general sense in order that they can be applied to a diversity of contexts and practice situations, to render some practice consistency. Secondly, theory provides explanations of why events or outcomes occur in certain contexts and what the specific contexts are. Thirdly, it provides accountability to clients/service users, managers and the public, by providing descriptions of general practice that are adequate to measure social work activities and check them to see if they are appropriate to the task; and fourthly, theory provides justifications for methods of intervention. Using theory reflectively, Payne (2000a) suggests that we should critically evaluate theories by measuring them against each other and assessing how well they account for the contradictions and complexities of practice realities. Critical sociology is relevant here because it entails comparison and critique of different sociological perspectives, which are often measured in terms of how well they account for reality.

Bryman (2004) suggest that theories are ways of describing and explaining the persistence of regularities in reality. In sociology there are three main types of theories:

- Grand theories (also known as meta-narratives), as the name suggests, explore issues on a grand scale – that is the whole of society. Examples of grand theory are Marxism or feminism.

- Middle range theories explore the middle range of interactions between wider society and micro- or individual level, such as racism, unemployment or deviance. These operate in a limited domain and focus on a specific area of social life.

- Micro-theories seek to explain individual or small-group behaviour. Goffman's (1968) study on asylums explored how a small group of people diagnosed with mental illness were stigmatized and treated because of this label.

D'Cruz et al.'s (2007) review of current social work literature identified how the terms 'reflectivity' and 'reflexivity' were often confused or used interchangeably in practice contexts. This led to the failure in practice to develop conceptual frameworks to examine the relationship between knowledge and power. Payne (2002) argues that reflectivity is crucial to social work and he defines it as the ability to reflect critically on the strengths and weaknesses of the theories, methods of intervention, and guidance social workers use in practice, as many of them are the subject of controversy and their effectiveness is open to question. He believes social workers need to be able to reflect critically because they need to discriminate and be able to identify which theories will and will not work in different practice contexts.

Reflection informs the theoretical and experiential dimensions of practice. Hence it is important for several reasons. First, it connects with the social work assessment, which tries to put together a full picture of what difficulties a service user faces from a host of fragmented sources. Secondly, it compels social workers to explore the sub-text or the deeper layer of meaning and interaction going on in a case. Boud and Knight's (1996) definition of reflection includes: returning to the experience, attending to the associated feelings connected with the experience, then re-evaluating the experience through recognizing its outcomes and implications. They also include reflection in action (which is thinking on one's feet, in practice, about the experience while you are engaged in it) and reflection on action (which is looking back and examining the experience later). Reflection helps recognition that most ideas in social work and its socio-political context are contested. Therefore, it is necessary to integrate knowledge of the law and social policy into the realities of practice in order to learn to be discriminating about which theories are most appropriate in a given context. Also, reflectivity offers rigorous ways of working, identifying biases and prejudices behind ideas, and it offers insights for the effective implementation of theories.

Adams (2002), however, argues that reflection on its own does not go far enough in informing social work practice and in creating an enabling and supportive relationship with service users. This is because reflection has a sense of 'here and now', which tends to limit the social work analysis to the existing context of practice. In such a situation it is difficult for students and practitioners to conceive of alternative futures or alternative forms of social organization in order to generate social change. Moreover, reflection does not place any requirement upon the social workers to modify their practice in response to the awareness of new and transformative knowledge.

In contrast, reflexivity requires social work practitioners to go a stage further than reflecting on the contradictions in society, the agency they work in, or the practice of other professionals. It requires them to be critical about their own practice and professional role and how they fit in with the wider world. Schon (1983) advocates practitioners having 'reflective conversations with the situation' in order to reframe the problem and develop alternative ways of dealing with it, but at the same time being 'reflexive' about their role in the case and the ways they contribute to or hinder the situation.

These approaches to reflexivity have been informed by developments within sociology in the twentieth century. These are illustrated in the work of Bourdieu (1996), and Delanty (2000).

Bourdieu's ideas on reflexivity were influenced by anthropological and sociological studies in French colonial Africa. He criticized what he termed the 'subjective reflexivity' in these studies, which he believed pretended to be objective, in which the researchers sought to reflect upon their role in the research. However, in reality, he argued, what happened was the anthropologist or sociologist remained at the centre of the process and the narratives and views of the people being studied were pushed to the periphery and their interests marginalized. 'Reflexivity' in sociology refers to the idea that sociology as a discipline should reflect upon its own biases and prejudices in its production of knowledge, not just those of society (Delanty 2000).

Payne identifies *praxis* as crucial to the development of reflexivity. Praxis is literally, the integration of theory and practice. Marxists use the term to describe a process where theory (in this case social scientific theory) raises people's consciousness of the systems of exploitation and oppression they are subjected to under capitalism. This is then coupled with strategies to mobilize political action to generate social change, and this aspect forms the practice.

Payne argues that praxis is a Marxist concept, which takes reflexivity a little further, because it emphasizes the influence of value-laden assumptions and subjective ideas on our reflexive processes. These in turn influence what we believe social reality is like. These subjective ideas cause us to have particular agendas, and praxis proposes that we allow our experiences of the world rather than these subjective ideas to reform our beliefs about it. He argues that praxis in social work suggests that social workers are forced by their own interactions with the clients/service users and their problems to think critically on *how* they respond to them. Praxis requires practitioners to think through the methods of intervention they use, and why they prefer certain types. It requires questioning of practice guidelines and agency procedures and continually modifying theories and approaches to new situations. It also requires social workers to understand how their relationship with clients/service users is influenced by how they experience the world.

In *The Pedagogy of the Oppressed* (1972), Freire argues for the use of a Marxist concept of praxis to raise clients' awareness of the systems of domination and oppression they are subjected to and to develop political action to obtain civil and welfare rights. According to Ray (1993), Freire's critical theory is a form of 'critical pedagogy' (pedagogy is a scientific principle or theory of how to teach) based on his social work practice with Latin American rural workers. Here the workers' reflexivity on the structural oppression they were subjected to led to new forms of consciousness raising – making them aware of the systems of domination and oppression in their society – and, as a result, compelled them to form trade union or civil rights groups to work for social reform and better work conditions.

Freire's form of praxis identifies the practical implications of people's oppression and he seeks to use his critical pedagogy for both social workers and clients so that they can then integrate theory and practice (praxis) in order to develop anti-oppressive practice (AOP) strategies. Implicit in the development of praxis is some understanding of the organization of society.

## Reflexivity and Society

Society, whatever we may conceive it to look like, is the context in which people interact with one another and live out their lives. It is centrally important that social workers have some understanding of the way their society is organized, because it determines a host of issues and factors which have practice implications. These include:

- The way social work practice is organized.

- How legislation and social policy are determined and implemented.

- The extent to which social workers can exercise power and autonomy in their professional roles.

- The level of resources they have, to carry out those roles.

- The ways social workers relate to clients/service users on the basis of gender, ethnicity, class, sexuality, disability or religious belief.

Thus, to appreciate sociology's practice relevance it is necessary to identify sociological theories of the 'social' and to examine how well they account for the structural and individual contradictions and complexities that create social work practice dilemmas.

Sociological perspectives on society enhance critical reflexive practice skills by getting social workers to reflect critically on what Billig (1995) terms 'banal nationalism' and Beck (2006), 'methodological nationalism'. These terms refer to the political and ethnocentric ways in which the term 'society' is frequently used. Very often people talk about 'society' as some kind of universal concept when they are really only referring to the society in their own country. Beck uses the term 'methodological nationalism' to show the bias of Western sociologists who assume the Western model of the nation state is the same everywhere around the globe.

When referring to the situation of global nation states, Giddens (2001) could be accused of adopting methodological nationalism because he uses various terms without critically examining the racist and ethnocentric assumptions they are imbued with. He uses concepts such as 'First World', 'Second World' and 'Third World' to describe the organizations of nation states at the beginning of the twentieth century. For social work students it is important to reflect critically on the value-laden nature of these terms and examine them in their historical context, in order not to conflate 'industrialized' with 'civilized' as is sometimes the case when comparisons are made between industrialized and non-industrialized countries.

The term 'First World' refers to the countries that industrialized first, such as the countries in Western Europe, North America, Japan, Australia, New Zealand, Tasmania and Melanesia. These countries operate free market capitalist economies and multi-party systems of government. 'Second World' countries are those that constituted the former Soviet Union and her allies in Eastern Europe. These included the former Yugoslavia and Czechoslovakia, Poland, Hungary, Romania and Bulgaria. These economies were run on communist lines, which were centrally planned by the state, with no private enterprise or commercial competition and a one party (Communist Party) system of government.

In contrast, 'Third World' is a term used to describe non-industrialized countries, some of which are former colonies of Western nation states in Africa, Latin America, Asia and the Caribbean. These include Haiti, India, Pakistan, Bangladesh, Burma (Myanmar), Singapore, Malaysia, Brazil, Belize, Algeria, Kenya, Senegal, Tanzania, Zaire and Ethiopia – all of which had gained independence by the 1970s. Many of these countries (such as Tanzania, Malaysia and Pakistan) are undergoing rapid industrialization, but they are still perceived as 'lagging behind' industrially. Doyle and Pennell (1979) and Cohen and Kennedy (2000) suggest that the uneven development of capitalism results in more than simply some 'Third World' countries 'lagging behind' in terms of industrialization. This uneven development is in part a legacy of the former colonial empires, which has had dire consequences for the living conditions in contemporary 'Third World' countries. Because Western nations industrialized first, they manipulated this advantage to colonize large parts of Africa, Asia and Latin America and to exploit the natural resources of these continents, in the form of oil, minerals, cotton and cheap or slave labour, which were virtually exhausted by the time many colonies gained independence. This process has impoverished many former colonies and they 'lag behind' in industrial terms, putting them in a position where they require foreign investment and loans in order to industrialize. This is illustrated in the *Global Poverty Report* (ESCR, 2001), which demonstrates how poverty is related to uneven capitalist development. In Africa since the 1990s the rate of economic growth has been insufficient to reduce poverty levels. In order for this to be addressed, most African nations would need a sustained rate of economic growth of 6 per cent per annum (UNECA,1999). It is estimated that 50 per cent of the world's population, some1.2 billion people, live in dire poverty, that is less than 2 US dollars per day. These people are concentrated in sub-Saharan Africa, Latin America and South and East Asia (Giddens, 2001).

Paradoxically, as many 'Third World' countries are experiencing economic hardship, other countries, such as Brazil, Mexico, Singapore and Taiwan, are experiencing rapid economic growth compared with their neighbours, and are referred to as 'newly developing countries' (NDCs), while India and China are emerging as economic giants at the start of the twenty-first century. These countries are experiencing growth rates several times that of many Western industrial nations while China's annual economic growth rate now rivals that of the US (BBC News, 27 November 2007). In the former countries of the Soviet Union the transition from communism to capitalist free market economies led to a large decline in aggregate output. Consequently the numbers of poor people in the region have increased sharply and aggregate incomes have fallen, though some sectors (particularly the professional and service classes) have benefited from private sector investment (World Bank, 2000). The biggest 'losers' in material terms have been the citizens of the Commonwealth of Independent States (CIS), where unemployment has increased and wages have been declining relative to inflation since 1995. For example, in the Ukraine by 1997, 80 per cent of the working population earned wages below the national subsistence level. By the end of the 1990s one-third of workers in the CIS were working in informal subsistence work compared with only 4 per cent in other Easter European countries like Poland (EBRD, 2000).

# Neo-Marxist Perspectives on Society

Marx attributed these periodic economic crises to the inherent contradictions of capitalism (a system where the production of goods and services occurs to accumulate capital or profit) that also led to alienation. The term 'alienation' refers to the loss of control the workers had over their labour and the products of their labour. He believed that by developing the concept of 'praxis' (the integration of a critical theory of society and political action to challenge systems of oppression and domination) he had found a way for people to address alienation. Thus, the function of praxis was to overcome alienation by raising working-class consciousness of its oppression under capitalism. Alienation results from exploitation within the class system. Marx believed capitalism was characterized by a number of contradictions, the main one being the contradiction in the relationship between the capitalist or ruling class and the subordinate proletariat (non-owning), or working class, and the exploitation of labour power. The contradiction exists in the fact that in exchanging their labour power for a wage, the workers only receive a tiny amount of what their labour power is worth, while the rest of their labour power is appropriated (taken possession of) and used by the capitalist to generate profit in the form of surplus value. The resulting inequality is a class inequality because under capitalism there are two classes: one that works for a wage and the other (the capitalist class) that lives off the profit derived from labour power. This inequality is responsible for alienation.

In addition to developing the concept of praxis, Marx used the concept of *dialects* in order to understand the contradictions between the economic and social spheres of society. A dialectic represents a unity of opposites, that is the economic, social, political and ideological spheres existing in the same space (society) but in contradiction, tension and conflict with one another. These contradictions and conflicts lead to crisis in the system, which results in power imbalances between the spheres, which then results in social change.

Delanty (2000) asserts that this concept of the dialectic prevents Marxist theory from becoming economic determinist (that is, reducing all explanations of social action to economic factors such as class) because he points out that, in Marxist social science, a crisis stage in the social system is a stage in which the contradictions between the different spheres do not necessarily lead to social transformation in the form of the collapse of capitalism and the rise of socialism. Despite this interpretation of the dialectic, Marx's theory has still been accused of economic determinism (Rojeck et al., 1988).

Neo-Marxists such as Gramsci (1988 [1936]) and Lukes (1974) in their different ways reacted to the criticism of economic determinism in Marx, by suggesting a change of sociological analysis. Instead of a critical analysis of how the economic and socio-political systems created inequality and oppression; they suggested a new critical analysis of how ideology operated. Gramsci (1988 [1936]) was an Italian neo-Marxist who tried to develop a more complex analysis of the contradictory way ideology operates in society and thus he developed a theory of hegemony. Ideologies are sets of ideas that are used to legitimate advantageous positions (Saraga, 1998, p. 32). The term 'hegemony' is taken from the Greek, which refers to an ideological lead given to society by its ruling classes or 'the leadership or predominant authority of one state . . . over others' (Oxford English Dictionary, 1989, p. 88). Gramsci, unlike Marx, did not see ideology operating in a crude way, creating a situation of 'false consciousnesses' amongst members of the working class. This is because he did not believe the capitalist class was able to impose false beliefs on the working class, because hegemony was never fully achieved in society. This was due to three factors affecting its success: first, the need for historic blocs; secondly, the need for the state to make concessions to the working class; and thirdly, the problem of dual consciousness.

Like the working class, the capitalist class was internally divided into different groups of capitalist interests all competing with each other to gain profit. Therefore, hegemony could only be achieved if two or more of these groups form an alliance. Thus, a successful alliance, which achieved a high degree of hegemony, was termed an 'historic bloc', but only lasted while the alliance did, and hence it was a constantly changing entity.

Another reason why hegemony is never total, is because the ruling class (in the form of the operations of the state) had to make concessions to the working class (manifest in health, welfare, education and housing reforms) owing to the inequalities capitalism produced and in order to gain consent to capitalist rule. In addition, a further factor precipitating the possible failure of ruling-class hegemony was dual consciousness. People's consciousness and perceptions of the world came from two main sources. One source which influenced them stemmed from ruling-class control over the institutions of civil society such as the schools, churches and judicial system. This could be manipulated to persuade them to think that capitalism was natural, democratic and desirable. However, people's perceptions of reality also came from their own experiences of inequality and oppression in the real world. These enabled them to see through the capitalist system and sometimes encouraged some of them to mobilize (by joining a trade union or a civil rights movement) and campaign for social reform. Thus, Gramsci's theory of hegemony provides a framework to explain the complex and contradictory processes through which ideologies operate in society in an attempt to secure a degree of social control.

Lukes (1974) is another Neo-Marxist sociologist whose theory of *power* is useful to the development of critical practice skills. He defined power in the following way:

> Power can be defined by saying that A exercises power over B when A affects B in a manner contrary to B's interests. (Lukes, 1974, p. 27)

This means that people can be affected or harmed by power whether or not they are aware that it is being exercised. Lukes argued that there are three faces or dimensions of power. The first dimension is *decision making*, the ability to act against someone's will, or force them to do something against their will, or to make decisions on an issue where no consensus exists or where different groups disagree over policy preferences. Acts of rape or domestic violence, or the invasion of a nation state, are examples of the first face. The second face of power is *non-decision making* (which is perhaps most relevant to social work in terms of agenda setting). This is where individuals or groups exercise power to prevent certain issues being addressed or specific decisions about them being taken. It is also the ability to redefine an issue so that it becomes less threatening to the groups undertaking the redefinition. The killing of John Charles de Menezes by police officers of the Metropolitan Police in the UK was framed by those in power into a health and safety issue. In this way they were able to shift the parameters of public debate on the subject, away from discussions as to whether the officers should stand trial for murder or manslaughter to a less threatening issue. It became an issue of accountability of a 'faceless' public body rather than a few individuals who potentially had committed a crime. The decision to re-classify the trial of the killers of John Charles de Menezes in the UK is an example of the second face of power. Here the trial was re-classified from a criminal trial against the police officers who shot him (and thus could possibly face manslaughter or murder charges) to an issue of health and safety in which, as a public body, the Metropolitan Police (not the individual officers) could face criminal charges. The third face of power is the ability to *shape desires*. This is the ability to manipulate the wishes, feelings or desires of a group and where some people may be persuaded to desire or accept something that is harmful to them. For example, owing to the power of the fashion and cosmetics industries to promote the 'perfect figure' many women have suffered from bulimia or anorexia nervosa in their pursuit of such an image.

Lukes' (1974) second dimension of power is useful for considering the process of agenda setting in social work practice, and Gramsci's concept of hegemony provides a more sophisticated analysis of the complex ways ideology secures forms of legitimation and hence social control than Marx's concept of false consciousness. The emphasis on the contested nature of consciousness provides a helpful conceptual framework to analyse the way different groups seek to secure a degree of hegemony over an issue. Dominelli and Cowburn (2001) use the concept of hegemony to show how the media rather than professionals have managed to secure an ideological lead over the ways child sexual abuse should be defined and addressed. This has been achieved by portraying it as a problem of 'stranger-danger' and of a lack of decisive action on the part of the police, social workers and medical professionals (in order to protect the public). This has served to reinforce the myth that child sexual abuse is caused mainly by a small group of 'invisible pacdophiles' and this, Dominelli and Cowburn assert, ignores the extent of child sexual abuse which is committed by relatives or carers that children know, in the assumed 'safe' domain of the family.

One of the significant contributions neo-Marxism has made is the way it has compelled social science to reframe knowledge. Adams et al. (2002b) point out that traditionally much social thought in Western society about the nature of reality was predicated on religious superstition. This in turn was replaced in society by rationality, based upon the scientific method. In contrast, neo-Marxism challenges the idea that society can be understood through rationality alone and compels us not to take for granted practices that are regarded as natural and given. For example, Marx (1970 [1867]) argued that people tended to treat capitalism as a natural and permanent feature of society, rather than a specific and (to a certain extent) person-made form of economic organization.

Neo-Marxist critical theory within social work was manifest in Radical Social Work Theory (RSWT), and is based upon Marxist dialectics. It sees people as being capable of a degree of agency, but at the same time constrained and shaped by society. Underpinning RSWT is a conflict model of society where interaction is seen as occurring between competing interest groups. It criticizes traditional social work practice by emphasizing social work's social control function, acting as an agent of social control and thus helping the welfare state preserve the status quo. In adopting the dialectical approach, Ferguson and Lavalette (2007) demonstrate how the agency of both clients/service users and social workers has been used to challenge changes in welfare. They have helped form advocacy groups to challenge the repatriation of asylum seekers in Australia and the UK, and to develop welfare rights groups in India and Argentina. In addition, Tsang (2000) has identified how dialectics have simplified the process of Kolb's (1982) learning cycle for social work students by identifying the contradictions and complexities between 'concrete experience' and 'abstract conceptualization' and by encouraging students to consider the difference between contextual learning (on placement or in the classroom) and holistic learning (wider lived experience).

There are, however, certain weaknesses in Marxism; for example, Marx's theory of praxis is contradictory. On the one hand he claimed that science was not a form of objective knowledge, but rather a culturally biased knowledge system of capitalism, yet on the other hand, he argued science had the potential to generate transformative knowledge by exposing the systems of domination, exploitation and oppression in capitalist society. In addition, Freud's (1933) work demonstrated Marx's limited view of class-consciousness by showing that human consciousness was individual, not a class-based and uniform entity waiting to be realized by praxis. In addition, Marx also had a very one-dimensional view of human need and assumed that capitalism was not able to meet it, because he treated 'need' as a homogeneous concept. However, human needs are not homogeneous owing to the diversity of human experience, history and culture (which social workers appreciate when undertaking assessments). Indeed, capitalism over the past 150 years has shown considerable diversity in adapting to people's changing and heterogeneous needs through development of mass consumption and the consumer society (Beck, 1992; Price and Simpson, 2007). In addition, despite the revisions of neo-Marxists, Marxism has never really 'shrugged off' the criticism of economic determinism and has been criticized by feminists (Dominelli, 1997) and postmodernists (Rojeck et al., 1988) for reducing all social interaction to class conflict and for its failure to consider adequately other forms of oppression such as sexism, racism, disablism, homophobia and sectarianism.

## Feminist Perspectives on Society

There are various types of feminism, such as liberal, Marxist, radical, black feminism as well as reflexive feminism and standpoint feminism. Standpoint feminism is based upon the idea that all forms of knowledge, including scientific knowledge within patriarchal society, embody a masculine bias or value system, and thus are based on knowledge from a male view or standpoint. Feminist standpoint sociology seeks to incorporate in its analysis an acknowledgement of the contribution of women's perspectives in its analytical frameworks.

Though they adopt differing perspectives on the precise causes of women's oppression, all forms of feminism locate female oppression within patriarchal society (a society that is dominated by male power). Feminist sociologists, who include Harding (1991), Stanley and Wise (1993) and Witz and Marshall (2003), argue for a form of reflexive feminist sociology. This approach continually reflects upon whether its methodology is egalitarian to all groups. They argue that social reality is a gender construction, and the aim of sociology should be to expose the oppressive dimensions of this gender construction and point to an alternative form of social organization, one that acknowledges women as autonomous social actors. They contend that science is not an objective discipline, but rather, the product of a masculine value system. Harding (1991) asserts that sociology needs to be re-oriented to acknowledge this sexist bias and give expression to women's experiences. This form of reflexive feminism is also known as 'standpoint feminism' and an extreme form of this perspective is the feminist standpoint epistemology of Stanley and Wise (1993), who argue that scientific knowledge is no different from any other form of standpoint knowledge based upon class, gender or ethnicity.

In order to explain women's subordinate position in society, feminists cite the ways work, or rather employment, is organized. The public world of work is that which takes place outside the home and this arena is dominated by men in terms of wealth, and of access to positions of power and prestige (McDowell et al., 1995). The private domain is the world of the family, which affords less social status and political power and is where women are largely found in their capacity as wives, partners and mothers. Feminists have pointed to the fact that these social categories have underpinned social divisions and have been central to the structuring of gender within Western society. Feminists distinguish between 'sex' (what separates us into males and females) and gender (i.e. what is masculine and feminine). They point out that gender is a social construct that various both historically and culturally. However, within patriarchy gender is often claimed to be a natural or biological given, to explain behaviour and to justify the power differences between men and women.

The public/private dualism is central to feminist critiques of patriarchy. The particular separation of the public and private spheres that developed in Western culture resulted in women's exclusion from the rights of citizenship. McDowell and Pringle (1996) suggest that the deconstruction of the taken-for-granted division between the public and private spheres is now a central notion of the social sciences and a major part of feminist re-theorizing. This has seriously strengthened sociology's critical capacity.

There are, however, problems in using the dichotomy of public/private uncritically. First, the separation of the public and private ignores the integration that exists between the two spheres. Secondly, it fails to account adequately for the nature of women's oppression outside the home; and thirdly, it leaves unchallenged the assumption that women's oppression exists purely in the private domain. An extreme example of this is manifest in the assumption that domestic violence only takes place within the private world of family and thus the tendency to reframe it as something else (i.e. assault) when it occurs in public (McKie, 2005). In addition the public/private or domestic/public opposition has tended to explain gender in psychological and functional terms and this masks the international diversity in the structuring and evaluation of gender.

Language is also a mechanism that secures women's oppression and one linguistic device, which stereotypes and hence secures the oppression of women, is the concept of dualism. Dualisms such as mind/body, reason/emotion, culture/nature, public/private are just some examples. Feminists argue these should be regarded cautiously because they link up to another dualism: male/female. There are two points to such dualisms. First, they are normally perceived as separate and opposed. Secondly, they contain an implicit value judgement. One side of the dualism, side 'A' (male), has positive value and the other side, 'B' (female), negative value, i.e. it is 'not

A'. Within patriarchal society, the first element in the set of pairs lines up with men, such as mind, culture, rationality, independence, and the second element with women. Women are seen as being closer to nature, controlled by their emotions and lacking a sense of independence (Pringle 1996).

Another form of legitimation for female subordination is 'naturalism'. Naturalism is the idea that there are biological and hence natural differences between the sexes, and this argument is often cited to legitimate the separation and exclusion of women. As Pringle (1996) points out, once something is defined as 'natural' it ceases to require social or political explanation and is regarded as a constant that can be taken for granted. The deconstruction of dualisms and the feminist critique of naturalism provide a useful theoretical framework that shows *how* women are defined and constructed by sets of social institutions, practices and values which construct gender divisions. For example, femininity is often defined in relation to masculinity. Such an analysis ignores the differences between women based on ethnicity, class, age, sexuality or disability.

Feminist perspectives have been crucial to social casework on a variety of levels by illustrating the ways in which women's exploitation and subordination occur, within the public world of work, the private world of family life (manifest in the unmasking of domestic violence and child sexual abuse), through the social constructions of masculinity and femininity and through the medical control of various natural female processes such as childbirth or menopause. Feminist sociologists like Pringle (1996) and Witz and Marshall (2003) point to the ways work is constructed to privilege men's experience over that of women. They identify the ways women have been denied access to work on equal terms with men. Central to patriarchal social constructions of femininity is the assumption that woman are 'naturally' equipped to care for others. The lifelong obligations to care for husbands/partners, children and dependent older parents is dubbed the 'triangle of care'. Feminists (Finch, 1988; Oakley, 1974; Williams, 2003) have examined how this social construction of caring equates with femininity and has been exploited to subordinate women. Dalley (1988) in her book distinguishes between 'caring for' and 'caring about'. Whereas men are permitted to care about without caring for, policy makers often assume that for women these things are one and the same.

Within social work, various forms of feminist analysis have been used. For example, Taylor and Daly (1995) examine the social construction of women's subservient role to men in law, medicine and religion. A different form of feminist constructivism has been explored by both Healy (2000) and McKie (2005) when examining gender differences in the construction of domestic violence.

Despite the ways in which these forms of feminist theorizing have informed critical reflexive practice, feminist sociology has been criticized for a number of theoretical weaknesses. Liberal and radical feminism, in reducing women's inequalities to culture or biology, ignore the structural dimensions of women's oppression, which have real material consequences. Black feminism tends to result in a dichotomy between white and black female experiences, which ignores the different experiences of racism and sexism based on ethnicity and not race, amongst other non-white groups (Anthias and Yuval-Davis, 1992; Anthias, 2001). Marxist-feminist analysis is a-historical, because patriarchy pre-dates capitalism and thus women's oppression cannot be reduced to capitalist class relations. Young (1980) expands on this point by arguing that in order to account for the dynamics of gender, Marxist-feminists have simply 'grafted on' the sexual division of labour to existing models of social organization, so instead of the Marxist analysis of production we now have the dichotomy of 'production/reproduction'. The problem of this approach is that it assumes that the economic organization that is peculiar to capitalism is the same in all societies. Similarly, post-modern or social constructivist feminist approaches have been criticized (Birke, 1996; Jagger, 1995) because in emphasizing the way femininity or masculinity are socially constructed they do not account for the realities of 'sex' and the material forms of oppression that result from being male or female.

Blackburn et al. (2002) argue that the idea of vertical segregation (where men are concentrated in managerial or higher-paid jobs and women in lower sections of the hierarchy in lower-paid jobs) in employment, which leads to women's oppression, is not supported by empirical evidence in countries like Sweden, Japan, or South Africa. In using this notion of patriarchy, feminists over-estimate men's agency and underestimate women's. In addition, the patriarchy argument fits badly with recent developments and changes in the labour market which are destroying traditional 'male' occupations such as coal, steel, shipbuilding and dock working and have adversely affected men's employment prospects, while the growth of the service industries has favoured women's.

# Postmodern Perspectives on Society

Postmodernism is known by various names including 'post-structuralism' and 'social constructivism'. Within social science, postmodernism did not really develop until the 1970s. It developed in France and Germany but quickly spread to the UK and US. Postmodern society is characterized in a general lack of faith in the inevitability of human progress, a lack of confidence in scientific rationality and technology to cure social ills, and disillusionment with the failure of traditional institutions of democracy to work for the benefit of the less powerful, and there is generally less certainty and confidence about the future. Within postmodernism, one key writer was

Foucault (1926–84). Foucault (1973) defined discourses as a series of language games in society through which power was exercised, and argued that the traditional sociological approaches of Weber and Marx were now out of date because they represented the main discourses of modernity. 'Modernity' or modern society is often associated with the ideas of the Enlightenment Movement and is characterized in a belief in the potential of human progress and the power of rationality to achieve such progress, and faith in the ability of science and technology to overcome social problems like famine, the rights of humans to self-determination, and a dependence on industry and commerce to provide goods and services to improve living standards.

Foucault argued that this modern society was one in which the dominant discourses of religion had been replaced by the discourses of science. These scientific discourses had in turn been superseded as modernism had been replaced by postmodern society. He asserted that discourses were the new forms of social control and that all forms of contemporary life were subject to surveillance and control by means of such discourses. This was achieved through the ways in which discourses permeated the operations of schools, prisons and asylums and through the ways the systems of ideas in these language games became diffused through society's institutions and practices. An example of how this process has the ability to mobilize power is through the various discourses which construct people's sense of 'self' and determine their identity, such as 'sexuality', 'gender', 'parenthood' or 'ethnicity'. Though he recognized the potential of human agency to resist these forms of control, the power of discourse, he argued, was secured through the ways it involved the creation of individual subjectivity using language to label, and hence define, all forms of personal identity.

Specific discourses are structured around central themes and these serve to set boundaries or limitations on the types of investigations or discussions that can occur on a given subject (Saraga, 1998, p. 38). Power is exercised in the way their central ideas become commonly accepted as the 'truth'. Discourse represents the intellectual organization of these ideas and their power is expressed through their diffusion through society's organizations. This is, however, a complex and contradictory process in which different discourses compete for dominance. The main ways such discourses assume power is through becoming institutionalized in the policies, practices and agency procedures in institutions like education or social services departments.

Postmodernism has been employed in various ways in social work, for example: Parton (1996) adopts a postmodern approach to criticize the efficacy of Marxist class theory in an understanding of anti-oppressive practice. In contrast, Nylund (2002) uses elements of postmodernism in his narrative therapy techniques when working with clients diagnosed with attention deficit hyperactivity disorder (ADHD). Healy (2005) uses discourse theory to critically analyse the impact of biomedical discourses in social work. She defines biomedical discourses as the contemporary and dominant approaches to medical science that have their origins in the biological sciences (p. 20). She argues that these discourses have had a profound influence on social work practice in the ways social work agencies define service users' needs, how they define the social work role, and through the ways, at times, they limit service user outcomes. In addition, these discourses have the potential to lead to oppressive practice. This occurs through the construction of the dichotomy of able-bodied/disabled, in which able-bodiedness is perceived as healthy and hence 'normal' and disability as 'abnormal' and deviant. Oppression results from the use of this dichotomy through attempts to modify the person with a disability rather than changing their environment to accommodate their needs.

Some of the weaknesses of postmodernism are identified by LavaLette and Ferguson (1999), who argue that the uses of postmodernist analysis will not lead to empowering practice with client/service users for several reasons. First, they assert, postmodernism's rejection of grand theory or meta-narratives means that social science (and indirectly social work), in adopting postmodernist analysis, no longer has a framework for analysing the structural causes of people's oppression. Postmodernism's emphasis on respecting everyone's narratives as equally valid, means that social work now lacks the capacity to distinguish the account of the oppressor from that of the oppressed. This means that it is reduced to describing rather then analysing and challenging the causes of people's oppression. This limits its ability to develop anti-oppressive practice (AOP) strategies to challenge poverty and discrimination and, as Lavalette and Ferguson point out, these things 'slip off the social work agenda' (1999, p. 32). If everyone's narrative is equally valid, how does the social worker distinguish the account of the racist from that of the racist's victim? Without any reference to grand theory, postmodernism lacks any adequate frame of reference to analyse the power dynamics that ensure that certain narratives and certain discourses retain dominance. Thus, the main problem behind postmodernism's emphasis on language is that it ignores the material conditions which reinforce people's oppression, and that exist behind the concept of identity politics. This concept does not explain why some people have the capacity to choose their identity (for example, middle-class philanthropists) while others (such as a person with a learning disability) have their identity ascribed, and why this ascription often entails a negative or low-status role in society.

# The Globalization Debate

According to some sociologists, such as Beck (1992) and Giddens (1996), in twenty-first-century notions of class and gender, inequalities have become superfluous because the debates within sociology have moved on to the *globalization* debate. Globalization can be defined by the feeling that the world is shrinking due to the impact of IT and satellite communications and the activities of transnational corporations, which make communication and international business transactions much quicker. Giddens (2001) attributes globalization to several factors: first, the decline of the Soviet Union and communism in Eastern Europe and the rise of capitalism here and in Asia; secondly, the growth of international government mechanisms, like the United Nations or the European Union; thirdly, globalization driven by intergovernmental organizations like the World Trade Organization, set up by a group of governments and responsible for the regulation of a particular activity which has international scope; fourthly, the impact of global information flows, thanks to the popularity of the world-wide web, which gives the impression that the world is shrinking. Giddens believes, however, that globalization is accompanied by some negative aspects such as increased global unemployment (as old industries and economies are replaced by new ones elsewhere around the world), increased ecological and health risks, and global inequalities and poverty. In addition, globalization is leading to a decline in the autonomy and power of the nation state to determine both domestic and foreign policy.

## Globalization Theory in Social Work

Villereal (2007), Yip (2005) and Mishra (2005) all consider how globalization can be used to inform the development of international social work education. Villereal examines how globalization has led to international investment in Guatemala's cities; however, this prosperity has not extended to the country's rural poor. He believes it is possible to use this investment and the international links that have developed because of globalization to develop an international social work model to address the welfare and educational inequalities the rural poor experience. Similarly, Yip (2005) identifies that one consequence of globalization is the dominant hegemony of American culture. He seeks to counter this hegemonic dominance by arguing for the development of cross-cultural social work education, which incorporates Asian cultural models as well. In contrast, Mishra (2005) identifies that one casualty of globalization has been international observation of human rights. She argues that international social work should seek to mobilize international support for an international standard on human rights, one that (unlike the current UN declaration) requires mandatory observation.

Many globalization theorists fail to acknowledge the influence of Western global capitalism and the negative socio-economic effects this is having. Noyoo (2000) identifies the socio-economic impact of globalization on sub-Saharan African nations, and the subsequent economic policies they have been forced to implement under pressure from organizations such as the World Bank and the International Monetary Fund (IMF) as a condition of their loans. This economic restructuring has taken the form of structural adjustment programmes (SAPs), which are in essence cutbacks in state spending on welfare and social services. These have contributed to economic stagnation in countries like Mauritania, Mali, Chad, Sudan, Eritrea and Ethiopia. As well as having some of the 1.2 billion of the world's poorest people (OEDC, 2000), these countries have seen their rates of economic growth average at a mere 3.4 per cent since 1961 (Noyoo, 2000 p. 455) and this has resulted in dire poverty and human misery for over one billion people. This poverty is exacerbated by lack of welfare and social services provision in many of these countries. For Noyoo the social practice implications are clear, in that professional social workers have a moral duty to develop paradigms to analyse the structural and material inequalities generated by SAPs and to start to develop critiques of government policies which fail to acknowledge the impact of SAP's, the lack of state expenditure on social welfare programmes and the vast migration out of sub-Saharan Africa (Noyoo, 2000, p. 460). Such failures in postmodernism to account for these structural inequalities have implications for its ability to account for the dynamics of social casework.

# The 'End-of-Class' Debate

An understanding of class is crucial to social work practice because class position affects quality of life in terms of the extent of poverty and social exclusion one experiences, educational attainment, pension rights and provision, and employment prospects. In addition, class has been implicated in health and mental health morbidity rates, with lower social classes experiencing higher rates of infant mortality, cardiovascular disease, depression and anxiety (Doyal, 1996; WHO, 2002). Moreover, there is a range of empirical research that identifies a strong correlation between class and incidents of child neglect and domestic violence (Calder, 2004; Evans, 2005).

Beck (2007) argues that class is no longer relevant to the study of contemporary society with its fragmentations and claims that everything is in a state of flux. He maintains that increased reflexivity and uncertainty has led to greater autonomy and increased individualization, where people have a multiplicity of statuses, not just class, and can self-define. Hence it is no longer plausible to talk about different classes or class conflict.

This argument has implications for social work practice on two grounds.

First, it is at variance with Jones' (2002) assertion that social work has always been involved with people positioned at the lowest ranks of the social strata, and more importantly, that social work colludes with hierarchical forms of social organization through its 'attempts to play down this class specificity' (Jones, 2002, p. 42). Secondly, if this 'end of class' argument has empirical validity, what of the material dimensions of class manifest in its relationship to poverty, ill health, homelessness, educational attainment and social mobility? Do all these material factors (which have an impact upon the extent of people's power and agency) simply evaporate into the 'ether' if, as Beck alleges, a person can now self-define and give primacy to other forms of identity? The 'end of class' debate has social work practice implications in two ways. First because there is abundant empirical evidence that global poverty and class inequalities are increasing, and secondly, there is an increasing focus, in social work practice, on particular groups of the socially excluded, namely those termed 'the underclass'.

The postmodern sociologists like Savage et al. (2005) criticize the 'end of class' thesis for the dangers it poses to critical sociology, and this too can inform critical practice skills. They maintain that contemporary sociological theories of class are too busy identifying and describing class, and thus they fail to address substantive questions relating to the exercise of power and social control in contemporary society. These substantive questions are still very important because class continues to be a dynamic in the experience of globalization and trade liberalization in Eastern and Central Europe, Asia and Latin America. In these countries since the 1990s there have been rising wage disparities between the skilled non-manual and semi-skilled or unskilled manual groups. Studies done in Brazil, Chile, Columbia and Venezuela (Cohen and Kennedy, 2007) as well as in Hong Kong, Japan and China (Wong, 2004; Hiroshi, 2001) illustrate this trend.

Savage et al. (2005) note that with the decline of the industrial working class, capitalist societies are experiencing the cultural dominance of middle-class discourses which are presented as the universal norm. The practice implication of this, for social policy, is further exploitation and social exclusion for those at the lowest end of the social stratum and their vilification in welfare and social work through the development of specific discourses on working-class families (Langan, 1998; Jones, 2002). Evans (2005) is highly critical of social work and other welfare responses to the class inequalities, and for the way things like gender, poverty and class are ignored in an analysis of domestic violence. She presents a series of empirical research studies which show the correlation between poverty or low income and the increased prevalence of domestic violence, such as the *World Health Report on Violence* (WHO, 2002), and research in the US and Canada. In her native Australia, she cites the rates of domestic violence in what they term 'central city poverty areas', at nine times the rate of more prosperous areas, while in New South Wales, crime statistics found that women living in poverty were seven times more likely to be killed by their partner or ex-partner than women occupying higher income groups.

Neo-Marxists such as Jessop (1990) and Ferguson and Lavalette (2007) have adopted Marxist class analysis to identify how the semi-skilled and unskilled working class around the globe have been the most vulnerable to the flexibility and deregulation of labour. As capitalism has taken on new global forms, neo-Marxists argue, new elements of the working class have developed such as an increasing number of dispossessed long-term unemployed people or casually employed groups of people (termed negatively by some, like Murray (1994) as the 'underclass'). Murray (1994) first identified what he saw as the problems presented by the underclass in the US before coming to Britain. He argued that the position of the underclass was not simply constituted by economic factors but was also a product of character, and claimed that the underclass was distinguished by the 'deplorable' or even 'deviant' behaviour of its members. For him, such deviancy was exemplified in a reliance on state benefits, the experience of lone parenting, a tendency to have children out of wedlock, homelessness, and engagement in criminal activity. He argued that the underclass threatened the social stability of UK society.

The neo-Marxist sociologist Macnicol (1987) provides a robust critique of such perspectives on the underclass by drawing historical parallels between Victorian portrayals of the 'residuum' and these contemporary references to the poor in UK and US welfare discourses. He notes that in the global economic boom of the 1950s and 1960s there was greater optimism that different forms of social work and welfare interventions could eradicate poverty. However, in the middle of the 1990s, primacy was once again given to the free market (in many Western democracies). As capitalism attempted to restructure in order to address the impact of world recession, the principle of self-reliance once again took hold and the poor were (as they had been in the great depressions of the 1830s, 1880s and 1930s) held accountable as the primary cause of their own poverty. The continuity in the nineteenth, twentieth- and early twenty-first-century discourses on the poor, as suggested by Shaw and Gould (2001) and referred to by Macnicol (1987), is manifest in the correlation between the state of the capitalist economies and the varying degrees to which the poor and unemployed are vilified within social policy and welfare practices. Jones and Novak (1999) identify how these discourses have begun to affect the organizational practices of social workers. This, they argue, is much in evidence towards those defined as 'poor' or the 'underclass', resulting in increasing surveillance and social work intervention in families defined as 'dysfunctional'. In addition, Bryan et al. (1985) note how this is perceived on the part of those families as oppressive and intrusive practice:

The social background of most social workers and the training they receive give them no real understanding of our different family structures, cultural values and codes of behaviour. It is so much easier for them to rely on loose assumptions and loaded stereotypes of us than to address the root cause of our problems.   (Bryan et al., 1985, p. 112)

Prandy (2002) argues that postmodernist perspectives on class fail to deconstruct these oppressive discourses about different classes because they do not recognize the material existence of a class system, and yet there is abundant empirical evidence that various social groupings consistently experience material disadvantage based upon their position in the social hierarchy. Postmodernists totally over-emphasize the extent of social fragmentation that has occurred in contemporary capitalist societies, while their emphasis on multidimensional analysis of class (based upon capital, assets and resources) fails to acknowledge the socio-economic structures that consistently reproduce these material inequalities. The consequence of postmodernism's approach using cultural capital is that class analysis is reduced to crude stereotypes. Commenting on stereotypes, Prandy observes the dangers in that they oversimplify reality and encourage people to avoid analysing the contradictions and complexities in real-life situations (Prandy, 2002, p. 589).

The reality of social work is, however, that in order to engage effectively with clients/service users, practitioners have to try to obtain an understanding of a more complex reality, and dealing with complexity and contradiction are part of the daily professional task. Thus, a structural analysis is important because for many service users the term 'class' means a specific relationship in society. For many people it involves a working class in opposition to the status quo, in which they are continually materially disadvantaged. The failure to recognize and attempt to make sense of such complexity can also lead to oppressive social work practice and the delivery of inappropriate services that fail to address clients'/service users' needs. For example, you have probably heard the controversies over cases where the decision has been made to remove children from 'poor' families. Under the auspices of concerns about neglect or deprivation, children have been taken into care when it would have perhaps been more empowering and therapeutic for the family to be given resources. This could have reduced the causes of deprivation which have an impact on parenting capacities.

Anthias (2001) criticizes traditional sociological perspectives on class for the ways they ignore dimensions of ethnic and gender inequality which interconnect with class inequality, and all three forms have material dimensions for women, affecting access to education, employment, health and social services. She criticizes neo-Marxist models of class, which reduce ethnic inequalities to a by-product of class inequalities, and neo-Weberian models using status (based upon market situation) because they fail to explain the material origins of class inequalities. The problem with status and the preoccupation with examining how things like honour and prestige are allocated is that this preoccupation fails to examine *how* material resource allocation and power are linked in society.

# Sociology and Social Casework

All these sociological theories are important to understanding the social dynamics in social casework. However, before discussing how they link in, it is first necessary to define what is meant by the term. This is important because the casework method is used internationally (Jones, 2002; Healy, 2001; Horner, 2006). It is considered a central feature of the client/service user–social work relationship, whether working with the clients/service users on their own or within the context of the family. Pearlman (1973) defines social casework as, a process where human welfare agencies assist clients with developing coping and problem-solving strategies (p. 4). Social casework is older than the social work profession itself. This method was first developed in 1857 by Mrs Ellen Raynard, founder of the Bible and Domestic Female Mission. This mission operated in a number of English cities, and bible workers worked with 'working-class' volunteers in poor districts organizing provident schemes and visiting the poor (Lewis, 1998, p. 75). A modern variant of the casework approach is noted by the US National Association of Social Workers (1993), which identifies casework as the main form of direct work with clients, which embodies a trusting and empowering relationship with the aim of restoring or consolidating the client's coping skills (1993, p. 3).

Horner (2006) points out that the casework model is central to practice because it continues to dominate contemporary fieldwork (2006, p. 23). However, despite its international popularity for its focus on the individual and for problem-solving capacities, it has come under criticism (Jones, 2002; Payne, 2005) for such a focus, which has the potential to 'victim blame' people for their problems. It is also criticized for the way it ignores the structural constraints and inequalities that have an impact on people's problem-solving capacities.

Jones (2002) argues that casework is a highly politicized form of social work practice, which tends to ensure conformity to the status quo through the regulation of the poorest members of society. The casework method gave legitimacy to the idea that a person's socio-economic status was the result of personal and individual effort and moral character. This type of casework orientation, according to Jones, reflected a conservative character (2002, p. 24). Similarly, Silavwe (1995) has criticized the concept of social casework for the way it is based upon individualistic Western cultural values, which are at variance with African cultures and the existing kinship mechanisms for the resolution of family problems and conflicts.

Whether casework is regarded as a viable method for engagements with clients/service users or an overtly political form of social regulation, socio-logical theories of society and class are crucial to practice. In addition, they inform an understanding of the ethical dilemmas that occur in practice.

# Reflexivity and Social Work Ethics

An understanding of ethics is crucial in order to practise in an accountable and anti-oppressive manner. Payne (2005) and Shardlow (2002) point out that, just as social work practice and methods are the subject of controversy, so too are social work ethics. Sociology in different forms helps practitioners to identify the contradictions and practice dilemmas raised by ethical considerations, thus informing critical reflexive practice skills.

Classical or traditional approaches to ethics in social work (Hugman and Smith, 1995) approach the issue of ethics almost as if it is an objective science. The idea seems to be that it is possible to (a) define the term 'ethics', then (b) set up a series of ethical principles, and then, (c) by adherence to these ethical principles, it is possible to practise ethically. For example, Davies (2000) defines ethics as:

> Professional ethics, comprise the more or less formalized principles, rules, conventions and customary practices, that inform professionals' treatment of their clients, each other, and their relations with society at large. (Davies, 2000, p. 272)

Clarke (2000), having examined a number of ethical codes around the globe, defines the core social work values and principles underpinning ethics in social work. These include respect for the individual client, the performance of the social work task in an honest and truthful way, ensuring the social work task is carried out using proper knowledge and skill, the use of care and diligence, respecting the client's trust in the professional, and ensuring that social work intervention is based on methods which have been demonstrated as effective and helpful. Equally, however, Pawar (2004) and Kaseke (2005) point to the Western ethnocentrism in these concepts of ethics and identify the practice dilemmas of their implementation in non-Western contexts.

The trouble with Clarke's (2000) approach to ethics in social work is that it tends to remove social work from its economic, socio-political and cultural context. Shardlow (2002) argues that such definitions of ethics are too narrow and ignore the complexity of the contemporary reality of social work practice. He maintains that any concept of ethics must consider the politics of professionalism (where different professions compete for status and prestige; Parry and Parry, 1997), which influence the direction of social work and have an impact on the development of ethical codes. For these reasons, he argues that when considering ethics, social workers need an operational knowledge of sociology (including structural and postmodern theories in order to analyse social work's function in society). He maintains that often discussions on social work ethics are not grounded in the concrete demands facing social workers on a daily basis.

Marxist social work academics such as Simpkins (1979) and Jones and Novak (1999) argue that classical approaches to ethics ignore the material position of people's experience and tend to divorce ethics from the contexts of clients'/service users' experiences of the social world, which are character-ized by poverty, homelessness, deprivation or oppression. Corrigan and Leonard (1978) takes a more extreme position and points to social work's unethical role in the production of a docile working-class labour force in capitalist societies, and hence, any question of ethics must be regarded in relation to social work's primary social control function.

In contrast, to avoid these forms of oppressive practice, the 'ethics-of-care' perspective (which is based upon postmodernist ideas) reframes the issue and offers alternative ways of conceptualizing social work practice and the caring role. It no longer sees the caring role as a product of a women's domain, but sees it rather as the responsibility of all citizens. This is premised on the recognition that all of us at some time or in some context will be vulnerable and require care; it is not just for children and older people. However, within this framework the ethics of care propose a new social worker–client/service user relationship. Rather than treating the client/service user as the subject of social work intervention, it argues for joint collaboration and an emphasis on communication, negotiation and the development of a dialogue. This, in conjunction with the use of reflex-ivity, is to enable both parties to see the discursive and political dimensions of the ways ethics tend to be applied and how they can be influenced by agency considerations. The 'ethics-of-care' position requires the social worker to develop what is termed 'reflexive solidarity' (Davies, 2000; Parton, 2003) with the service user. This is a process of negotiation and communi-cation between the professional and the service user. In this process, both have the potential to change their perspective of the situation through collaboration and communication. In this way they are able to negotiate and identify solutions to address the difficulties arising. The significance of this 'reflexive solidarity' is that the power is shifted away from the social worker as 'expert' and a more collaborative and egalitarian approach is adopted through discussion and negotiation of different perspectives.

## Summary of the Main Points

● An understanding of theory and the differences between reflectivity and reflexivity is important to the development of critical reflexive practice skills.

● Sociology informs the development of reflexive practice skills by providing various conceptual frameworks such as discourse theory, hegemony, Lukes' three dimensions of power, and Marxist praxis.

● Three key sociological perspectives on society are Marxism, feminism and postmodernism.

● Marxism identifies how inequality and oppression are secured through class divisions and the contradictions in the capitalist–worker relationship.

● Feminist analysis identifies how patriarchal society secures the subordination of women.

● Postmodernism in the form of discourse theory has informed social work practice by deconstructing oppressive medical and welfare discourses.

● Sociological critiques of Beck's (2007) 'end-of-class' thesis help social workers avoid oppressive practice by identifying:

    (a) the fact that class inequalities are increasing;

    (b) how class affects quality of life in terms of income, employment, educational attainment and health;

    (c) how it correlates with child abuse and domestic violence;

    (d) how underclass discourses are beginning to influence the organizational context of social work (Jones and Novak, 1999).

● The 'ethics-of-care' perspective seeks to develop a more collaborative role between social worker and service users which no longer privileges social work knowledge as 'expert' over the knowledge.

## Conclusion

This chapter has begun to identify sociology's contribution to social work by examining how it informs an understanding of reflexivity, praxis and critical reflexive practice. It demonstrated how sociological theories of society help simplify the complexities of the social work practice context by identifying how sociological concepts of power, class, ideology and discourse theory can unpack complex case dynamics. It illustrated the relationship between knowledge and power in social work and how different types of sociological theorizing can underpin an awareness of ethics. It also identified the three levels of sociological theory, i.e. grand theory, middle-range theory and micro-theory (which will be examined in Chapter 5), and provided some illustrations of how they help an understanding of the different levels of human interaction. Marxist dialectics and concepts of praxis provided insights into the structure/agency relationship and how reflectivity, praxis and critical reflexive practice are linked, while Bourdieu's (1996) and Delanty's (2000) concepts of reflexivity helped simplify the complexity over reflectivity and reflexivity as well as providing some illustrations of how both can enhance anti-oppressive practice strategies. In addition, feminist analysis of dualisms, the separation of the public and private spheres, the organization of work, the use of naturalist arguments, all enhanced a critical sociological analysis. All of these approaches could be used to identify the existence of gender divisions in society and how they affect clients. Some of these perspectives will be explored in more depth for their practice implications in Chapter 2, which opens Part 1 of the book, 'Contexts of Social Work'.

## Case Study

Sharon is a 20-year-old white English woman who is pregnant, and who lives with her mother in a two-bedroom council flat. Her parents divorced when Sharon was a baby and Sharon has not seen her father since she was three. Sharon has been assessed as having a moderate learning disability and has been out of school for just over a year. She attends a local day centre two days a week and goes to college three days a week where she is studying to be a hairdresser. Sharon's boyfriend James (21), who is also white English, and has been assessed as having a mild learning disability, has been attending the same college as Sharon, which is where they met. James wants Sharon to move in with him. Mrs Smith (Sharon's mother) is very concerned as she thinks Sharon is too young and too vulnerable to leave home. She is also concerned because Sharon has diabetes and is quite overweight and needs a lot of support managing her condition.

Sharon has referred herself to the Community Disabilities Team for support to find accommodation and help to look after her baby when it is born. The social worker who has been allocated the case is Sally Daventry.

Sociology could assist Sally Daventry with determining the nature of intervention because different sociological perspectives would emphasize different aspects or levels of analysis of Sharon's situation. For example, a postmodernist approach would examine the discourses implicit in the medical model of disability, which constructs able-bodiedness as 'normal', and disability as a form of abnormality or deviance. It would examine how this dichotomy results in Sharon's oppression by the way she is targeted for professional intervention. A different approach would be adopted by a reflexive feminist perspective, which would stress that under patriarchy there is a distinct separation of the public sphere (the world of work and civil life) and the private sphere (the

## Case Study (*cont'd*)

world of family). This private sphere, which emphasizes the feminine roles of 'mother' and 'housewife', entails less power, status and prestige than the public domain, which is dominated by men. This approach would examine how the welfare state (through welfare legislation) exploits the unpaid labour power of women as carers, and would consider how a lack of access to the public domain in the form of employment, resources and access to child care would reinforce Sharon's role in the private domain. Neo-Marxism, on the other hand, would examine the structural inequalities and contradictions in Sharon's life by exploring her class position and, using praxis, seek to raise Sharon's consciousness of the oppression and discrimination she faces by emphasizing that as a member of the working or subordinated class (she might possibly be negatively labelled as a member of the 'underclass') she has only her labour power to sell. Thus, her oppression is manifest in the way she is socially excluded owing to her lack of employment opportunities, which results in poverty and affects her access to housing, health and education.

# Further Reading

Adams, R. (2002b) 'Developing Critical Practice in Social Work', in R. Adams, L. Dominelli and M. Payne, *Critical Practice in Social Work* (Basingstoke: Palgrave Macmillan).
This chapter presents an excellent synopsis of the importance of combining reflectivity with reflexivity in critical practice.

Freire, P. (1972) *The Pedagogy of the Oppressed* (Harmondsworth: Penguin).
In this book Freire demonstrates how the Marxist concept of praxis can be used in a practical way in social work to generate AOP.

Saraga, E. (1998) *Embodying the Social: Constructions of Difference* (Buckingham: Open University Press in association with Routledge).
This provides an excellent, simplified summary of Foucault's use of the concept of discourse, and using poverty, shows how discourses influence the institutional practices of social work.

Jones, C. and Novak, T. (1999) *Poverty, Welfare and the Disciplinary State* (London: Routledge).
This book identifies the increasing surveillance and social control aspect of UK social work, when dealing with those defined as poor.

# PART I
# Contexts of Social Work

# 2
# The Changing Welfare Landscape

## Introduction

Some further dimensions of critical reflexive practice skills are now explored as the focus shifts to examine competing perspectives on the welfare state. Several sociological perspectives are presented, beginning with neo-liberal and social democratic approaches. These will be compared with Fordist and neo-Marxist approaches, in terms of how well they account for the operations of the welfare state. The chapter will then move on to consider feminist and anti-racist critiques of these approaches. A fourth and important dimension is added through the contribution of the perspectives of Islamic Political Economy (IPE) as presented by some Muslim sociologists. This is useful in identifying the Western ethnocentric nature of traditional sociological perspectives on the welfare state, and pointing to alternatives.

## Key Words

the welfare state, power, social policy, Islamic Political Economy (IPE)

## What is the Welfare State?

According to Hughes and Lewis (1998), the term 'welfare state' refers to a distinct set of institutional arrangements organized specifically for the efficient delivery of welfare. Key components amongst such provision would be a system of social security, education, health, social services and the near universal provision of basic health and welfare needs (Hughes and Lewis, 1998, p. 7). Other sociologists (Williams, 1995; Taylor-Gooby and Dale, 1981) consider the welfare state as a key concept underpinning the academic discipline of social policy – which explores social problems and the welfare state's responses to those social problems. Implicit in this model is the presumption of state control and state provision of welfare. Wright-Mills (1959) argued that this approach suggests social policy is a form of objective science. However, he argued that what happens in reality is that powerful groups in society set the agenda on what becomes a social problem worthy of state intervention – and he argued that some aspects of social policy could be regarded as forms of social control of poorer elements of society.

Global trends in welfare state expenditure are relevant to social work practice because these determine the amount of resources that are allocated for social services. Hill (2006) suggests that there is sufficient empirical evidence to demonstrate that the amount of state expenditure on welfare provision for unemployment, sickness and disability benefits, health, education, social services and housing services, is directly related to the extent of national prosperity, with notable exceptions in the case of Japan, USA, Canada, Ireland and South Korea. The average gross domestic product (GDP) spent on welfare is 9 per cent, with countries like South Africa and Argentina spending between 13 and 14 per cent and Indonesia and Taiwan spending between 2 and 3 per cent (OECD, 2004). The trend seems to be that many countries are getting poorer and cutting back on welfare expenditure. This poverty is reflected in Kaseke's (2005) research, which has identified that welfare states (as predicated upon Western social democratic lines) are poorly developed in Africa and this is manifest in the fact that the majority of African nations do not have comprehensive insurance and welfare schemes. In Tanzania, Uganda and Zambia, governments have transferred their provident schemes into social insurance schemes; however, these only cover 20 per cent of the population. The International Labour Organization ILO (2000) noted that only thirteen countries in Africa provide any health insurance schemes, while countries like Cameroon, Ghana, Tanzania and Tunisia have implemented structural adjustment programmes with financial support from the International Monetary Fund (IMF). However, this policy has tightened the criteria and actually increased need and there is no real state- funded social services provision. In South Africa there is a universal national health and social insurance scheme, state-funded pensions, child benefit, some form of state-funded health and education. However, since 1998 the newly elected government has reduced public spending and the welfare budget for 1998–2001 actually declined by 9.5 per cent (Triegaardt, 2004), resulting in cuts in social services spending.

Pawar (2004) notes that most Asian-Pacific countries do not have well developed state-funded social services provision but rely on informal, family and community support networks. He believes a Western welfare model is difficult to replicate and is impractical in Asia-Pacific countries because of cultural differences in attitudes to family solidarity and kinship networks.

He argues that informal family and community welfare support networks would be undermined by any formal social welfare systems and he points to the fact that many Western nations are moving away from this model, opting for more means-tested benefit systems and more private and voluntary organizations involved in social service provision.

Walker and Wong (2004) argue that contemporary social policy notions of 'the welfare state' are based upon Western capitalist, social democratic or neo-liberal models and are ethnocentric. They note that countries like China are neither capitalist nor adopt institutions of social democracy but have for many years since 1945 had a comprehensive state-funded welfare system, which has also contributed to vast reductions in China's poverty levels. This welfare system is only now experiencing strain as a consequence of the Asian economic crisis of 1997–8. In view of the complexity in these countries, Gough and Woods (2004) question whether it is appropriate to talk about 'welfare states' as a global, unified and homogeneous term.

## Social Democratic Perspectives on Welfare

According to Kearns (2001), the discourse of the social democratic perspective underpins common assumptions about the organizations of Western democracy. The social democratic perspective defines the state as 'A set of institutions in which public power is located' (Kearns, 2001, p. 21).

The social democratic perspective attributes the development of the welfare state to three things: the impact of the industrial revolution, the expansion of democracy in Western Europe in the nineteenth and twentieth centuries and the rise of a large industrial European working class. The negative aspects of industrialization were mass urbanization (resulting in overcrowding), poverty, unemployment, disease and appalling work conditions, which according to social democratic theorists required a collective response by the state. At the same time, electoral reforms presented an increasing social challenge from a large industrial working class. Underpinning these developments was the social democratic perspective on rights. Social democrats are committed to the notion of rights and freedom based upon the principle that humans can think and exercise free choice. This also extends to a belief in welfare rights, as social democrats believe that it is only through a democratic state that liberty can be guaranteed to the maximum number of people.

The main criticism of the social democratic state is reflected in the fact that, in most industrial nations, it failed to relieve poverty and had an inefficient welfare system for targeting the poor. Often this system was far too complex, with a variety of administrative agencies, qualification criteria, types of benefit and methods for collecting finance (manifest in complex tax and national insurance contribution systems). Moreover, it lacked any coherent goals and, worse, it created a *dependency culture* by creating a series of disincentives to work. Social democratic perspectives are also criticized for their ethnocentric bias, and this has social work practice implications.

Berman (2006) argues that the modern industrial welfare state is a peculiar Western idea, and many of its problems in alleviating deprivation have more to do with cultural perceptions than with the extent of a nation's industrial or economic development. He cites Alaskan Native Americans and Negev Bedouin Israelis, who are both marginalized from welfare and social services in their respective countries. The main barriers to accessing services are not just their remote geographical locations (isolated from the welfare infrastructures of large towns and cities) but also what Berman calls the 'cultural incompatibility' between providers and recipients (Berman, 2006, p. 97). In other words, many of the customs and lifestyles of both the Negev Israelis and Alaskan Americans do not fit comfortably within the usual service-delivery model of most Western welfare states.

# Neo-liberal Perspectives on Welfare

Neo-liberalism, on the other hand, is predicated on the notion of *methodological individualism*; that is, the idea that there is no such thing as 'society' or 'the state'. These institutions are only real in the sense that they are made up of the activities of a host of individuals engaged in interaction with each other based on a set of legal or contractual obligations (in a methodical way – hence the term 'methodological individualism'). Through these arrangements individuals pursue a set of collective outcomes. Thus, it is not the state, but the free market that is the most important institution in society. Neo-liberals believe that a free market unencumbered by state intervention is the most efficient mechanism for creating wealth. In relation to the market they view labour as a commodity like any other and therefore consider wages to be determined by the laws of supply and demand for labour. Further, they argue that free from state intervention, unemployment will find its natural level and there will be very little involuntary unemployment.

Neo-liberals argue for a form of negative liberty that is that every one should have political rights but not civil or welfare rights. Political rights mean voting rights and freedom from coercion. They reject the social democratic notion of welfare rights in terms of health, employment, education and housing assistance. They assert that to claim that people have an automatic entitlement to such things will lead to the government (in the form of the state) having to decide between competing claims to these rights and competing claims for scarce resources. In terms of the nature of scarce resources in society, neo-liberals adopt an absolute concept of poverty and argue that there is very little poverty in most modern industrial societies. Equally, they argue that the best mechanism for eradicating poverty is the market, by providing employment opportunities so the poor can work their way out of poverty.

According to Lavalette and Pratt (2001), neo-liberal approaches to the market and welfare states have failed to halt the continual drift towards global economic stagnation in the 1990s. In contrast, Clarke and Newman (1997) adopt a different approach by examining the restructuring of welfare states along market lines since the 1980s and the social control functions this served. Under successive New Right governments the control of public spending has led to the creation of new delivery systems for welfare. Using the concept of 'managerial dispersal' they explain how central government's restructuring of welfare states has secured more than just a series of mechanisms to coordinate welfare functions. The extension of state power has been achieved through managerial dispersal. 'Managerial dispersal' refers to the reduction of state intervention in the economy but at the same time its increasing involvement in civil society through the state's commissioning, financing and control of more private and voluntary social service providers (Clarke and Newman, 1997, p. 29). Moreover, dispersal has subjected bureau-professions like social work to forms of power beyond the welfare state in the form of 'citizens-as-consumer', empowered to make choices and demands regarding service standards and performance. At the same time it has increased state control over these professions through intensified central government control secured by tighter fiscal control and an increasing audit evaluation. Using the concept of managerial dispersal, Clarke and Newman identify the ways traditional theories of the state fail to see *how* the extension of the mixed economy of welfare has actually increased the movement of state power into civil society.

# Neo-Marxist Perspectives on Welfare

Neo-Marxism is predicated on the view that the state is not a neutral arbiter of power that works for the benefit of society as a whole. For its followers, neo-Marxists, the state performs a number of functions but its main function is to secure the conditions for the maintenance and expansion of capitalism. The state achieves this in a variety of ways, through the development of a legal framework that protects business interests, and through direct economic activity to support national currency or to protect domestic production from foreign competition. In addition, the state engages in activities to keep capitalism supplied with a steady and healthy labour force by ameliorating the worst aspects of poverty and deprivation faced by the working class during periods of economic slump. Also, by developing social policies both to support and to discipline different groups within society, the state partly legitimates capitalism and partly controls those groups who threaten the economic workings of the system. These contradictory roles at times involve the state in a conflicting relationship with the capitalist class. This is because the state needs to secure conditions for the maintenance of capitalism, and at times this will conflict with the interests of a specific group within that class. Thus, neo-Marxists reject the term 'welfare state' as it implies the idea of a concerned, benevolent, caring socio-economic system. Moreover, they point out that the development of the welfare state has not reduced class inequalities. These are exacerbated during times of economic recession and crisis because the welfare state becomes a major economic contradiction for capitalism (due to its financial cost) and a source of political tension and conflict.

In understanding the operations of the welfare state in the twenty-first century it is useful to consider Lavalette and Ferguson's (1999) neo-Marxist analysis, which seeks to explain the functions of the state by accounting for the contradictions between human agency and structural constraints in the formation of social policy. Often the mismatch between welfare objectives and outcomes can be examined in terms of the contradictory and compet-ing influences on social policy, which all vie for predominance. Social policy is a contradictory, complex and fragmentary process under capital-ism, which encapsulates the structural needs of capitalism, the political and human agency of various classes and social movements for reform, and the need to maintain legitimacy and the social cohesion of society. Seen from Lavalette and Ferguson's perspective, the incongruity between social policy's objectives and its outcomes will depend upon the contradictions between the economic and socio-political spheres of society, the demands of service users, and the power and agency they can mobilize to assert those demands.

Williams (1995) argues that this neo-Marxist analysis contains several weaknesses. Neo-Marxist models of welfare states ignore the interconnec-tions of race, class and gender, in the social regulation of labour. For exam-ple, the dynamics of gender relations are subsumed under notions of 'family'. Thus, rather than attributing any changes in the family to increas-ing female agency, neo-Marxists simply identify such changes as emerging from the family unit itself. In addition, in examining questions of decom-modification (the degree to which welfare services are free from market pres-sures and thus being provided free to all (Giddens, 2000, p. 686)), they ignore the contribution of women in the provision of those services. For example, while decommodification may have enhanced male workers' capacity to enter the labour market on their own terms, this capacity is enhanced only by the unpaid domestic labour performed by women as housewives and carers. Furthermore, neo-Marxist analysis fails to include the patriarchal, gendered and racialized nature of social insurance schemes in many Western welfare states or in welfare provision in general. This analysis ignores the fact that welfare state provision is bolstered by the unpaid labour of female and black workers in the caring services they provide to families and by their role in welfare states in the poorer or lower-waged ranks of the health and social services. This issue is made invisible by neo-Marxist analysis, which tends to generalize the white–male experience. Consequently, this veers towards a-historical, non-specific, structurally determined analysis, where no sense of agency is given to gender or class.

Williams (1995; 2003) also points out how neo-Marxists totally ignore the degree of agency ordinary people have exercised against pressures from the welfare state. She notes that the restructuring of global welfare states was not only a response to the crises in capitalism, but also a reflection of the challenges to and accommodations made to the balance of power in society around issues of ethnicity, class and gender. Therefore, notwithstanding the merits of neo-Marxist analysis, a key feature of such an account of welfare states is the failure to locate class antagonisms in the wider international context.

# Fordist Perspectives on Welfare

Fordism is a form of capitalist accumulation and is believed by sociologists such as Jessop (1990) to have increased its dominance over world economies form the end of the nineteenth century to the end of the 1970s. It was characterized by a highly efficient mode of industrialization both at national and international level and was predicated on Henry Ford's model of factory organization that he developed in his plants in Detroit between 1880 and 1916 (Cohen and Kennedy, 2000).

The golden age of Fordism's dominance within global economies appeared to occur from the end of the Second World War to the 1970s. Very broadly this was a period of unprecedented and sustained economic growth and prosperity based on the dominance of mass production and consumption, a large semi-skilled industrialized workforce, and labour relations predicated on industrial bargaining over wages. This by implication necessitated an increased role for large-scale capital and organized labour, while, on an international front, Fordism was based upon a free market economy and stable exchange rates.

However, by the 1970's the economic growth that the Fordist society was built upon was slowing down, and by the mid-1970s, global recession had started to occur. The ensuing economic crisis was exacerbated by the oil crisis in 1973–4, and the recession that followed undermined the collective bargaining relationship between the working and capitalist classes that had underpinned Fordism. Fordism was also jeopardized by the growth of international competition from rising economic powers like Japan, which pursued a policy of mass exportation of mass-produced consumer goods, and by the growth of Japanese transnational corporations (TNCs) like SONY, Mitsubishi, Honda and Fuji, who established plants in Europe and North America.

Global capitalism's response to the crisis of Fordism was the restructuring of the welfare states by New Right or neo-conservative governments around the globe (Esping-Anderson, 1996) in order to cut public expenditure to ensure conditions for capital accumulation and to increase the flexibility of labour. This flexibility of labour is characterized by global job insecurity due to technological change and economic pressures. Global capitalist production has increased competition between firms, particularly in the fields of clothing, shoe and electronics manufacturing, as well as increasing global poverty and unemployment as robots have replaced human labour in many industries (Cohen and Kennedy, 2000).

Pierson (1991), Parton (1996) and Howe (1996) all identify what is termed the 'hollowing out' of welfare states as a response to the crisis of Fordism and this has had an impact on social work. This 'hollowing out' takes the form of cutbacks in public expenditure, leading to the scaling down of social services provided by the public sector and increased private and voluntary agency provision of services. In addition, free market principles have been introduced in the public services sector as well as flexible labour and organization patterns, the growth of managerialism and the shift from the 'client' to the 'service user' or 'consumer' of services.

Clarke (1996) criticizes the Fordist analysis on three grounds. First he questions whether the concepts of mass production and consumption can be applied so easily, and so simplistically transferred from the industrial and manufacturing sectors of the economy to welfare and public sectors. Secondly, it is debatable whether any real empirical evidence exists for Fordist society. Thirdly, there is controversy as to whether Fordism was such a global phenomenon as Fordists claim, even in heavily industrialized countries in Western Europe, North American and Japan. He argues that the diversity in the global economies is often ignored or glossed over by Fordists in their attempts to identify it as an international form of capitalism:

> Esping-Anderson's work on different welfare regimes identifies different varieties of expanded state (social democratic and residual) all of which obtained in countries which have been assumed to operate Fordist regimes. The assumed consequence of Fordism as a systematic structure of production, consumption and state form downgrades questions of political process and the diversity of their outcomes in favour of economic and technical determinism.   (Clarke, 1996, p. 39)

# Feminist Perspectives on Welfare

Hallett (1995) identifies the key differences between the views of liberal, Marxist and radical feminism on welfare states. Liberal feminists are concerned with equal rights and access to education and employment. They believe reforms are possible within the welfare state, whereas Marxist feminists attribute oppression to structural inequalities and social relations either of capitalism or of patriarchy, which are expressed through the relationships of welfare. Marxists differ in the extent they attribute oppression to ideology or material conditions however, central to all Marxist-feminist perspectives is an analysis of the role of capitalism and the welfare state in particular in the reproduction of gender inequalities. These inequalities are manifest in the ways welfare states exploit the unpaid domestic labour of women and their role as carers of dependent children, or sick and/or older relatives, and in doing so abdicate responsibility for proper state-funded welfare provision in these areas (Abbott and Wallace, 1997).

In her analysis of this oppression by the state, Williams (1995; 2003) incorporates various feminist perspectives. The examples she cites of different feminisms include liberal and libertine feminism. The weakness of libertine or right-wing feminist approaches, she argues, is that they ignore structural inequalities by stating that increased competition in a free market rather than reforms within the welfare state is the best way to end women's oppression. Williams points to the 'class blind' individualism of this approach. Similarly, liberal feminism seeks to obtain women's equality by working for reforms through the system, via legislation on pay, employment and education. This idea is predicated on the social democratic belief in the state as a neutral arbiter and guarantor of individual freedoms. However, it also underemphasizes structural constraints limiting women's equality. In addition, difference feminism in the form of Ramazanoglu (1989), and Muslim feminists such as Hasso (2005), adopt a different approach, which highlights the weakness of white Western feminisms' ethnocetricism, which is reflected in the failure to recognize the different experiences of black, Asian and non-white groups of women and thus renders their experiences invisible. Equally, Eastern and Muslim feminists criticize what they see as the racism of Western feminism and this will be discussed further in the section on 'Anti-racist Perspectives on Welfare'.

# Anti-racist Perspectives on Welfare

These perspectives identify the ways the welfare state reflects the dynamic relations between imperialism, capitalism and patriarchy and argues that, as a result, the welfare state is an extension of those dynamics, and part of the racism of society through the way it operates via reproducing racial divisions and through the second-class welfare provision it offers black and non-white groups in society as well as through the maintenance of immigration controls. For example, Williams (1995) combines a feminist and anti-racist perspective to demonstrate the interconnections between racism, sexism and classism in the operations of the UK welfare state. She criticizes traditional social policy analysis for the way it fails to acknowledge the marginalization of black and Irish citizens by the welfare state during the twentieth century. These policies were legitimized through particular social constructions of 'family', 'nation' and 'welfare', which were constructed around notions of 'family' predicated on a white, heterosexual family, while the idea of 'nation' was based on British values and British culture (Williams, 1995, p. 7).

Williams (1995; 2003) maintains that traditional social policy analysis fails to examine the way that black people have been marginalized from UK welfare. Moreover, it tends to categorize the problem not as one of racism but as one of race relations, and hence solutions are either to change the prejudices of white people (through various Race Relations Acts) or to change the cultures of black people through assimilationist or integrationist policies. However, she provides a host of empirical evidence in educational, welfare and employment policies, which demonstrate that the emphasis was on assimilationist rather than integrationist principles. This problem was exacerbated because the traditional focus of social policy from 1945 onwards was on class inequalities and it was only in the 1970s that feminism and anti-racist critiques began to develop and challenge this approach.

Similarly, a number of Middle Eastern and African feminist economists and sociologists, who include Minh-Ha (1989) and Hasso (2005), criticize what they regard as Western feminist and ethnocentric approaches to social policy and women's issues in Middle Eastern, African and Muslim countries. They argue that many of these feminist prespectives, in relation to the success of Middle Eastern, African and Muslim women (in particular) over social welfare or employment issues, have adopted two methods: either they have homogenized the female populations of Muslim women in 'Third World' countries as the hapless victims of Islam (thus lacking agency and capacity for political mobilization) – a very paternalistic approach; or they have adopted a stance of orientalism within feminist writing. The paternalistic and ethnocentric nature of this kind of stance is summed up succinctly by Bahramitash (2007):

> Orientalist feminism has two important characteristics: first it assumes a binary relationship between the West and the Orient with respect to the situation of women. The progressive West is the best place for women, in direct contrast to the backward and uncivilized Muslim world which has the worst conditions for women.   (Bahramitash, 2007, p. 87)

In reality this negates the agency of Muslim women and social workers in developing political strategies to mobilize political activity and to generate welfare services in a number of Muslim countries. For example, Farman Farmaian set up social work in Iran in 1958 and developed a host of community programmes working in poor areas, providing counselling on family planning and literacy. The School of Social Work also established the Family Planning Association, introducing family planning in Iran (Healy, 2001). However, Farmaian was asked by the Iranian authorities to leave the country during the revolution in 1979. Now Iranian social work takes the form of the activities of non-governmental organizations (NGOs) mainly run by Iranian women. There are more than 60 NGOs in Iran dealing with minority issues, offering women's and children's education, addressing child abuse and setting up 40 pre-school centres, and in 1997 with UNHCR funding, various programmes were set up to create child care centres. In addition, many Iranian social workers are taking an international and practice developmental lead in designing and running community programmes for the victims of Iran's recent earthquake disaster in Bam in 2003, by identifying the practice needs of social workers in such emergency situations and developing specialist training (Aghabakhshi and Gregor, 2007; Javadian, 2007).

# Regime Theories of Welfare

Esping-Anderson (1996) has sought to address some of the problems of ethnocentric approaches to welfare state analysis by developing a regime theory and has identified three distinct kinds of welfare states. Countries such as Norway, Sweden and Denmark have sought to expand employment in the welfare sector and these are what he terms 'social democratic' because they are characterized by the principles of universalism and attempts at decommodification of social rights (Hill, 2006, p. 28). In countries such as the US, Canada, UK, Australia and New Zealand, successive New Right or neo-conservative governments have opted for a more neo-liberal, free market approach, by deregulating wages and labour markets, and by cutting back on welfare state provision and developing means-tested systems of benefits. The third regime of welfare he refers to as 'conservative' in the sense of state led development of social policy, and of countries that were dominated neither by neo-liberal ideologies nor by social democratic movements. These have included Japan, Finland, Italy, Germany, France, Austria, Belgium and the Netherlands. In Germany, France and Italy, governments have sought to reduce welfare employment, whilst at the same time maintaining existing social security standards. In contrast, the emerging welfare states in Latin America and East and Central Europe have implemented private provision from the outset (Esping-Anderson, 1996).

This model has been criticized by Western and Eastern sociologists and economists alike for a variety of reasons. Castles and Miller (2003) argue that it assumes a causal link between social democracy and a universal welfare system, while communist countries like China and Cuba, have demonstrated that it is possible to have universal welfare provision without social democracy or capitalism. They also point out that the correlation between social democracy and welfare in Esping- Anderson's work causes him to misrepresent the type of welfare regimes in Australia and New Zealand. Castles and Mitchell classify these countries as belonging to a fourth regime called 'welfare capitalism' in that it was not the impetus given by the Left or left- parties in Australia and New Zealand that led to the funding of universal welfare provision, but rather, tax transfers from the more affluent middle and working classes. Secondly, this theory does not account for anomalies like China or Cuba (who are neither capitalist nor social democracies) and thirdly, the limitation of regime theory is that (like Fordism) it tends to provide a high level of generalization by combining a diverse range of countries in a necessarily limiting set of regime types.

## Muslim Perspectives on Welfare

Muslim sociologists and economists, who include Anjum (2006), Choudhury (1999) and Aliyev (2007), argue for Islamic Political Economy (IPE) in creating more holistic welfare provision in Muslim countries. In a similar way to the Marxist dialectic, IPE sees human interaction in a totality but with a spiritual dimension. It identifies the fact that Islamic teaching is not only a religion but a whole belief system that incorporates the values of humanitarianism, concern for the welfare of others, and universal solidarity, and these values Muslims seek to integrate as a code of conduct in religious, economic and social behaviour, in order to create equal opportunity for all society's citizens. This is not to suggest that Muslim societies do not have a stratification system with wealthy and poor classes. However, wealth is seen as a personal responsibility (to be used for the benefit of society as a whole and for eradicating poverty) as much as being a source of personal gain or success. Choudhury (1999), for example, uses IPE to argue against both neo-liberal Western capitalism and European Marxism. He criticizes Western capitalism for the damaging effects of its principle of self-reliance, and European Marxism for its lack of spiritual dimension in economic affairs. Unlike capitalism, IPE is not based upon the exploitation of labour power, and unlike socialism, it has a spiritual base, which is shared by everyone in society, and thus it does not rely on the socio-economic and political impetus of just Communist Party members. Such a political economy is therefore more holistic as it is predicated on the well being of all society's members and it embodies Islam's concern with equal resource allocation. Using this approach, Anjum (2006) argues that this can lead to the efficient management of Muslim nation-state economies and welfare systems. He cites the failures of globalization that have increased global poverty and unemployment, and escalated global conflicts between nation states. He argues that this form of globalization is merely the contemporary form of Western capitalism and economic and political colonial expansion. To support this argument he provides empirical evidence by citing the activities of intergovernmental organizations such as the EU, the World Trade Organization (WTO) and the North American Free Trade Agreement (NAFTA). The activities of these institutions account for two-thirds of the global market.

Like Choudhury, Anjum maintains that IPE has the potential to create universal and comprehensive welfare systems and he suggests these could be achieved in countries like Pakistan and Malaysia (two countries that have been impoverished by globalization) by dispensing with what he sees as the Western emphasis on self-reliance, which is selfish and characterizes neo-liberalism. He points to the fact that IPE is based upon the values of human universalism, equality, respect based upon the principle of self-help, but combined with universal cooperation in pursuit of human development. In this way IPE can achieve:

> progressive humanitarian policies of realizing human development, economic growth, need fulfilment, full employment . . .   (Anjum, 2006, p. 174)

He highlights the successes of the Islamic revolution in Iran. This success in welfare provision is supported by OECD figures that have identified the benefits of state-funded universal welfare reforms, which have resulted in improved literacy rates, a rapid decline in poverty and infant mortality rates, and improved employment rights and protection as well as increased civil liberties. Similarly, Aliyev (2007) argues, IPE could be used in the Muslim states of the CIS as they make the transition from communism, and to address the poverty, unemployment and deprivation that has occurred as a consequence of this transition. He points out that Islam is not simply a religion but is also an holistic belief system embodying a specific spiritual, socio-political, cultural, moral and behavioural code. This underpins not only religious behaviour but economic and political behaviour as well, as it seeks to ensure all human behaviour is conducted according to ethical premises.

Thus, in IPE those who lose out from market reforms (i.e. the poor) must (Anjum argues) have more state intervention to ameliorate their poverty and deprivation. He believes that adopting IPE can help transform the welfare system of his native Azerbaijan and reduce poverty there. Other

Muslims (especially Muslim feminists), however, argue that IPE has not yet been successful in creating equality of opportunity and they cite the fact that the Iranian revolution has not improved the lot of the poor. Bahkramitash (2007) points out that under President Khatami in the 1990s welfare rights (particularly the employment rights of women) took a retrograde step. As oil prices plummeted in the 1990s and Iran had to rely on foreign loans from the World Bank it was forced (as a condition of the loans) to adopt neo-liberal economic policies which resulted in a reduction in subsidies on fuel, food, shelter, while many other social programmes saw their funding cut back. Then in 2005 President Ahmadinejad was elected, and attempts are now being introduced to produce a more universal welfare system on Islamic lines, however this has had limited impact because President Ahmadinejad does not wish to alienate the business and professional middle classes by increasing taxes to fund the welfare budget. At the same time women's civil and employment rights have been curtailed by this more conservative government (Bahkramitash, 2007, p. 89). In addition one of the failures of IPE is that it tends to underestimate the global context of neo-liberal capitalism, which countries like Iran have to operate in and the external pressures of trying to implement IPE while competing in the global capitalist export market.

# Globalization and Welfare States

Mishra (1999) argues the impact of globalization has implications for social democratic ideas on welfare states. This is because the logic inherent in globalization conflicts with the logic of the national community and democratic politics. Social policy emerges as a major issue of contention between global capitalism and the democratic nation state. The long-term effects of these trends are an increase in global unemployment and the 'hollowing out' of welfare state systems.

In contrast, Kleinmann (2002) suggests that, with regard to EU social policy, in many areas nation states still have considerable power to determine their own social and welfare policies free from the effects of globalization. He cites a host of examples to show how nation states have been able to set the agenda when it has come to social policy, by adopting the principle of subsidiarity (which gives primacy to nation states' policy over EU policy) and through the ability of various nation states to opt out of EU agreements. For example, the UK has done this over elements of the social charter. Another example of nation state power compared to EU power was reflected in the failure of the EU to secure monetary union in the form of single currency by 1999.

The ways different nation states organize their welfare provision has social work practice implications, but this is a complex and contradictory process even within similar welfare regimes and the global dominance of neo-liberal approaches to welfare. Take, for instance, the US and Japan. Both countries, I would argue, could be described as adopting neo-liberal or conservative approaches to welfare by giving primacy to the market and fostering the development of private and voluntary organizations in the provision of welfare. However, as Segal (2004) notes, the ways these two countries have developed their children's services are very different. Whereas the US has state-funded and regulated social services departments, which cover home-based care, fostering and adopting, residential care and child protection investigation services, much of the actual administration and provision of services is in the hands of private organizations. In contrast, Japan (owing to concerns about falling birth rates) has launched a massive state-funded child development and welfare programme with vast state subsidies going into public (as opposed to private and voluntary) children's services.

Different cultural as well as socio-economic contexts have determined the organization of welfare. In Asian-Pacific countries like Singapore, Thailand and Taiwan the lack of state expenditure in welfare has led to social workers taking a more direct and networking role in what are termed 'communities' informal care and welfare systems' (CICWS). Pawar (2004) notes that welfare states (along Western social democratic lines) are non-existent in most Asian-Pacific countries, and in many respects at variance with the Eastern cultural values of family and community solidarity. However, due to the impact of global capitalism (in the form of neo-liberalism) on Asian-Pacific countries, particularly with respect to employment patterns, and urbanization, many of these community and family networks are breaking down, exacerbating welfare needs in local communities. His research has sought to develop social work intervention strategies with social workers taking a lead role in helping clients/service users re-kindle these community networks in order to develop informal systems of welfare. He and his colleague have developed a series of professional training packs for professionals, government and non-governmental organizations to develop CICSW approaches in Asian-Pacific countries in terms of community development (Pawar, 2004, p. 447).

Sociologists and social work academics such as Pawar (2004) and Vogel (2006), amongst others, highlight the potential of these forms of welfare and social services around the world. For example, Vogel (2006) explores the economic dimensions of charitable donations made by various US institutions such as USAID, the Rockefeller Institution, or the Carnegie Trust, and argues that global donations for humanitarian charities and NGOs totalled 6.2 million dollars in 2004 and this is helping projects contributing to the extension of civil society. In Nigeria and New Zealand, Lucas (2001) and

Walker (2007) identify the different degrees of success social work advocacy has had in community development and in NGO projects. Lucas (2001) shows how NGOs like the Country Women Association of Nigeria have been instrumental in promoting the labour and civil rights of rural Nigerian women, and social workers have been facilitating women's leadership in community development projects. This has been able to promote their increased economic participation and to develop social policy initiatives involving rural women. In New Zealand there has been a collaboration of the Ngai Tahu Maori Law Centre (NTMLC) and the Dunedin Community Law Centre (DCLC) combining and working with local Maori communities to develop their own self-run social services.

In non-capitalist countries like China, the impact of global neo-liberalism has compelled the government to embrace free market principles in the running of the economy and this was precipitated by the Asian economic crisis of 1997–8. This highlighted the problems facing China's older population and the lack of welfare provision due to deregulation policies. In 1995 the population aged over 65 was 6.7per cent, which is 81 million people (Leung and Wong, 2002, p. 205). In relation to those Chinese citizens over 80 years of age, some 86.2 per cent have no pension provision or state income and rely on children for economic support (State Statistics Bureau, 1995, p. 66). Generally in China, public welfare services for older people, apart from institutional care, are limited. There is a lack of day care centres, home help provision and nursing homes. Public expenditure is minimal and as a result, revenue comes from factories, businesses, hotels and fee-charging public and welfare services and lottery funding. Thus, in the bigger and more affluent cities the services for older people are much better. In some areas they rely on charities or revenue from public donations, or profits from welfare organizations (Wong, 2004, p. 211).

Countries of the former Soviet Union also have to contend with the problems of global neo-liberalism in the wake of the demise of communism. In Russia, the transition to capitalism has meant that comprehensive welfare provision has been eradicated and families have to rely on their own networks and resources. Ironically, the increasing public recognition of social problems such as alcoholism, poverty (running at 39 per cent of the population: Tregoubova, 2000), unemployment, a 'brain drain' (for better salaries in the West), domestic violence and increasing crime rates, have all stimulated the growth of social work as a profession and the inception of the first training programme in 1991. Despite the developments in the Russian social work curriculum and the practice innovations being developed by many Russian social work academics, the welfare state it operates within is 'cash strapped' (Templeman, 2004), and owing to the lack of welfare funding there is insufficient money for social work services, education and training, and many Russian social workers lack a formal social work qualification.

# Summary of the Main Points

- The diversity of welfare regimes around the world means it is no longer plausible to talk about 'the welfare state' but instead it is necessary to talk about 'welfare regimes'.

- Different sociological perspectives of the welfare state inform critical reflexive practice by highlighting the socio-economic, political and ideological factors affecting the delivery of social work services.

- The main sociological perspectives on welfare states inform the development of anti-oppressive practice.

- The controversies between these competing perspectives highlight

  (a) the discursive nature of social policy analysis;
  (b) the racist, sexist and ethnocentric bias of traditional perspectives, which have been highlighted as being culturally inappropriate for implementation in a variety of Eastern countries.

- The global impact of contemporary neo-liberal capitalism is forcing nation states to radically reorganize welfare provision, leading to cutbacks in social services.

- Islamic Political Economy criticizes Western neo-liberalism, in particular its failure to locate poverty in the structural inequalities produced by capitalism and for the ways, under the guise of globalization, it has reinforced Western imperialism and colonial expansion.

# Conclusion

The main emphasis in this chapter has been to reinforce the development of critical reflexive practice skills by examining competing sociological perspectives on welfare states and considering them for their implications for social work practice. This required examination of the interconnected strands of socio-economic, political, ideological and cultural influences that affect the organization of welfare. This in turn helped unmask the dangers of traditional approaches to social policy, which highlight the functional nature of social policy and welfare provision. These focus on description at the expense of prompting critical reflection on social policy's discursive, politicized and oppressive dimensions. In doing so it identified the practical utility of sociology to social work. First, it provided theories which identified the contradictory nature of the operations of states and welfare regimes. Secondly, it explored perspectives which examine the dialectics in the structure and agency relationship. Thirdly, it incorporated frameworks to account for the interconnections between global nation states in terms of trade and the production of global inequality, poverty and unemployment. The focus has therefore been at the level of grand theory, looking at national and international welfare regimes for the impact on social work as a whole. This approach will be continued in Chapter 3, which examines social work potential for advocacy within the context of poverty, social exclusion and citizenship.

## Case Study

Reza Hassan and his friend and colleague Gassan Rouhifar are two social workers who live and work in the city of Al-Hillan in the Babil province, Iraq. The two are discussing Reza's new job working for a NGO project funded by the Ministry of Social Affairs. Reza is very excited about the project. The project's brief is very large and diverse. It includes helping the local medical services provide cholera vaccinations (following the recent outbreak) to the local residents, the coordination and development of services to facilitate drug rehabilitation support services, food centres, housing assistance, services for older people and their carers, literacy clubs and support to street children, orphans, and people with mental health problems. There is also the remit to provide therapeutic services to those residents traumatized by recent violence between coalition forces and Iraqi groups. In contrast, Gassan is not so optimistic that the project will be able to provide the right kinds of social services for the local community as it is led by foreign NGO officers (who have little understanding of the local community culture and the problems it faces). Also, Gassan believes the only way to get the right social services is for the government to overhaul the country's economic infrastructure so Iraqis can develop their own health and welfare services and be more autonomous.

Sociological perspectives can provide a critical analysis of both social workers' perspectives on NGOs. Reza might point out that in the last year there have been 140 similar NGO projects developed by Iraqi social workers, funded by the Iraqi Ministry of Affairs and UNICEF and developed by Iraqi social workers using Freire's (1998) sociological model of Marxist praxis on consciousness raising to develop projects with the involvement and leadership of local community members. He might also cite the fact that success in this approach comes from developing a strengths model of local community resilience, skills, resources and expertise that the project can tap into (Roff, 2004). He could identify the range of skills and roles social workers offer within NGOs, which include providing a variety of services, such as relief and development projects, human rights and advocacy for peace, development work, health education, children's education, adult literacy and numeracy, international exchange networks for social workers, welfare programmes such as HIV/AIDS counselling, social policy advice and the development of child protection services, and food assistance as well as work in domestic welfare agencies.

In contrast, Gassan might argue that Reza's approach is very individualized an optimistic about the power of human agency to generate change. He adopts a sociological structural perspective in his critique of local arrangements and the failure of the government and coalition forces to put sufficient resources into restructuring the health

## Case Study (*cont'd*)

and welfare infrastructure. Also, his reference to 'foreigners' running the project has echoes of popular criticisms of many NGOs for their Western ethnocentric bias and the way they tend to develop services that are inappropriate for non-Western contexts. In addition he may cite the research of Islamic Political Economy (IPE), which argues that both neo-liberal capitalism and European Marxism are culturally inappropriate in developing the health and welfare services of Muslim countries. Neo-liberalism emphasizes self-reliance and self-help, which is at variance with Muslim cultural and spiritual values of mutual support and cooperation, and using prosperity for society as a whole. In addition, as far as IPE is concerned, European Marxism lacks a spiritual dimension altogether and thus would have difficulty in harnessing the communitarian and humanitarian resources of the Iraqi people.

# Further Reading

Aliyev, F. B. (2007) 'Problems of Interaction between the State and Economy under the Post-communist Transition: the Perspective of Islamic Political Economy', *Humanomics*, vol. 23 (2), pp. 73–82.
This article provides a very good critical appraisal of neo-liberal and neo-Marxist perspectives on welfare, and identifies their Western ethnocentric bias. In addition, it provides a useful summary of the basic tenets of IPE.

Lavalette, M. and Pratt, A. (eds) (2001) *Social Policy: A Conceptual and Theoretical Introduction* (London: Sage).
A particular strength of this book is the way it identifies and simplifies the contradictory operations of welfare states. This makes it a very accessible read for students new to sociology and social policy.

Williams, F. (1995) *Social Policy: A Critical Introduction*, 2nd edn (Cambridge: Polity).
In this, Williams provides a very articulate critique of both neo-Marxist and traditional social policy approaches to welfare. She also locates the importance of interconnections between ethnicity, gender and class in the operations of the state. The focus on assimilationist policies is particularly good for identifying which groups come to be marginalized with welfare and social services provision.

# 3
# Poverty, Social Exclusion and Citizenship

## Introduction

Poverty, social exclusion and citizenship are all connected to an understanding of social policy and welfare. In addition, they are often linked in *specific* ways in social policy initiatives and welfare discourses. The ways this is done are important because they have implications for the quality of life clients/service users experience and the quality of services they receive. Moreover, access to citizenship rights affects the resources and capacities of social workers to promote the interests of service users. One of the key features in understanding professional social work's relationship to poverty is to consider one of the recurring themes in the poverty discourses over the past 150 years. Whether these discourses embody neo-liberal or social democratic thinking as employed by governments in the latter half of the twentieth century, such discourses have entailed the notion that those defined as poor are in part to blame for their situation. Such discourses attribute the causes of poverty to 'flaws' of character, rather like the Victorian notion of the demoralized poor. Consequently, such an approach has tended to ignore structural inequalities that have an impact upon the poor. The ideas behind such a view have been subtle and covert, and at other times extremely overt and pathologizing. These ideas have, in turn, shaped social workers' thinking about poor clients/service users and have had implications for the development of empowering practice. We will examine the development of such discourses later in the chapter. However, first it is necessary to consider why the issue of poverty is so important to social work practice.

> ## Key Words
>
> poverty, social exclusion, citizenship

# Pathologizing Poverty

Poverty is a central feature of social work practice because it affects most of the people social workers engage with. Lavalette and Ferguson (1999) point out that poverty is seldom addressed on the social work curriculum; however, in practice, it is strongly associated with the absence of power, autonomy and social and political influence (Jones and Novak, 1999). Poverty is not simply an economic phenomenon but entails important psychological dimensions affecting a person's sense of self-esteem. A plethora of research over the past ten years has identified a host of factors that demonstrates the ways poverty has a negative impact upon clients/service users. The OECD (2004) estimate that 1.2 billion people around the globe live on less than 2 US dollars per day. Other research has found that the poorest neighbourhoods tend to be the most susceptible to crime, and to a lack of facilities and services, and tend to be cut off from the labour market (SEU, 2002; Evans, 2005). According to Wilkinson (1996), being poor means that you are likely to have a shorter life expectancy, your children are at greater risk of serious illness or accidents, you are more likely to be the victim of coronary heart disease or cancer and you are more likely to experience the more demeaning (and lowest paid) forms of employment, if you are employed at all. In addition, you are likely to be exposed to the most stigmatizing depictions of your life and character.

The social work value base, which was critically evaluated in Chapter 1, requires social workers to take action to counter all forms of inequality including poverty, and indeed many welfare states around the globe were founded on the ideal of eradicating the worst excesses of poverty and deprivation. However, the issue of poverty has proved to be an extremely difficult one for governments to address. One of the main reasons for this is not simply conflicts within social policy debates on the best ways to tackle poverty, but also because any definition of poverty and the extent to which it exists, is such a contentious issue.

Saraga (1998) makes an important point about the competing theories of poverty. Whether sociologists adopt an absolute definition of poverty (taking it to mean an absolute lack of resources for subsistence) or a relative definition of poverty (that is, measured as relative to the average living standards of a particular society), this still leaves the problem of *how* to interpret the data. She suggests, therefore, that a social constructivist approach would be useful to help 'un-pack' competing theories of poverty. Of those who adopt an absolute definition of poverty (Murray, 1994: Saunders, 1993) there are those who see poverty as either natural or inevitable. This idea is based on the argument that some people are born more talented or work harder and will naturally succeed. This in turn creates inequalities, which is why some people are poor. Others see poverty as a product of biology (Bosanquet, 1902; Hill, 1893) in the sense that some people have innate character 'flaws' in that they are lazy or shiftless, or inadequately socialized into self-reliance, and these characteristics make them more predisposed to poverty. In contrast, there are those who subscribe to a relative definition of poverty (Townsend, 1997; Byrne, 2002) and argue that poverty is caused by the interplay of economic and socio-political factors, which results in low incomes or cuts in public expenditure.

One of the useful aspects of Saraga's (1998) social constructivist approach is the way it can be used to critically evaluate what she terms 'common sense' views on poverty such as 'nobody needs to be poor'. She identifies the implicit assumptions this comment makes about 'society' (full of opportunities) and behaviour (people make bad choices). She notes the implicit value-judgement in the statement 'poor people make bad choices' and then, through the process of 'othering' (unlike us non-poor who make good choices), a judgement is made that poor people should not be helped because they make bad choices. Behind these discourses she also identifies the social processes through which they secure power over poor people:

> Discourses in this sense are also about relations of power. They organise positions and places in a field of power so in relation to poverty, they empower . . . state agencies to monitor, assess or intervene in the lives of poor people. They empower some agencies (both state and voluntary agencies) to evaluate 'worth' or 'desert' of some people.    (Saraga, 1998, p. 36)

This notion of evaluating 'worth' or whether a person deserves a service has continuities with the poverty discourses in the nineteenth century. Lewis (1998) has identified the continuities in the UK between nineteenth-century Victorian philanthropy and New Right academics and politicians in the 1990s. These continuities are reflected in the modern reassertion that the poor are largely to blame for their situation. Moreover, within these statements there is a strong moral tone. This relates to the separation of those who con the system (paupers) and the deserving poor who have a legitimate right to be helped. This is at variance with the humanitarian definition of poverty adopted by the UN.

The UNESCO definition of poverty (1995) refers to the absence or 'severe deprivation' of life's necessities such as unpolluted drinking water, adequate sanitation, shelter, an adequate standard of health, and access to education and information. In addition, it stresses that poverty is not just the absence of income. This definition extends the notion of poverty to non-material concepts such as access to decision-making, and links to the concept of social exclusion.

# Criticism of the 'Absolute Poverty' Model

The 'absolute poverty' model has been criticized for its assumption that there is a minimum standard of 'necessities', which is common to all societies irrespective of culture or lifestyle. Needs for drinking water and nutritional needs vary from society to society, depending upon things like lifestyle, occupation, geographical location and climate. In terms of cultural necessities such as 'adequate education', this will also vary depending on the economic mode of society, i.e. whether it is agricultural or IT based. Also, the problem with concepts like cultural necessities is that they tend to reflect the culture and bias of the assessor.

Poverty affects people in a myriad different ways and there are differences in terms of gender, ethnicity and disability. Around the world there are 1.2 billion people who live on less than 2 US dollars per day. These are found largely concentrated in sub-Saharan Africa, and South and East Asia, while women tend to outnumber men in cases of global poverty. Sinclair (2003) suggests that there are a number of social factors that account for gender differences in poverty rates. First, women are more likely than men to be lone parents. Secondly, women tend to out-live men on average. Thirdly, the majority of single pensioners are women. Fourthly, women are more likely than men to be unpaid carers; and fifthly, female workers on average still only earn 88 per cent of their male counterparts' wages around the globe (Hill, 2006).

In addition, people with disabilities are also likely to experience poverty. Having a disability can increase the chances of being poor due to the increased costs of transport, the cost of housing adaptations or the cost of paying for assistance. Algunick et al. (2002) found that in the UK 46 per cent of people with a disability were living in poverty in 1996–7, when figures were adjusted to take account of these additional costs.

Global poverty increased in the 1990s with the end of the Cold War. Also, with the demise of the Soviet Union, a number of African nations with communist regimes such as Angola, Mozambique and Ethiopia, saw a loss of economic support. This occurred at the same time as they experienced a withdrawal of Western investment to the more established markets in Asia and some of the new Eastern European republics. Paradoxically, many of the new countries of the former Soviet Union such as Azerbaijan and the Ukraine saw poverty levels increase with high levels of unemployment, falling wages and increase in part-time or casualised work (Anjum, 2006; Hill, 2006).

Kempson's (1996) research examined the negative effects of poverty, which included poor diet, poor health, and social exclusion, financial problems leading to marital conflict, domestic violence and family breakdown. Of particular concern in the research was the ways poverty was linked to poor health.

The research cited examples of older people with severe arthritis cutting down on heating (even in the coldest conditions) to save money on fuel bills. The study also found that being poor meant that people were more prone to living in poor housing or being homeless, and having debt problems.

# The Redistribution of Poverty

There is a host of global research on urban poverty in Latin America (Gilbert and Gugler, 1992), in the US (Massey and Denton, 1993), on the urban poverty amongst indigenous Australian's (Swain and Cameron, 2007) and in sub-Saharan Africa and South and East Asia (Giddens, 2001; Noyoo, 2000). The globalization of free markets together with increased diaspora has exposed the vulnerability of rural workers and small farm producers around the world who cannot compete with giant agricultural corporations and supermarket chains. For example, small farm producers of bananas in the Caribbean have been unable to compete with these companies and to meet the demands by supermarkets in rich countries for a more standardized banana product at lower prices. Over the past twenty years, global free markets have also had an impact upon the older industrialization of Western economies. Between 1974 and 1983 approximately eight million relatively highly paid manufacturing jobs, representing a crucial volume of purchasing power, disappeared. The job losses occurred mainly in Europe, with Britain and Belgium bearing the brunt. By 1985 well over two-thirds of the manufacturing labour force had migrated to the service industries while their wages failed to rise, in real terms, for more than twenty years (Cohen and Kennedy, 2007). The downsizing of many firms and industries together with a trend towards flexible specialization and increasing temporary and part-time labour went some way towards deindustrialization.

With the onset of global capitalism and mass industrialization many poorer countries are constituted by rural communities that cannot provide self-sufficiency for their population. As a result, many rural poor flock to the cities. Harrison (1982) estimated that global urban migration rose from 1.85 million in 1845 to 770 million by 1975. By 1997, China had a rural population of 470 million, of which, 70 million had migrated into urban areas. For instance, there were 330,000 urban immigrants a day moving into Shanghai and 170,000 daily in Beijing (Cohen and Kennedy, 2007).

# Competing Theories of Poverty

Wallerstein's (1974) world systems theory (WST) explains global poverty by examining the mechanisms of capitalism. As capitalism expands globally it creates a structured hierarchy of markets. The dominant countries will have markets which place them at the core of capitalist production and trade, the semi-periphery economies are in the middle, followed by those countries that form the dependent periphery. The semi-periphery countries are less technologically advanced and wealthy than those at the core, while those countries at the periphery tend to be very poor and technologically less developed. A country's position in the hierarchy is not fixed, as Japan's rise from a periphery economy in 1890 to a core economy by 1970 illustrates. Though the situation is dynamic, the chances of an economy moving from the periphery to the core is becoming increasingly difficult under global capitalism. This is because, according to Wallerstein, capitalism has its own logic of accumulation and hence tends to protect the economic interests of the major players – the countries at the core. As capitalism expands on a global scale it creates an integrated global economy dominated by capital accumulation and free markets. At the same time, those countries on the periphery experience unemployment and the creation of large populations of marginalized and displaced poor.

Some critics of world systems theory, such as neo-Marxists, argue that it tends to suggest some objective set of global structures divorced from any political power or agency in the creation of poverty. They argue that historically, the spread of capitalism was due to the economic and military might of Western nations and their desire for colonial expansion to secure more markets for capital. Their military power enabled them to impose forced labour and unequal trading terms on these colonies.

Criticizing the limitations of WST, are those who adopt the New International Division of Labour (NIDL) perspective. They argue that global TNCs have located some manufacturing processes in what are seen as cheap labour havens; yet they have done little to enhance the living standards or invest in the infrastructure in those poorer countries affected. At the same time, the new international division of labour does not fundamentally alter the ability of core countries to dominate the global system. The weakness of this theory is, as Cohen (1987) suggests, that it underestimates the agency of some nation states in developing countries to resist the economic pressures from the core. New industrial countries such as Singapore and Malaysia have successfully managed to avoid these pressures from the core capitalist countries.

An alternative perspective on the causes of global poverty is presented by the Thai economist Bello (2001; 2002). He argues that poverty is caused by the contemporary dominance of neo-liberal free market approaches. In these markets the wealth and power is held by the already rich business elites, international banks and TNCs who have the power and freedom to invest anywhere in the world without being held accountable for the social and environmental impact of their policies. He cites additional forces in the causes of poverty. These include the economic and hegemonic power of the US, which the US government has used since the 1980s to protect the interests of its corporations. It has used its control as the single largest contributor to the IMF and the World Bank to exploit the situation and to push through a neo-liberal agenda within the IMF to the detriment of the world's poor. This agenda does not simply cause global poverty in the sense of lack of income and resources, but also causes deprivation in the form of social exclusion in a variety of forms.

## Poverty and Social Exclusion

Byrne (2002) suggests it is significant that social democratic governments like New Labour in the UK have linked poverty to social exclusion, because it results in a major shift in ideology. The link, in a less pejorative way, performs the same function in policy as the ideology of victim-blaming and the 'dependency culture' performs for neo-liberal administrations. He cites Mandanipour et al.'s (1998) definition of social exclusion:

> Social exclusion is defined as a multidimensional process in which various forms of exclusion are combined: participation in decision making and political processes, access to employment and material resources, and integration into common cultural process. When combined, they create acute forms of exclusion that find a spatial manifestation in particular neighbourhoods. (Mandanipour et al., 1998, cited in Byrne, 2002, p. 2)

Byrne argues that the term 'social exclusion' has replaced the more stigmatizing American term 'underclass', but its consequences (in terms of social policy outcomes) are no less damaging for those defined as poor. This is done by inviting the public to re-conceptualize the underclass as embodying an individualized discourse that blames the poor for their own poverty. He distinguishes between poverty and social exclusion by pointing out that social exclusion goes beyond poverty. Poverty refers to a lack of material resources necessary for survival, whereas social exclusion includes a host of dimensions in which people can be excluded. These range form exclusion from society to exclusion from employment and exclusion on the basis of age, gender, ethnicity, disability, religion and sexuality. Byrne also points out that a significant dimension of social exclusion is that it entails the exercise of power. Social exclusion is something done by some people (usually powerful groups) to others (less powerful).

Byrne distinguishes between weak and strong definitions of social exclusion. Strong definitions of social exclusion entail an analysis of the power imbalances resulting in material inequalities and the need to address these inequalities and the social structure that produces them. In contrast, weak definitions of social exclusion emphasize individual responsibility and agency and ignore the material constraints. Hence individual perspectives on social exclusion do not require any increase in equality to address it. This definition of social exclusion is based on the notion of individual rights and according to Byrne, ignores the democratic socialist project of collective social change. Thus, in many ways, New Labour's concept of social exclusion can be seen as a weak definition.

Views about the usefulness of the concept of social exclusion are divided. Some sociologists, like Nolan and Whelan (1996), regard the concept as a regressive step because they believe it distracts attention away from dealing with poverty and it enables governments to abdicate responsibility for helping the most disadvantaged. They point out that one of the primary reasons for its adoption into EU social policy debates was because the then UK Conservative government of the time was unwilling to accept that poverty was a large-scale problem in Europe, and the term 'social exclusion' was far more nebulous. They also suggest that the concept of social exclusion can be used to legitimate benefit cuts (especially for the unemployed, because this provides incentives for their integration or social inclusion).

Lawson (1995) disagrees and adopts a progressive view of social exclusion. He defines social exclusion as becoming detached from the broader socio-economic and political experiences of mainstream society. Social exclusion is progressive because an analysis of this entails more than exploring income inequality; rather, it involves other forms of social inequality and social injustice resulting in people's marginalization.

In contrast, Marxist sociologists emphasize strong definitions of social exclusion because they locate the causes in the structural inequalities of capitalism. There are various neo-Marxist interpretations for these causes of social exclusion, ranging form the deployment of a reserve army of labour as a form of social control (Friend and Metcalf, 1981), to regulatory theories of social exclusion (Nelson, 1995), to Byrne's (2002) theory of underdevelopment. Friend and Metcalf's version of social exclusion relates to the way the reserve army of labour gets 'sucked' into the labour force during times of economic boom (and thus it makes a contribution to the surplus value) and the ways it becomes unemployed during times of economic slump. This reinforces the dynamic nature of poverty in that it is not simply contingent upon being unemployed, but rather it is a result of the continual, dynamic movement back and forth from unemployment to insecure paid work. The significance of the reserve army lies not in its role in disciplining those in work, but in the fact that it is crucial to the process of restructuring when capitalism is in crisis. It forms part of the social conflict and class struggle that develops. Nelson's (1995) version of the regulation of the poor as a form of social exclusion provides a good account of the organization of the new low-wages service sector in the US. In this sector there is a division of labour between the highly 'credentialized' and high-waged management sector and the low-waged insecure workforce.

In terms of underdevelopment, Byrne (2002) argues that this is a useful theory to describe some of the social processes that constitute social exclusion. For example, Harrison (1981) describes underdeveloped neighbourhoods within the city of London within which the conditions are so disadvantaged, that despite their close proximity to London's more affluent areas, they have more in common (in terms of squalid living conditions and lack of amenities) with some of the slums and ghettos of the most impoverished cities in the developing world. In relation to this type of social exclusion, Bessis's (1995) definition of social exclusion refers to the corollaries between today's UK poor and their Victorian ancestors and argues that social exclusion has replaced exploitation:

> the concept of social exclusion has come into even greater use with the deepening social crisis. Contrary to what occurred in the Industrial Revolution of the last century, the rich now have less and less need for the labour power of the poor. Exclusion seems to have replaced exploitation as the primary cause of poverty. (Bessis, 1995, p. 13)

The significance of Byrne's (2002) analysis is the way he has used urban sociology to explore various dimensions of social exclusion, from poverty, unemployment, low-paid employment, to the use of space. He identifies the ways that the social control of the poor in the inner cities occurs via their exclusion from the decision-making process in urban regeneration schemes. Also he identifies the way space has been divided up in the post-industrial city. He points out that people from ethnic minorities, older people and lone mothers are more likely to live in deprived inner city neighbourhoods with high crime rates, few public services or amenities, and few community support networks. This problem is compounded by the way the poor have been excluded from the decision-making process in European urban regeneration projects such as the Single Regeneration Budget Schemes and the Urban Development Corporations (UCDs). These were supposed to promote social inclusion through the involvement of local communities in the planning process. However, in reality such decisions are largely taken by the private investors, who exploit the public purse in the form of subsidies they get for regeneration projects, and develop the areas to their own personal designs (Byrne, 2002, p. 123). He identifies how in modern Britain, in cities like Glasgow and Sunderland, those living on what he calls 'outer estates' are living in socially excluded space.

For Byrne the significance of the dominance of the neo-liberal discourses is the way it affects the whole 'poverty and social exclusion' debate. This is because the discussions of citizenship in the twentieth century have been predicated upon abstract nineteenth-century philosophical notions of civil rights, from which it is difficult to develop coherent political strategies with which to ground the collective political struggles of citizens for civil and welfare rights. Because of the dominance of neo-liberal discourses in the debate on citizenship, all discussions of citizenship abandon the collective socialist element.

# Social Exclusion and Citizenship

Most twentieth-century discussions of citizenship in Western democracies refer to T. H. Marshall's (1950) definition of citizenship. According to him, a person required three sets of rights in order to be accorded full rights of citizenship. These were civil rights (such as individual liberty, freedom of speech and thought, and the right to justice), political rights (which included the right of participation in the political process) and social rights (such as the right to a modicum of economic security, welfare, a shared standard of living and shared heritage). These rights were to underpin the welfare state. Thus, state provision in welfare was part of this package of social rights, which were to be granted to all citizens. This in essence makes all citizens stakeholders in capitalist society without effecting a fundamental redistribution of wealth in society across the classes.

The main weakness of Marshall's social democratic notion of citizenship is its failure to recognize that these social rights are not the product of a neo-liberal concept of rights, but rather secured through the collective political agency of ordinary working-class citizens. Moreover, the version of citizenship being predicated upon neo-liberal methodological individualism ignores the wider structures of society, which constrain human action and thus provide the *context* in which people experience their citizenship.

Wilson (1999) argues that the problem is that citizenship is a contested notion and it relies heavily for its survival on the capacity of any state to mediate and balance the socio-economic and political forces in society, which, in the late 1970s Western European welfare states found this difficult to do owing to the crises of late twentieth-century capitalism. The result was cutbacks in welfare state expenditure and large proportions of the population excluded from welfare rights.

Both Pateman (1989) and Williams (1995; 2003) examine how women and black people have traditionally been excluded from citizenship. For Pateman this has been achieved through the neo-liberal concept of liberty, which divorces the issue of access to rights from issues of power in society. She identifies the ways women have historically been excluded from the public domain, the site where most forms of power are located. For

Williams, black people have been excluded by the specific notion of 'citizen', which was based on the interrelated themes of 'family ' and 'nation', which was a highly racialized and gendered construction, predicated on the white, heterosexual family, with a traditional sexual division of labour, and based on notions of a British nation which did not include black people. Lewis (2003) takes the argument a stage further and argues that the neo-liberal notion of citizenship actively results in social processes that serve to exclude certain groups. This occurs through the ways that certain state institutions legalize forms of discrimination, such as various immigration and asylum acts and the restrictions on benefits rights for asylum seekers, to deny citizenship. This exclusion also takes the form of the denial of cultural diversity, in the form of censorship on dress codes, which is used to deny Muslims citizenship rights, and this has occurred in both the UK and France (Lewis, 2003, p. 330).

## Social Exclusion and Citizenship Around the Globe

On 9 June 2006 the United Nations High Commission for Refugees published its annual report on global refugee trends, which examines the plight of the millions of refugees, asylum seekers, internally displaced persons (IDPs) and stateless people. In concluding its analysis of the progress on resettlement the report concluded:

> Local integration, an important durable solution to the plight of refugees, is a legal, economic and social process. In some countries refugees have the opportunity to integrate locally because the host country has provided them with access to land or the labour market, while in others they remain confined to camps where they depend on assistance from the international community.   (UNHCR, 2006, p. 6)

Repeatedly in discussions about citizenship, whether in sociology, politics or social policy, the issue of citizenship rights is linked to access to waged labour or the economy (Pateman, 1989; Williams, 2003; Sullivan, 2003; Byrne, 2002). Both Williams' concept of citizenship and Byrne's dimension of social exclusion are useful in informing an understanding of the ways global refugees, displaced citizens and asylum seekers are denied the ability to exercise these rights in various ways.

Sullivan (2003) points to the importance of social constraints and contexts affecting people's experience of citizenship and this relates to the 8.4 million people who were granted refugee status in 2005. Cohen and Kennedy (2007) note that the legal definition of 'refugee' status enshrined in the 1951 Geneva Convention and the 1967 Bellagio Protocol (which was signed by over 190 nations) involves the duty to make every effort to extend protection to people who are outside their country of nationality due to a realistic fear of persecution as a consequence of their race, religion, nationality, political views or membership of a particular social group (2007, p. 249). Unfortunately, determining who is deemed to qualify for refugee status was left to individual nation states, which have increasingly sought to narrow the criteria for refugee status. It is this context in which many refugees and other vulnerable people experience citizenship rights. In 2005 there were 8,394,500 refugees, of which 2,571,500 came from Africa, 2,476,300 came from CASWANAME,* 564,300 from the Americas, 825,600 from Asia-Pacific and 1,965,800 from Europe. In addition to these there are those whom the UNHCR terms 'people of concern', who are people who are outside the current mandate of the UNHCR but to whom it extends protection and/or assistance. As at 2005, it estimated that there were nearly 10 million people in this category. Afghanistan had 2.6 million people, Columbia 2.5 million, Sudan 1.6 million, Pakistan 1.1 million and Somalia 839,000. In addition to these there were a further 1.5 million Afghans living outside their country of origin in camps in Pakistan receiving no assistance from UNHCR and 4.3 million Palestinians not included in the refugee statistics because they were receiving assistance from other international organizations.

On age and sex there is a lack of precise data, but of the 10 million people of concern to the UNHCR, 49 per cent are women, 40 per cent are children aged between 0 and eighteen, and 6 per cent are adults over 60. In relation to these people, 16 countries reported resettlement of a number of refugees and these included the US (58,800), Australia (10,400), Sweden (1,300), Finland (770), and Norway (750). In terms of naturalization and being afforded citizenship the full figures are not known, because there is an underreporting by nations of the numbers of people being granted citizenship. During 2005 the US granted 58,900 citizenship applications, Kyrgyzstan 3,400, Armenia 2,300, Belgium 2,300, Mexico 1,200 and Ireland 580.

In terms of asylum seekers, as at December 2005 there were 680,000 applications lodged for asylum around the globe. Though the UNHCR does not have the figures for how many were accepted, the breakdown was as follows: there were 374,000 registered in Europe, 125,000 in Africa, 75,000 in Asia-Pacific, 72,000 in the Americas and 22,000 in CASWANAME. For many of these people, both refugees and asylum seekers, their rights to citizenship are curtailed by lack of access to the labour market (as they are not permitted to work), their movement is controlled through their being confined to

---

* CASWANAME is an acronym which stands for Central Asia, South-West Asia, North Africa and the Middle East.

refugee camps, and denying them citizenship rights makes them ineligible for welfare benefits and reliant on UNHCR or other international aid. Much research demonstrates that in terms of access to citizenship rights in most host countries asylum seekers fare less well than accepted refugees. For instance, in Austria they fared less well in accessing economic integration and jobs, while in the UK they suffered higher rates of mental health problems (Allen, 2003), and there was a gender bias in some countries, in terms of deprivation suffered, with women experiencing higher instances of poor health (Kennedy-Lawford and Murphy-Lawler, 2003 study in Ireland). Added to this there is an ethnic dimension with 1.5 million Afghans in Pakistan receiving no UNHCR assistance and 4.3 million Palestinians in the Middle East without assistance from any nation state.

Another group of people who receive no citizenship rights are those termed 'internally displaced people' (IDPs) those who have been displaced by war or ethnic conflict. Conversely however, in 2005 UNHCR noted that many countries were witnessing a decrease in the number of displaced persons. In Liberia 261,000 IDPs were resettled, in the Russian Federation the figure was 164,000 and In Bosnia-Herzegovina 126,500 people were resettled. Nonetheless, Columbia continued to have 2.5 million IDPs and Azerbaijan 578,000; however, the UNHCR argue that the number is likely to increase, with 62 countries reporting the existence of IDPs.

Given the close relationship between economic power and access to citizenship, it is easy to see different forms of social exclusion experienced by different people around the globe and here Byrne's (2002) multidimensional analysis of social exclusion is relevant, with its emphasis on the control of space, low-paid employment and the enforced movement of rural populations. In China the rural workers migrating into the city lack economic power in the form of access to the labour market and regularly experience violations of their citizenship rights. They have been banned from employment in 23 industries, the police have destroyed the temporary accommodation and shanty-towns they were living in. In addition, many have been repatriated to their territories and others have been detained and forced to work in labour camps. Moreover, over one million people in China have been displaced from the land because of the Yangtze Dam Project, while 16.4 million people have been displaced in India because of dam projects there.

Recently sociologists have discussed citizenship rights in relation to the power of TNCs to reinforce the social exclusion of populations in countries where they invest. Major corporations like Shell in Nigeria have continued to exploit oil with noticeable indifference to the local communities, who have witnessed the Nigerian government appropriate land on behalf of the company. At the same time Shell argues that the pollution caused by its refineries in the fishing grounds and villages is more than compensated for through the taxes it pays. It further suggests that the Nigerian government should invest this more efficiently to address the issue.

Similarly, the incident at Bhopal in India in which 2,800 workers died and 20,000 people were injured is still ongoing, with the parent TNC Union Carbide Corporation (US) stalling the legal proceedings. Thus, through a combination of global poverty, war, ethnic cleansing, human-manufactured ecological disasters, and the vast increase in refugees, asylum seekers and displaced people, many populations around the world experience social exclusion and infringement of citizenship rights.

A number of sociologists, such as White and Harris (1999) all argue that Marshall's concept of citizenship actually results in social exclusion from full citizenship rights for a host of groups, not just refugees and those seeking asylum. It also affects those who officially have citizenship as members of a nation state. Modood et al. (1997) argues that British Muslims are socially excluded from full citizenship in the form of 'cultural racism' and this is manifest in their under-representation in mainstream social institutions and the masking of their social disadvantage by using generic terms in survey research such as 'black' or 'Asian'. White and Harris (1999) argue that current EU conceptualization of social citizenship linked to employment, based on Marshall's (1950) social democratic model, is a weak model of citizenship because it ignores the power exercised by the state in relation to social services users and because of its lack of concern with individual need. Equally the neo-liberal model based on a consumerist model of citizenship does not really address the individual service user's needs, but paradoxically it has the potential to extend citizenship rights because of the contestation between social service providers and citizens-as-consumers:

> Across Europe, the social services provide myriad sites on which issues around oppression, discrimination, empowerment, inequality, and individual need are being played out.   (White and Harris, 1999, p. 10)

White and Harris also point out that for any concept of citizenship to address those who are socially excluded it must be conceptualized as a fluid entity, which has to be understood in the context of the changing and multiple situations people experience, and it must incorporate the civil rights aspirations of new generations of European citizens (White and Harris, 1999, p. 8).

Both new neo-liberal and social democratic governments in the 1990s and 2000s have sought to extend citizenship rights through the ways they have restructured state-funded public services and emphasized consumerism in the market. Many commentators have questioned whether this new concept of consumerism (signified in the UK by New Labour's notion of a 'stakeholder society') really renders greater citizenship rights. Sanderson

(1992) argues that there is a fundamental difference between the conditions in local government and those in the private sector. In the private sector owing to the level of competition, monopolies are rare and the power of the consumer is supreme. This power stems from the wide access to resources, the ability to exercise choice and the efficiency of competition between firms responding to consumer demand. By contrast, the 'consumer' of social and welfare services is limited by lack of information about services, the possible difficulty of expressing need due to educational, cultural or linguistic difficulties, and the lack of alternatives. Thus, the discussion of the power of the consumer is often oversimplified in market models of welfare. This is because the issue is taken out of its proper context, by focusing on the market. In this way the neo-liberal perspective ignores the plurality of interests that exists in local communities. People's lives are not one-dimensional and they can be service providers and consumers of services at the same time. They can be local government employees (as social workers, nurses or teachers) and at other times service users (as council tax payers). Consequently, this generates a wide range of stakeholders in society with their own definitions of need and personal interests. These disparate interest groups affect the power of the state, in the form of welfare and social services, to generate citizenship.

The global issue of migration and the plight of temporary workers either with documentation ('legal aliens') or without visas or documentation ('illegal aliens') exposes the failings of both neo-liberal and social democratic models to create an inclusive and contemporary definition of citizenship. The issue of global migration is highly relevant to social work practice because it challenges social work values of respect for the individual, promoting social justice, challenging all forms of discrimination and oppression and promoting inclusiveness. Social workers who work in NGOs with migrants around the globe face the daily contradiction of working within legal parameters on immigration and promoting the citizenship rights of migrants. This practice dilemma is brought out forcefully in the research by Martinez-Brawley and Gualda (2006) in Spain and the US, and Ingamells and Westoby (2008) in Australia. Their research identifies the global problems faced by migrants and the social workers who work with them.

In comparing Spain and the US, Martinez-Brawley and Gualda note that immigration policy is now a global concern and they identify the problems of addressing the needs of over 1 million undocumented migrant workers who came to Spain over the last decade, and 10 million in the US with over 1.37 million working in agriculture and 44,000 being undocumented or illegal aliens. In the US many migrants are from Mexico, while in Spain they are constituted by diverse populations from the countries Spain has entered into bilateral agreements with such as the Dominican Republic, Ecuador,

Colombia, Morocco, Poland, Romania and Bulgaria; 39 per cent of migrant workers are from the EU and 55 per cent from Africa (Martinez-Brawley and Gualda, 2006, p. 64). The situation of migrant workers is complex and contradictory. For the host nations, many commentators argue that their agricultural businesses, hotel, catering and construction services could not function without migrant labour. On the other hand there are those who view the migrant population as the main reason for the depressed wages for indigenous workers. The controversy is heightened by the fact that many temporary workers in the US and Spain out-stay their visas or temporary works permits and disappear.

In both countries there are a range of protection rights for temporary migrant workers, and health and welfare support services (in the form of the state and voluntary and charitable organizations); however, these services are contingent upon migrants adhering to the terms of the temporary visas or work permits. Social workers are involved in both state social service departments and NGOs providing a range of services including educational services for migrant children, humanitarian aid, personal hygiene programmes (including facilities for bathing and washing clothing), translation services and legal advice on immigration and labour procedures. However, for many, professional practice is hampered by the lack of local knowledge about immigrants in both local and global contexts and of research on the depressed conditions of migrants (Martinez-Brawley and Gualda, 2006, p. 62). This problem is exacerbated by the fact that the response of the majority of nation states to undocumented migrant workers is to tighten the law, placing increased restrictions on them.

In Australia, Ingamells and Westoby (2008) identify similar forms of exclusion from citizenship rights for adolescent refugees. The situation here is equally complex for social workers trying to support young refugees in dealing with the traumatic experiences they have had (as a result of leaving their homeland) and to address their social and welfare needs.

Approximately 12,000–13,000 refugees are accepted in Australia from countries such as Vietnam, Cambodia, Myanmar, Bosnia, Serbia, Croatia, Kosovo, El Salvador, Chile, Somalia, Eritrea, Ethiopia, Sudan and Iran. The vast majority of the refugees are from Sudan and Sierra Leone (Ingamells and Westoby, 2008, p. 2). Unlike the US where status is determined by documentation in terms of visas and work permits, in Australia the primary categorization relates to the manner in which a person enters the country. This can be either 'on-shore' or 'off-shore'. Off-shore applicants are eligible to apply for protection provided they meet the Australian definition of the Refugee Convention. On-shore applicants can apply for asylum provided that they have the right legal documents, and can be given 'bridging visas' while their applications are being processed. However, those without such documentation are only given temporary protection and are held in detention and evaluated every thirty months. These applicants will be encouraged to return to their country of origin if it is deemed safe. Ingamells and Westoby point out that the welfare imperative and immigration rules represent two competing and conflicting discourses for social workers. These create problems when seeking to engage and support young refugees and this causes confusion and hampers advocacy work:

> Social workers encounter refugee young people and their families within schools, housing support services, employment and health services, statutory child protection, generalist welfare services, neighbourhood centres and counselling services, as well as in settlement services. Whatever the context, responsive practice needs to be holistic, and this often means ecological approaches. Yet, if this is possible at all within the current socio-political environment, then it entails working against the grain, or beyond the confines, of welfare reform trajectories. (Ingamells and Westoby, 2008, p. 3)

## Summary of the Main Points

- Sociological theories of poverty are important to social work because of poverty's relationship to social exclusion, and citizenship rights.

- Whether sociologists adopt a relative or absolute definition of poverty, there is still the problem of *how* to interpret the data (Saraga, 1998).

- There are continuities between nineteenth-century and twenty-first-century discourses on the poor, which have practice implications, because both social democratic and neo-liberal approaches to welfare entail the notion that those defined as poor are in part to blame for their situation.

- Byrne (2002) argues that social democratic notions of social exclusion legitimate the decision to foist responsibility for getting out of poverty on individuals.

- There are strong and weak definitions of social exclusion. Weak definitions of social exclusion emphasize individual responsibility and agency and therefore do not require any increase in equality to address it. Strong definitions locate social exclusion within the structural constraints of capitalist society and examine the material conditions that produce it.

- The social democratic definition of social exclusion is a weak definition because it is based upon individualism. This denies the collective struggles of working-class men and women around the globe to claim civil and welfare rights. It also fails to consider how these rights have been ignored in social policy.

- 'Stakeholder society' represents a weak definition of social inclusion because the power of the citizen-as-consumer is oversimplified in market models of welfare. It ignores the plurality of competing interests in local communities, which affects how much power the citizen-as-consumer has.

# Conclusion

The promotion of citizenship rights is a complex issue, inextricably linked to issues of poverty and class. Many of the contemporary social constructions of poverty and social exclusion (with their emphasis on individual self-reliance) have important implications for the international plans to eradicate poverty and in tailoring service provision to meet the needs of marginalized groups and promote their citizenship rights. This is because strong definitions of social exclusion not only demonstrate the dimensions of exclusion and deprivation that the world's poor face, but they also identify the fact that social exclusion has a more complex relationship to poverty and citizenship than the simple mismatch of the excluded and opportunities for inclusion. Despite the neo-liberal rhetoric about the need for all citizens to recognize their responsibilities to develop their skills and qualifications for social inclusion in the global market, the underpinning discourse continues to entail neo-liberal notions of the 'deserving' and 'undeserving poor'. The focus continues to be on the individuals and not the structural inequalities that produce their situation; therefore, their poverty and social exclusion and hence exclusion from citizenship will continue. This has implications not only for their social and welfare rights but also for their legal rights as citizens. This will be examined in Chapter 4, which examines the legal context of social work.

## Case Study

Wihyu Murtago is an asylum seeker from East Timor who has fled to London, UK, claiming he had to flee for his life from the Indonesian authorities there. He has contacted local social services because he is sleeping on the floor at a friend's flat and he has no money, and no job or way of earning a living. He reports that he stays in the flat when his friends go to work because he has been the victim of racist abuse in the past, but this means he feels isolated. He also told the social worker he feels depressed about the racism he has encountered since coming to the UK.

## Case Study (*cont'd*)

Sociological perspectives can help his social worker address some of the power imbalances and forms of oppression that Wihyu faces. This can be done by critically examining notions of citizenship and social exclusion and planning social work interventions accordingly.

Marshall's (1950) model of citizenship is predicated on a link with employment, which is being adopted by the European Union; it is limited by the current organization of welfare states, which are predicated on a neo-liberal model. The economic dimension limits the access to citizenship of a number of social clients/service users groups because it fails to consider the power of the state in relation to service users or to acknowledge individual need, hence it cannot address the disadvantages of service users manifest as 'cultural racism', as in the under-representation of Muslims in social institutions (in many Western countries), asylum seekers denied access to employment, or older people socially excluded from civil and political forms of participation. Moreover, it is a static model, which is unable to keep pace with the diversity of citizenship needs arising out of global migration. The works of Martinez-Brawley and Gualda (2006) on migrant workers in Spain and the US, and of Ingamells and Westoby (2008) on refugees and asylum seekers in Australia, identify a set of common barriers faced by migrants and refugees in accessing citizenship rights and the problems facing social workers in seeking to support their citizenship rights. Such problems are how to reconcile the international social work value of human rights with national immigration laws and welfare policies, which emphasize the social regulation of foreign nationals, and reductions in welfare expenditure.

Social exclusion is a useful concept in trying to understand the barriers to citizenship because it includes poverty but also examines a range of material and non-material factors (such as social isolation) as well. However, social workers need to be aware of the differences between weak definitions, which only explore social exclusion at the individual level, and strong definitions, which locate social exclusion in the structure of society and the material inequalities that cause it. In this respect, one strong definition that is useful is that of Byrne (2002). He adopts an urban sociological perspective and identifies how social exclusion results in a form of social control. This occurs by people's exclusion not simply from the labour market and from a decent income, but from services and amenities that most people would consider an essential part of daily life. He cites how in cities like Sunderland and Glasgow many (mainly older people, ethnic minority groups and lone mothers) exist on the periphery of cities in run-down neighbourhoods with few local shops, and few amenities in the form of health, welfare and public transport services.

# Further Reading

Bello, W. (2001) *The Future in the Balance: Essays on Globalization and Resistance* (Oakland, CA: Food First Books).
Bello provides a very good analysis of global poverty and a sophisticated critique of various Western sociological perspectives on the issue.

Byrne, D. (2002) *Social Exclusion* (Buckingham: Open University Press).
This book provides another dimension of social exclusion by exploring the impact of spatial exclusion.

Williams, F. (2003) 'Social Policy: Culture and Nationhood', in P. Alcock, E. Erskine and M. May (eds), *The Student's Companion to Social Policy* (Oxford: Blackwell Publishing).
Williams demonstrates the interconnections between ethnicity, gender and racism, this time by examining the issue of immigration.

# 4
# Sociology, the Law and Social Work Practice

## Introduction

> For all social workers the law provides the framework within which services are offered: it is impossible to practice without coming up against the law and it is impossible to practice effectively without an in depth understanding of how the law affects everyday social work practice. (Johns, 2003, p. 167)

As Johns (2003) points out, there is a distinct difference between the need of social workers to understand the law and integrate it into their practice, and that of members of the legal profession. For a start, social workers are not involved in the same way lawyers are (for example, they are not engaged to defend or prosecute anyone). For social workers, understanding the law underpins their work in the promotion of human rights. It underpins the intervention in people's lives to protect them from themselves or other people. It relates to the protection of people's rights in terms of access to information, confidentiality, assisting with entitlements to services. It also informs the provision of advocacy services and working in publicly accountable organizations (Johns, 2003). All these tasks require reference to the law.

## Key Words

civil law, criminal law, legal reasoning, precedent, legal realists, natural law theory, human rights, international law

# Sociology in a Legal Context

Sociology makes a useful contribution to understanding *how* the law operates in any given society. Sociologists see the law as an indicator of macro-relationships: relationships that are part of the 'bigger picture', because the law relates to society-wide concerns such as social control, crime, industrial relations, the welfare state, and state intervention in families. In addition, sociology is concerned with inequality and power at both the structural and the interpersonal levels and so it focuses upon the interconnection between law and changing social intuitions. This is in order to see how power and inequality are manifest in society. Increasingly in the twentieth and at the beginning of the twenty-first century the law has been used as an instrument of social change around the world and the potential of the law to achieve this has been a source of heated controversy between sociologists.

Roach-Anleu (2002) suggests that sociology can be useful to the study of law by exploring specific aspects of the law in terms of what they tell us about society. Through the law it is possible to gain insight into

- The specific social conditions in which laws emerge and change.
- The extent to which the law can promote social change.
- The kinds of values and belief systems the laws embody.

To get to grips with these issues students do at least need to have some basic understanding of how the law operates. This can be done by distinguishing between *criminal law* and *civil law*. Criminal law is concerned with behaviour that is deemed a threat to society and it provides sanctions or penalties for breaking the law. This is to ensure conformity and prohibit certain types of behaviour. If a person is found guilty of a criminal offence, it also entails a conviction, which goes on a person's record. Civil law, on the other hand, is concerned with legal wrong which results in harm to someone for which they seek redress, compensation or some other course of action. It does not involve punishment. Most social workers, whatever their specialist area, are generally involved in civil cases involving advocacy of peoples rights, and protect the health and welfare of children or older service users. However, at times, as in cases of abuse of children or vulnerable adults, a criminal offence might also have been committed, which will entail criminal proceedings.

*Legal theory* deals with abstract issues such as the nature of laws, the structure of legal systems and how the law relates to complex, abstract notions like 'justice' or 'morality'. Intrinsic to legal theory is *legal reasoning*, which is usually identified with the process by which rationality and the existence of legal doctrines are maintained. Legal reasoning tries to generate consistency in the law, and this is only achievable if similar cases are determined in a similar way with similar outcomes. The main ways this consistency is achieved is through *precedent*. Precedent is a process where the higher courts make decisions and, in similar cases, the lower courts feel bound to observe those decisions owing to the higher courts' superior position to them in the judicial hierarchy.

Decisions are often reached through *reason by analogy* – that is, comparing the facts in different cases, identifying the rules or principles underpinning the decision in a prior relevant case (known as *ratio decidendi* or reason for deciding) and applying these to the new facts of the new case. However, reasoning by analogy suffers from the subjective process of interpretation, and assessment of *ratios decidendi* are often complex, contradictory and lacking clear structure. Consequently, they have to be identified or socially constructed. Furthermore, reasoning by analogy entails a fair degree of flexibility because judges can interpret precedent narrowly or as widely as possible in order to render a particular outcome.

## Sociological Perspectives on the Law

There are three main sociological perspectives on legal theory: positivism, legal realism, and natural law theory. *Positivists* argue that the scientific method can be applied to the study of society. Positivist legal theorists regard the law as an objective and neutral body of knowledge that entails a logical and structured system of rules that govern behaviour in society. The criterion for determining whether a statute or new rule has validity and is therefore legal, is determined by whether the statute conforms to procedural and substantive rules. This criterion for validity is what, according to positivists, makes the law objective and value neutral. This model, however, has been criticized for tending to ignore the human dimension in the legal process, whereby interpretation inevitably entails value commitments, with individual judicial biases and broader social factors affecting legal decisions.

*Legal realists* reject the positivist idea of objectivity in judicial decision-making and argue that the law is value laden and political. They reject the positivist idea that rules are certain and that their application in specific cases is a rational technical task. In contrast, they point to the unpredictability of legal outcomes despite the law of precedent and the role of the human personality within it. As a consequence legal realists advocate greater practical training for law students prior to completion of their legal training so that they become acquainted with the complexities and ambiguities of judgement making. One of the main problems with the legal realist approach is the inherent relativism. If, as legal realists assert, there is no independent or external means of evaluating the law outside of what judges say, then it is impossible to evaluate the kinds of decisions judges make when they support totalitarian regimes, such as when ruling on legislation resulting in racial segregation in the US and apartheid in South Africa.

*Natural law theorists* on the other hand, argue for the *existence* of *a priori* moral and universal principles that establish *absolute standards* of human justice that can be uncovered by human reason. They argue that when a society's substantive laws deviate from these higher principles they can be deemed unjust laws and therefore not legally binding. This poses a moral dilemma for citizens when their governments impose legal obligations that are contrary to natural laws, as was the case with Nazi policies during World War II. However, natural law theory leaves unanswered significant questions like determining the nature of 'humanity' and what exactly are these universal moral precepts that can be uncovered by reason.

Parsons (1962) maintained that the law was the main social mechanism for addressing social integration. The law is especially crucial in modern industrial society where there are so many competing interest groups. In order to secure integration, the law (in order for it to establish society's rules) must address four main problems. First, it must be accepted by members of society as legitimate, i.e. people must accept the authority and power of the law as right and just. Secondly, it must address and have a degree of monopoly on *interpretation* – that is, it must identify which legal rules govern which specific contexts and which legal rights they define. Thirdly, it must have the power to impose sanctions to discourage non-conformity (such sanctions can vary, involving either inducement or coercion), and lastly, it must be able to establish legal *jurisdiction* – that is, both the power and the ability to determine in what contexts a given set of legal rules apply.

Parsons argued that a universal legal system was essential to integration in a modern, complex heterogeneous society. This was because such a highly differentiated society would require a mechanism for balancing an array of competing interests. Thus, he asserted that the law served as a focal point to balance the competing interests of law, politics and other aspects of society.

Like most positivists, Parsons saw the law as an objective and neutral arbiter of conflict in society, serving the interests of all citizens equally. In this he was heavily criticized by C. Wright-Mills (1959), who saw Parsons' theory of the social system (and the law within it) as simply reflecting the core values of liberal American society.

Habermas (1996) is a critical theorist who also explores how the law secures integration in society. However, unlike Parsons he adopts a dialectical approach and believes that the law can be at one and the same time both oppressive and democratic. This is because he believes that the law achieves social integration by regulating conflict in the economic, political and social spheres of society as well as on a more one-to-one level between individuals. He traces the history of Western society and shows how the law has embodied a tension between the rights of citizens and the rights of a monarch or the ruling classes. For example, in the European bourgeois state in the seventeenth and eighteen century, the law was instrumental in facilitating the transition from feudalism to capitalism. It did this by enshrining individual freedoms such as negative liberty, granting property rights, and establishing the principles of a legal code and the concept of a legal person. It also established civil law to regulate transactions between citizens. However, civil law was secondary to the coercive force of the state manifest in the absolute rights of monarchy as the legitimate government. In the nineteenth century the bourgeoisie constitutional monarchy and state was manifest in countries like Germany, when there was some constitutional regulation of executive authority, with some legal rights for citizens. These included individual rights to liberty, life and property but not voting rights. Moreover, the sovereign determined national and foreign policy. In contrast, democratic constitutional states like the UK and US after 1789 were characterized by increased democratization, where citizens gained civil and voting rights. This increased throughout the class system in the UK with various electoral reforms between 1832 and 1928.

The modern social democratic state of the twentieth century embodies full civil and democratic rights and increasing welfare rights including shorter working hours, freedom of union affiliation, social security rights and limited universal education and health service provision as well as legislation on working conditions. The legislation of the welfare state is the positive side of the law in that the law is functioning to protect citizens against the worst effects of capitalist market relations. The negative dimension of the law is that the evolution of the welfare state also results in increased state intervention in the private sphere of the family: for example, through the establishment of social services to provide therapeutic assistance, which results in increased state intervention into people's private lives.

Though this is a useful analysis for understanding the dual nature of the way the law operates in contemporary societies like the UK, this model of the law and the claim that it secures integration via increased democratization has been criticized by both feminists and postmodernists. They argue that it fails to recognize that the law in Western societies reflects a particular dominant value and belief system which is patriarchal and ethnocentric.

# Postmodernist Perspectives

Postmodernists such as Bourdieu (1996) adopt a social constructivist approach to examine how the law operates. For Bourdieu, the law is not about 'social rights', or 'justice', or 'objectivity'. Rather, it represents the outcome of struggles between competing social actors for the right to determine the law. In these struggles different social actors have different levels of legal competence in terms of their ability to interpret legal texts, procedures, statutes etc. and different skills and abilities in terms of getting their interpretation of the law accepted and ratified in the courts. Hence, the law is the outcome of this competitive process.

Bourdieu observes that the law appears neutral in the way it is often presented as codified, structured, and based on legal precedent, logical rules and legal argument, and administered by the legal agencies of the state in an objective, disinterested way. However, he points to the way that the interpretative process can be manipulated in judicial decision-making, as Roach-Anleu (2002) has summarized:

> The legal technique of distinguishing cases on their facts and extending or restricting precedent ensures that cases can be used in many different ways. . . . Given the elasticity of texts, which can be entirely ambiguous or, at best contradictory, the process of declaration or judgement entails considerable latitude.   (Roach-Anleu, 2002, pp. 55–6)

This idea has some resonance when examining the way that legal professionals operate in the courtroom. Legal professionals secure their dominance over legal interpretations of cases by the way they manage the legal process in court. The court system is an adversarial one in which people give their testimonies and are cross-examined, with the defence and prosecution sides vying for interpretative dominance. This means that lawyers compete in the courtroom with a range of other professionals including social workers, probation officers, educational welfare officers, psychiatrists and doctors, who all provide expert evidence. Legal dominance is secured by destroying or discrediting the credibility of other professionals or trying to prevent their evidence being admitted (Abbott, 1988).

Bourdieu's analysis of the way the law is socially constructed by the legal profession and different state agencies is directly relevant to social work practice. For instance, Johns (2003) notes with interest that there are far more mandatory or statutory pieces of legislation regarding children than there are for other potentially vulnerable service user groups such as people with physical or learning disabilities, people with mental health problems or older people. While on the one hand this reflects the citizen's right to self-determination, conversely the law provides a form of justification by which the state can legitimately abdicate responsibility for potentially vulnerable groups of people.

# Neo-Marxist Perspectives

In contrast to postmodernists, neo-Marxists are more concerned with the wider dimensions of the law and examine it within the context of capitalist society and the management of class conflict. This perspective can be broadly categorized by two approaches. The first adopts an economic determinist approach (Poulantzas, 1976; Quinney, 1975) which sees the law as functioning to secure the economic and political interests of the ruling class. The second 'correlation view' (Lavalette and Ferguson, 1999; Jessop, 1990) sees the operation of the law as far more complex. This view argues that the state, when exercising the operations of law, cannot simply act as a crude instrument of capitalist class rule. Rather, the legal system is an effective mechanism for the maintenance of capitalism because specific laws have an affinity with the conditions for capital accumulation. At the same time, the state retains relative autonomy from direct intervention in either the economic or political spheres.

The illusion that everyone is equal before the law reinforces the inequalities produced by capitalism, but often seems plausible to the majority of people because certain legislation, i.e. on employment or trade union organization, actually runs counter to the interests of the capitalist class. However, one example of the way the law reinforces capitalist inequalities is the law on private property. For example, the notion that property laws apply equally to all has resonance to property owners, be those people who own a mansion or a one-bedroomed flat, whereas the laws on vagrancy or homelessness apply to only a minority in society.

A development from the neo-Marxist legal perspective is *Critical Legal Studies*. Critical Legal Studies (CLS) was a social movement that emerged in the 1970s from a broad alliance of lawyers, teachers, social scientists and legal academics who were all committed to exploring the relationship between legal theory and practice and social reform for a more egalitarian and humane society. CLS is not a single coherent theory but a movement whose ethos includes a radical reappraisal of the legal process and the law as a bastion of objective technical and legal–rational knowledge. In this respect ,CLS rejects the idea that the law can be separated from politics (in the sense that politics represents a struggle for power) and argues that judicial decisions simply codify and rationalize political decisions in any society.

One of the weaknesses of the CLS movement is that its members disagree on the ways to generate social change. Some think it is enough to demystify legal processes and educate people into considering alternative approaches to the law. Others point to opportunities within the court arena as the forum for an alliance of ordinary citizens, lawyers and other legal professionals to reshape the ways people conceptualize the law and their roles within it.

CLS is useful to our understanding of how the law operates in society through the way it integrates legal theory with critical social theory and the way it reassesses the link between law and politics in contemporary society. This is particularly important in terms of the link between legal reasoning and the reproduction of social and economic inequalities. Conversely, however, the CLS movement has failed to develop a coherent theoretical position to develop an alternative theory of the law necessary to generate the types of social change its members desire. Also, the movement is internally divided between those who adopt a neo-Marxist critical theory perspective or a postmodernist perspective. In addition, it has also (particularly in the US) been criticized for being an almost exclusively white, male and middle- class and professional elite movement.

# Feminist Perspectives

Like CLS theorists, feminist legal theorists are concerned with how the law serves to reproduce inequalities, but they are mainly concerned with those pertaining to women. Feminist legal theory points to the ways that the law in practice discriminates against women and the way the legal profession remains a predominantly male bastion. In addition, they examine the ways legal institutions and discourses reflect male concerns and priorities. They cite the liberal notions of rights and citizenship, which allegedly apply to all citizens but in reality are socially constructed in a peculiarly masculine way through the way they are linked and are contingent upon waged labour. There are, however, differences within feminist legal theory. One of the main differences is between liberal and radical legal feminist theorists. Liberal feminists believe the law can incorporate women's experiences and aspirations and that it can be used to eradicate discrimination. Thus, Gilligan (1982) argues that the feminist legal project should be to ensure that legal knowledge and practice incorporate female values and concerns as complementary to men's concerns.

In contrast, radical feminists disagree that the masculine nature of the law can be changed simply by increasing women's participation in the legal profession or by placing more value on female concerns. Rather, they argue that it is necessary to deconstruct the law, which reinforces male ideologies and values, which are then used to maintain male domination through the ways the law reproduces patriarchal power relations. For example, in some societies, the traditional laws on rape require four male witnesses to the rape, or in other societies, the law on rape in marriage denies the possibility of it occurring (owing to the rights of men within the marriage contract). These are typical examples of how the law secures such domination. Feminists cite the way that in the early twentieth century the courts often interpreted the word 'person' to mean man, and reinforced the notion of the separate spheres of the public and the private to justify the exclusion of women from the legal profession.

MacKinnon (1989) argues that the state, through the law, secures male power. Citing the way men and women are socially constructed in a dichotomy she identifies the essential characteristics that are associated with 'male' in the male/female dichotomy, such as rationality and objectivity, and the essential features of the male perspective, which are seen as equality, liberty, privacy and freedom of speech. The adoption of these values, she claims, reproduces gender divisions under the guise of neutrality and justice.

The extent of violence towards women around the globe has been extensively researched (US Common Health Survey, 1998; WHO, 2002; Evans, 2005; McKie, 2005). The US Common Health Survey identified 3 million women experiencing domestic violence, while a survey undertaken on behalf of the Inter-American Development Bank in 1997 found that there was an increasing proportion of GDP spent on health care, in relation to addressing domestic violence. In Columbia it was 5 per cent, in El Salvador 1.8 per cent, Brazil 1.9 per cent and Venezuela 0.3 per cent. In addition, Finland spent 9 million euros annually addressing domestic violence, while in Scotland the issue accounted for 136,000 GP consultations, and £5 million was spent on projects in the London Borough of Hackney. Worldwide, there are over 500,000 rapes reported in South Africa; 250,000 women and girls are trafficked from countries of the former Soviet Union for the domestic and sex industries of Europe. There are over 10,000 honour killings in countries including Turkey, Pakistan and India, while over 130 million women and girls have endured genital mutilation (WHO, 2002).

Feminists have drawn attention to the ways the law on rape and domestic violence around the globe have often been interpreted to disadvantage or oppress women. In the UK the common law definition of rape was 'carnal knowledge of a woman above the age of 10 without her consent and with a woman under the age of 10 with or without her consent (Sexual offences Act, 1956). This initial definition of rape meant that only women could be raped, and only outside in marriage. It was not until 1996 in the UK that the law recognised rape in marriage. However, many countries including the UK have reformed the rape laws, either by making the crime 'non gender specific' (Roach-Anleu, 2002, p. 182) or by replacing the term 'rape' with sexual assault predicated upon the harm done to the victim.

With regard to the crime of rape, the rules on corroborating evidence in the UK and the US are different from the rules that empower a jury to convict on the testimony of one witness. However, there have been some modifications to the law in that defence councils are no longer allowed to cross-examine the victim about his/her previous sexual history in an attempt to discredit their testimony. Nonetheless, the court can permit such a cross-examination if it deems it of sufficient relevance. In relation to this point, feminists continue to question the assumption that the sexual past of the victim is relevant to the issue of consent. In countries such as Pakistan, the law requires four Muslim male witnesses of good character to verify a woman's claim of rape. If the woman is unable to provide witnesses to the incident she can, under Hudood Ordinance, be sentenced to imprisonment or corporal punishment for adultery (Sahibzada, 2007).

Reform of the law on domestic violence, as with that on rape, has been largely the result of campaigns by the women's movement. However, while multi-agency working (including that by the legal profession) to address this problem has improved and many professional bodies, including the police, support mandatory arrest in battery cases, there is often a large discrepancy between policy and practice. Research Dobash and Dobash (1979) on the UK, Evans (2005) on Australia and Canada, and McKie (2005) on England, Scotland and Sweden, indicate that in a number of cases the police continue to trivialize domestic complaints, sometimes operating from the belief that violence is a way of life for some couples. Often they are reluctant to intervene owing to the low chance of securing a conviction. Police are sometimes unwilling to make arrests for domestic violence unless both parties are present, the victim demands an arrest and signs an arrest warrant, and/or the victim alleges violence and alcohol consumption on the part of the perpetrator.

Sociological perspectives are crucial to an understanding of the issue of domestic violence through focusing upon how violence is normalized in society, or minimized by ignoring the gendered nature of domestic violence and redefining it as 'couple violence' (McKie, 2005), or through the operation of gender stereotyping and the dominant discourse of hegemonic masculinity (Giddens, 2001; Dominelli and Cowburn, 2001).

More recently, criminal law has focused more on the issue of dealing with survivors of domestic violence and for those who kill their abusive partners the law has been accused of being quite oppressive. Feminists argue that the legal doctrine on self-defence used in many Western legal codes is based upon men's experiences and perception of dealing with violence and is unacceptable and inappropriate because female defendants must fit into an existing masculine frame of reference. Successfully arguing self-defence has sometimes resulted in acquittal but defendants need to show that the use of force was commensurate with the imminent danger. Sometimes demonstrating provocation reduces murder to manslaughter, and this requires the defendant to show that the victim's actions caused him/her to lose self-control and act in the heat of the moment and thus, the killing was not premeditated. However, the sexist bias in the interpretation of the law is manifest in the way judges have been far more likely to recognize female ridiculing of male sexual prowess as sufficient provocation in cases of male murder of female partners (Howe, 1991) than to accept a cumulative pattern of violence and abuse over a period of time as legitimate reason for female murder of male partners (in the UK, *R* v. *R*, 1981: 321).

Some courts have accepted the battered woman syndrome as a legitimate defence and this approach is regarded as remedying the limitations of conventional defences because the killing is then interpreted as an unavoidable or an inevitable response to extended periods of abuse and violence. However, this can also lead to a 'medicalization' or 'psychologizing' of the woman's response, thus undermining her sense of agency.

Scotland has been at the forefront in introducing legislation on domestic violence in Europe. The Protection from Abuse (Scotland) Act came into force in 2001, which enhances protection for victims of domestic abuse, while a change in the terminology from 'domestic violence' to 'domestic abuse' has widened the remit of behaviours and offences that can be addressed by recourse to this law. In addition, the Sexual Offences (Scotland) Act 2002 has reinforced protection legislation, most notably around sexual offences. Moreover, in 2003 the Scottish executive introduced a national strategy aimed at introducing multi-agency and multi-professional preventative work on domestic violence. This initiative included attempts to stop the abuse before it happened by targeting and re-educating children and young people on attitudes which seek to condone domestic violence. This was known as 'primary prevention' and included 'secondary prevention' strategies which entailed work with women and children who had experienced domestic violence and work with men who had perpetrated domestic violence.

In this respect, McKie's (2005) sociological approach to the issue of domestic violence is useful to a social work understanding of the law. This is because she examines how traditional social constructions of domestic violence in medical, legal and social work discourses have affected the implementation of policies to address domestic violence. She notes the impact of the lack of an internationally agreed definition as to what constitutes domestic violence:

> The failure to agree a definition works to the benefit of abusers and reinforces the ad hoc manner in which policies and services respond (Kelly, 1999). There is no agreed definition of domestic violence between nations, nor within the UK: legal, police and related services work with a range of definitions. This means that the collection of data on prevalence and incidence is highly problematic, thus making concerted policy and service development complex and potentially difficult. (McKie, 2005, p. 24)

The weakness of both liberal and radical feminist legal theories is that they tend to treat 'men' and 'women' as discrete homogeneous categories and thus to underestimate the importance of other social divisions and inequalities based on class, ethnicity, or national and regional differences within these groups. Also, the emphasis on the way the law reinforces patriarchal dominance belies the contradiction in the way the law sometimes empowers and enhances women's human rights and at the same time minimizes the contribution of women's struggles to gain legal and social reform.

In contrast, postmodernists examine the law as a series of discourses in order to analyse how the law is an expression of power in society. This is achieved through the ways the law *exercises* power. This is not simply in the way it determines what is legally valid, but in the way it can disqualify other knowledge and experiences as less valid via the insistence that they must be translated into legal issues before they can be processed by any legal system. This is what Saraga (1998) (see Chapter 1) means, when she states 'discourses define what is worth knowing [about a subject]'. Thus, through its dependence on a 'rights' discourse the law places limitations on women's movements, anti-racist movements, disability rights movement and gay and lesbian movements because their everyday experiences of conflicts around various forms of oppression must be translated into a rights discourse. This discourse is highly individualized and this enables the state (through the law) to exercise power and mediate such conflicts. In this respect the law is limited because as a mechanism of social regulation the law is linked to property rights, which historically has undermined the needs of these various social movements. For example, under slavery black people by law were considered the 'property' of white slave owners; women historically have fought the presumption in law that their bodies were the property of men through marriage. Similarly, gay and lesbian people have fought long and hard against the medicalization of homosexuality as a disease, in order to avoid becoming the property of medicine and psychiatry.

Increasing globalization, diaspora, migration and the rapid increase in the number of stateless people have increased reflection on the issue of human rights and the law as opposed to the more nation-state-specific concept of citizenship and the law. Turner (1993) has attempted to develop a universal concept of human rights predicated on the commonalities of human existence. This includes the frailty of the human condition in terms of life-span, exposure to social risks of war, famine, disease and ecological disasters, and increased frailty and dependence in older age. Roach-Anleu (2002) argues there are serious weaknesses with trying to develop universal concepts of human rights. First, the notion of 'humanity' is contestable and limitless in terms of how it can be applied. Secondly, it is difficult to identify what the term 'human rights' means in any real sense outside of any local, social, economic and political context. This is because perceptions of what is desirable with regard to human rights are influenced by the convergence of socio-economic, political, cultural and historical factors, which occur in a society at any given time. Lastly, there is often considerable disparity between the ideals embodied in any human rights declaration or convention and their implementation in people's experience. Moreover, for many sociologists (Said, 1997) the development of human rights definitions entails a peculiarly Western slant and is underpinned by political and economic agendas.

## Islamic Legal Theory

Both Muslim and non-Muslim legal theorists criticize the contemporary debates on human rights for the ways they either ignore Islamic law, or stereotype Islamic law as oppressive, archaic and hence unable to contribute to any international law on human rights. For instance, Weichman et al. (2001) criticize what they regard as Western prejudices and assumptions about Islamic law and its portrayal in Western media, particularly after 11 September 2001. They cite the fact that there is no separation of 'church and state' as such in Islamic law, but different Muslim nation states interpret this relationship differently. For example, Turkey has had a secular legal system since the time of Mustafa Kemel Ataturk, while Iran reverted to an Islamic legal system following the introduction of an Islamic republic in 1979. In Egypt there is a formal parliamentary process, which has a formal code based on Islamic principles. In contrast, in Saudi Arabia judges are allowed to set the punishment on Ta'zir (lesser) crimes.

In most Muslim countries provisional governors appoint judges and in a number of countries, such as Saudi Arabia, the Ministry of Justice appoints them. They are known as Qidis. Just as in Western nation states, many undergo a formal legal training beforehand accompanied by a period in a pupillage or internship (like Western lawyers). In addition, Shari law is based on the Qu'ran, Sunna, Ijmas (consensus legal findings reached by a religious scholar or 'Ulama') and Qiyas. These three forms of legal rules make for a very flexible legal system that gives judges a great deal of flexibility to find solutions in cases where there are less serious crimes. Also, the burden of proof in *Had* cases (that is cases based on breaches of the Qu'ran) is very strict and a Had punishment can only be imposed if the defendant confesses to a crime or there are at least two witnesses (four in cases of adultery).

Using Bourdieu's theory of discourse and his concept of sexuality, Dupret (2001) examined Islamic law in Egypt in relation to two cases of sex change operations and one case of female circumcision. He noted the changing discourses within Egyptian society on issues of sexuality. He discussed how, although discourses on sexual morality are still dominated by what he terms 'Islamic normativity', this was not the only influence on the legal judgements. His research showed that judges had a lot of professional discretion to interpret moral precepts in each of these cases. The verdicts reached demonstrated the changing nature of moral discourses in contemporary Egyptian society and the diversity and flexibility in legal rulings, contrary to Western stereotypes of Islamic law.

In contrast, however, Carroll's (2001) research on inheritance and adoption laws in India and Pakistan, and Sahibzada's (2001) research on rape laws in Pakistan, both question the extent of diversity and flexibility in Islamic law. Sahibzada identifies the punitive and gendered nature of Hudood Ordinance, under which rape victims can be imprisoned or subjected to physical punishment if they are unable to prove the rape. Similarly, Carroll noted how in Pakistan, Islamic law was used to appeal against the legal requirements of the 1961 Muslim Family Law Ordinance, which gave inheritance rights to orphaned grandchildren. She noted how the proposed Adoption Bill in India was shelved following Muslim opposition (due to concerns over inheritance) and argues that this will greatly affect the legal rights of orphans and prospective adoptees in India and Pakistan in future. Similar controversies and concerns have been associated with laws on rape, domestic violence and adoption in Europe and the UK (McKie, 2005; Allen, 2003).

# The History of Human Rights

A universal declaration of human rights was established by the UN in 1948 under the 'Declaration on Human Rights', which identifies fundamental human rights that all men and women are entitled to without discrimination. These rights cover civil, political, social, economic and cultural rights and are based upon a universal concept that all humans are rational and moral beings and therefore entitled to certain rights and freedoms. Article 1 of the Declaration asserts that all humans are born free and equal and should act towards one another in a spirit of brotherhood. The rights include a right to life, liberty, security of person; freedom from enslavement, torture or inhuman and degrading treatment; a right to fair trial; freedom of movement; political affiliation; freedom of expression; the right to own property and to participate in government. In addition, the UN has established a Human Rights Committee and the International Declaration on Civil and Political Rights to monitor the implementation of the Convention.

In practical terms, one of the biggest issues regarding the implementation of the Convention and hence the enforcement of international law concerns the question of armed intervention in a nation state to prevent human rights violations. Traditionally the consensus view has been that such intervention represents a breach of international law, which has been shaped by the UN Charter. This suggests that negotiation, rather than the use of force, is the preferred option and is commensurate with the UN Charter and the principle of non-intervention in the affairs of a sovereign state. However, numerous contemporary international conflicts entailing repression and ethnic genocide heighten the tension between state sovereignty and the human rights of citizens.

The problem is exacerbated because the human rights debate does not occur in a political vacuum, but rather in the context of a very uneven playing field between superpower nations such as the US or China (who have the socio economic and political power to act unilaterally) and less powerful, newly industrialized nations, who have come under pressure from institutions such as the World Bank, which have linked the terms of national loan repayments to socio-political conditions on human rights. In addition, for many critics the whole concept of human rights as articulated by the UN Declaration is founded upon Western liberal ideals and values, which are anathema to the more communitarian ideals of many non-Western nations and cultures (Ghai, 1994).

In practice, international law often does not 'square' with domestic law. The general principle is that where the two are seen to be in conflict, then international law should take precedence. However, in reality, this is seldom the case with regard to human rights. Parsons' (1962) sociology of law is useful in understanding the barriers to international law enforcement, particularly in the area of human rights. In identifying the four key problems to be addressed before a rule-making system could become a body of law, he identified the power of *jurisdiction* and the power to impose *sanctions* as crucial in order that the law achieve its integrative function. Held (1995) argues that the UN has historically failed in this respect because it has been unable to develop a new model of international relations and to create a new model of international law (and hence identify its jurisdiction). Therefore, it is relatively weak against powerful nation states (namely the five permanent members of the UN Security Council, the US, Russia, China, Britain and France). These nation states can, and often do, use their power of veto to set the agenda, thus limiting the power of the UN to impose sanctions, particularly where there are human rights violations.

# Legal Discourses and their Impact

The law has played a crucial role in the construction of homosexuality. One of the many difficulties for social workers in promoting the civil and political rights of lesbian, gay and transgendered service users is that in many countries there are strict laws prohibiting homosexual relations. Moreover, it is difficult to assess accurately a country's views on the issue because the laws are not necessarily indicative of social attitudes. A number of nations have laws prohibiting homosexuality and have had them for years, but in practice such countries may be far less oppressive than their laws suggest. These laws may be a residue of an earlier more oppressive period. Equally, countries that have laws prohibiting discrimination against gays and lesbians may have a hostile culture towards homosexuality and persecute gays and lesbians in other ways. In a number of countries the laws on homosexuality stem from Judaism, Christianity and Islamic teaching and are sometimes used in various countries to legitimate sanctions against gay and lesbian relationships even when there is no legal prohibition. Examples of this include the Vatican City and Egypt. A further complication is that in many countries in Africa, Asia, Oceania and Central America there are laws prohibiting gay relationships but not lesbian relationships. There are also different degrees of punishment for breaches of the law. For instance, 25 African nations, 14 Asian, 13 Oceanic, 5 Central American and 1 South American country prohibit homosexuality. Of these, in Mauritania, Sudan, Iran, Saudi Arabia, United Arab Emirates and Yemen, a maximum conviction carries the death penalty, while in India, Bangladesh, Guyana, Sierra Leone, Tanzania, Myanmar, Singapore, and Barbados the maximum sentence is life imprisonment. Paradoxically, however, 28 countries legally recognize civil or registered partnerships between same sex couples, while Canada, some states in the US, Belgium, Spain and the Netherlands all legally recognize same sex marriages (Kitzinger and Wilkinson, 2004). In a number of countries including the UK, Canada, US and Sweden, the adoption laws have changed to allow gays and lesbians to adopt and foster.

However, in all these areas discrimination, civil partnerships, marriage and adoption – the situation is complex and contested and the relaxation of legal codes in any one country does not readily translate into civil and political rights for gay and lesbian service users. A number of sociologists (Ryan, 2000; Weeks, 2004; Holt, 2004; Clarke and Finlay, 2004) all identify the ongoing discrimination and the violation of civil and legal rights that gays and lesbians continue to experience.

A number of European countries have signed up to the European Convention on Human Rights, which is an attempt to adhere to the 1948 UN Declaration. However, as Johns (2003) points out, there is a problem with this:

> This [convention] has not been adopted by all countries, is not a code of law as such. Hence it is not possible to complain to the courts that action in a particular case breaches the Declaration on Human Rights. (Johns, 2003, p. 23)

Johns suggests that the Declaration and other UN declarations and conventions are used as 'benchmarks' against which countries can be assessed regarding the extent to which they comply with human rights. One of the best known conventions in relation to human rights is the UN Convention on the Rights of the Child, which the UK government ratified in 1991. Every five years the UN International Committee assesses a nation's performance in respect of this convention. Similarly there have been case examples and practice examples cited by advocacy groups, of concerns about the ways the human rights of mental health services users have been violated. Article 5 of the European Convention on Human Rights (ECHR) concerns the right to liberty and protection of persons of 'unsound mind'. The legal definition sets out very specific conditions regarding the medical issue of 'unsound mind' requiring the establishment of a true mental disorder, warranting compulsory detention and incarceration, and regular monitoring of the validity of confinement. Above all, it entails the presumption of a medical assessment as a prerequisite to detention. In relation to the question of detention it is useful to consider Bourdieu's concept of the 'elasticity' of judicial interpretation to understand the diversity of court rulings regarding mental health service users and the question of compulsory confinement. For example, in the case of *Aerts* v. *Belgium* (1998: 29 EHRR 50), where the breach of human rights was considered to apply because no medical treatment was offered. Conversely, in the case of *Anderson, Doherty and Reid* v. the *Scottish Ministers and the Advocate General for Scotland*, the definition of treatment was expanded to include a need to protect the public, and cases where therapeutic treatment was considered palliative. Broadening or narrowing the legal definition of 'treatment' has also been connected with breaches of Article 3 (which concerns degrading or inhuman treatment). In recent legal discourses the narrowing of the definition of 'inhuman' or 'degrading' has occurred where the courts have decided that so long as the treatment is necessary the Convention is not considered to apply, as in the cases of *Herczegfalvy* v. *Austria* (1992: 15 EHRR 473) and *Grare* v. *France* (1993: 15 EHRR CD 100).

In Habermas's (1993) sociological analysis of the law, he identified its dialectical nature when operated in relation to rights and social justice. He noted that the establishment of a welfare state in many European countries in the twentieth century represented increased democratization for many working-class people in the form of increased welfare and social security rights, but at the same time increased forms of social control in the form of state intervention in the private sphere of the family. To support this point he cites in particular the therapeutic support services of social services departments. This contradiction is exacerbated by the contradictory way the law operates in many Western societies as it seeks to regulate the conflict between those competing for rights versus social control in order to secure integration.

In Chapter 2, Kleinmann (2002) identified the relative weakness of international organizations like the EU in controlling social policy in the face of individual European nation states' ability to assert their sovereignty and pursue their own domestic policies. Although the European Convention on Human Rights is absolutely nothing to do with the EU (which is in essence an economic partnership) and was signed by Britain and the other 44 members of the Council of Europe, the workings of the European Court which presides over the human rights violations, are influenced by the relationships within the EU. In this respect Kleinmann (2002) argues that bodies like the European Commission and the European Court of Justice are beginning to make some progress on issues like human rights in some countries, but they are hampered by the power and autonomy of individual nation states. This probably explains why governments can in principle commit themselves to passing legislation that is commensurate with the spirit of the UN Convention but at the same time why the requirements of the Convention are not absolute and can be exploited using legal 'loopholes'. The limitations of the ability of international bodies like the UN or the EU to address the global problem of human rights violations and to call nation states into account is reflected powerfully in the UNHCR's statement on the 10.6 million people it defines as being 'of concern' (UNHCR, 2006, p. 10).

# Sociology, Law and Social Change

Roach-Anleu's (2002) sociological analysis demonstrates the contradictory way that the law operates around the globe, which means it is at one and the same time a source of both empowerment and social control. For instance, numerous social movements have successfully used the legal system to obtain changes in the law to further their civil rights. The mental health advocacy groups in the US and UK have obtained changes in the law on rules and conduct regarding patients/clients who are detained, over issues of informed consent and guardianship of their property or finances. The National Association for the Advancement of Colored People (NAACP) in the US has secured the introduction of laws repealing racial segregation in the areas of housing and education. Moreover, despite national limitations, over 190 countries have signed up to the UN Convention on the Rights of the Child, while a number of European countries have introduced legislation allowing gay and lesbian people to adopt. In Australia, Roach-Anleu cites the way indigenous Australian social movements have successfully advocated for changes in constitutional law which prevented widespread flooding of wilderness areas in Tasmania and the adoption of race and sex discrimination legislation (Roach-Anleu, 2002, p. 119).

Conversely, however, the law has also been a crucial element of social control with specific regard to marginalized groups. In the UK for example, elements of the 1989 Children's Act can be used to undermine the agency of children (particularly section 47 governing child protection procedures and duties to investigate significant harm) and can be used in ways that contravene the principles of Articles 8 and 12 of the UN Convention on the Rights of the Child. Roach-Anleu also examines the use of the Family Group Conference (FGC) model in New Zealand, which was introduced under the auspices of the *Children, Young Person's and Their Families Act 1989*, and notes that despite its attempts at diverting young offenders from the court system it has failed to involve young people pro-actively in the decision-making process (Roach-Anleu, 2002, p. 157). In a similar fashion, aspects of Pakistani law can be argued to maintain the gendered status quo, as in the case of allegations of sexual assault and witness corroboration (Sahibizada, 2007).

Roach-Anleu uses Weber's concept of the relationship between the law and domination to examine the ways the law acts as a form of social control. She argues that in contemporary societies the law as a social control mechanism is equated with the criminal justice system. The two basic models of the criminal justice system are the *crime control* model and the *human rights* model. The crime control model is predicated upon the control of criminal activities through the punishment of those who commit offences. It assumes that those who instigate criminal proceedings will base their assessments on systematic investigations and evidence and that those who are not guilty will be processed out of the system while those who are assessed as guilty will be moved on to the next stage. In contrast, those who emphasize a human rights model of criminal justice focus on due process and correct legal procedures being followed. Here the focus is upon legal procedure rather than whether the person is 'guilty' as alleged. It stresses the considerable power of the police and the criminal justice system and argues that given the potential of this power to subject citizens to criminal punishment, there needs to be very thorough scrutiny of the actions of the police and the court system; also, that such action should be controlled and curtailed by the law. This perspective highlights the need for safeguards to accommodate doubts about the accuracy and impartiality of police investigations, the procedures for the protection of suspects, and policies and protocols regarding searches, use of interrogations, weapons, and access to legal counsel (Roach-Anleu, 2002, p. 142).

## Summary of the Main Points

- Sociology informs social workers' understanding of law by:

  (a) identifying the social conditions under which laws emerge and change;

    (b) examining the extent to which the law contributes to social change;

    (c) exploring the values and belief systems of the law.

- Postmodernists like Bourdieu argue that justice has very little to do with the law; rather, it is simply a reflection of the power of those legal professions which have achieved discursive dominance.

- Critical legal theorists provide a conceptual framework for understanding how the political and economic dimension of law-making is useful in an understanding of social policy and social work.

- Neo-Marxists argue that the law operates to ensure the efficient operations of capital by addressing the competing needs of welfare legislation and of passing laws which facilitate the efficient accumulation of capital.

- Feminists identify how women are subordinated by a legal system and how it reinforces patriarchal power relations.

- Islamic legal theory provides insights into the complex and diverse nature of the relationship between 'church' and 'state', as well as the diversity and flexibility of the Islamic legal code.

- Parsons' notion of the four main problems that need to be addressed before a rule-making system can become a legal system helps clarify the difficulties of law enforcement around human rights and the problems facing the UN.

- Habermas provides a framework for understanding the complexities between the legal rights of citizens and their responsibilities to adhere to the sovereignty of the state.

# Conclusion

This chapter has outlined the varieties of ways in which sociology informs an understanding of the law in a social work context, and promotes a critical reflexive approach to legal considerations. First, it demonstrates how the law relates to issues of deviance and social control. Secondly, it informs an understanding of the relationship between inequality and power on both an individual and a structural level. Thirdly, it illustrates the connection between the law and various social institutions in society. Similarly, various sociological theories (Bourdieu,1993; Habermas, 1996) inform an understanding of the politicized and dialectical nature of the law and help explain why at times it has the potential to be both empowering and oppressive. In contrast, Roach-Anleu's (2002) sociological analysis of the law provides insights into what specific conditions give rise to particular laws, such as

anti-terrorism legislation in the wake of '9/11' and '7/7', and provide indicators of how the law promotes social change (either positive or negative). In
addition, the sociological analysis of the law presented here helps to explain
the power imbalance between international organizations such as the UN or
EU and individual nation states, and how that imbalance influences
progress on human rights around the globe.

   All these dimensions of sociological analysis of the law enhance critical
reflexive social work practice through the ways they inform an understanding of the autonomy and advocacy dimensions of the social work role. This
aspect is relevant to all kinds of social work, whether social workers are
involved in NGOs, community development, protecting vulnerable children, supporting older people in retaining their independence or assisting
mental health service users or refugees in gaining access to services which
enhance their human rights. This latter issue will be examined in more
depth in Chapter 5, which examines some of the practice dilemmas of
balancing human rights with legal constraints when working with
clients/service users.

## Case Study

Gerhardt is a social worker discussing with his manager whether or not to apply for a
court order in a case involving a man who has badly beaten his ten-year-old son. He
tells his supervisor that he is worried because generally the parents of this child provide
good care for their son and he does not want to get the father into trouble, but on this
occasion the father would not accept the social worker's concerns about the violence
used. A discussion ensues between social worker and manager, and the manger
suggests that Gerhardt needs to look at law in a more dynamic and critical way.

Sociological perspectives would enable Gerhardt to do this by providing different
models of the law, and demonstrating its social work practice implications. The crime
control model and the human rights model illustrate the contradictory and dynamic
way the law operates in society, and at times it can be used by social workers (who
need to work within the law to carry out their professional duties) to advocate for
service users' rights. The crime prevention model focuses more on the punitive and
social control aspects of the law with its emphasis upon punishment, and its faith in the
scientific objectivity in criminal investigations and the capacity to obtain sound corroborating empirical evidence. (The debate on the accuracy of DNA sampling in the
Madeleine McCann investigation illustrates the complexity of this problem.) It also
identifies the reductionist way that non-offenders can be screened out from offenders.
In contrast, the human rights perspective emphasizes the importance of due process in
investigations, interviews and the processing of suspects, and the rule of law ensuring
transparency and regulating the actions of the police and ensuring a fair trial. This argument has been used successfully by human rights lawyers and advocates around the
globe to address the treatment of Iraqi prisoners by US and UK armed forces personnel, and the treatment of people suspected of terrorist offences.

## Case Study (*cont'd*)

However, the human rights model has been involved in the debates about the efficacy of incarceration and the move to increased use of non-custodial sentencing. This has included supervision orders, attendance centre orders and an increasing array of professionals including psychiatric, social and welfare services, social workers and probation officers. While some have pointed to the benefits of non-custodial sentencing in terms of cost savings, opportunities for rehabilitation, less disruption to family life and work commitments, others have criticized this approach for its failure to lead to a reduction of incarceration rates, and instead leading 'to the expansion of control and surveillance under the veneer of welfare and assistance' (Roach-Anleu, 2002, p. 166).

# Further Reading

McKie, L. (2005) *Families, Violence and Social Change* (Buckingham: Open University Press).
This book highlights the global nature of violence as well as providing a new definition of domestic abuse, which can inform AOP strategies with families.

Roach-Anleu, S. L. (2002) *The Law and Social Change* (London: Sage).
This book provides an excellent synopsis of the differences between civil and criminal law. It also provides a host of case examples, which help students understand the practical application of the law.

Weichman, D., Kendall, J. and Azarian, M. K. (2001) 'Islamic Law: Myths and Realities', electronic source http://ireland.iol.ie-afifi/Articles/law.thm (accessed 2 October 2007).
This is an interesting article in two ways. First it dispels some Western popular myths and stereotypes about Muslim cultures, and secondly, it provides some practical knowledge about the application of Islamic law to everyday social problems.

# PART II
## Arenas of Practice

# 5
# Work with Service Users

## Introduction

Sociological theory from grand theory to micro-interpretivist and social constructivist perspectives can inform direct social work with clients/services users. In order to demonstrate this, various interventions with some different service users' groups will be considered. These are, children and their families, older people, people with learning and physical disabilities, and people with mental health problems. Reflection upon sociology in relation to these service user groups is undertaken to demonstrate how these theories can be employed as a means of engaging with them and understanding their problems. In considering these different dynamics the chapter will evaluate critically the competing tensions between client/service user agency and the structural needs of service provision. These will be examined within social work's socio-political context to see how they contribute to the contradictory nature of the social work role.

> ## Key Words
>
> model coherency, Social Role Valorization (SRV) theory, sociology of childhood, spurious interaction, mortification of the self

## Sociology and Children

The chapter begins with children simply because childhood comes before adulthood in the life cycle. Sociological theories not only inform an understanding of child abuse and neglect (as discussed in Chapter1) but also enable social workers to reflect upon the efficacy of child development theories. The 'sociology of childhood' model as manifest in the work of James et al. (1999), Thomas and O'Kane (1998) and Punch (2002) differs from the more traditional sociological models of childhood. These traditional models ignore children's agency (the power to act or take decisions), by locating childhood firmly within the confines of the education system or the family, virtually making children invisible. What the sociology of childhood perspective seeks to do is to locate child development models within both their biology and their structural contexts. This is to see how child development is culturally and socially constructed in different societies. Within the sociology of childhood four main models are used to examine the ways the issue of childhood has traditionally been explored:

- *The developing child* – in this model the child is regarded as incomplete and lacking in status.

- *The tribal child model* – this model views the child as competent but part of an independent culture that can be studied. However, this child does not form part of the mainstream culture of the adult world.

- *The minority child* – this approach points to the ways children are marginalized from adult society like other minority groups.

- *The socially developing child* – this model questions whether there exist biological and universally applicable models of child development. Instead it identifies childhood as a social construct and the product of a specific history and culture.

Edwards and Aldred (1999) argue that the new sociology of childhood seeks to empower children by recognizing their capacity for independent thought and autonomous social action. A variant of this approach is the 'child as social actor' perspective, which regards children as having different (though not necessarily inferior) competences from adults. These approaches have sought to critique traditional models of child development, which regard the 'child as subject' as needing to be studied from an adult-centred perspective. For instance, James et al. (1999) criticize Piaget's (1927 [1972]) model of the socially developing child. They take issue with the way Piaget classifies childhood as an incomplete state of human existence, which functions to secure adult maturation (p. 17). Using Archard's (1993) research they assert that it is debatable whether there exists 'natural', biological and universally applicable stages of child development. In addition, Archard points to the Western ethnocentric bias in Piaget's model. He maintains this is based on Western models of scientific rationalism and Western science in the form of Darwinism. Using these to assess children's competences (James et al., 1999, argue) can lead to ethnocentric and oppressive practice.

James et al. (1999) and Punch (2002) identify how adult-centred discourses in society (which dominate social work practice) secure the marginalization of children. This is achieved through imbalances of power

(Punch, 2002), the structuring of children's space, play and time, the control of children's finances, and adult presumptions about children's competences (James et al., 1999).

The extent to which the 'sociology of childhood' model presents a plausible framework to examine social work practice, is the extent to which it acknowledges that children are not passive receptors of universal models of child development (which do not exist). Instead it recognizes that children are autonomous social actors. For example, James (1993) noted in her research that gender divisions in the friendships and play of young children may be a consequence of the school system itself. In the home or in the street, children may socialize much more in group settings. She cites Qvortrup's (1990) study which demonstrates how often children are rendered invisible in a lot of adult research. This is achieved through the absence of child-specific statistics. Data on children are either amalgamated with those of the family or placed under the ambiguous euphemism 'for children under 16'. She shares his concern that this may serve to deny a child the rights of citizenship or lead to the misinterpretation of a child's experiential position within the research, as a member of a different age group within the social structure.

Often psychodynamic theories like Piaget's (1972 [1927]) tend to present children as a homogeneous or unified group, as if generalizations about their development or behaviour can be drawn from the small experimental samples used in the research. In other words, it is assumed that by studying some children we can identify patterns across the children and young people in all cultures and societies.

## Social Work Practice Implications

Adult discourses on childhood have influenced the conduct of childcare practices, which ironically have been designed to promote the inclusion of children. For example, in the UK Thomas and O'Kane (1998) conducted research into the participation of children within the public care system (Looked After Children). They discovered that these children were marginalized in various ways. There was a lack of independent advocates. Children talked about the ways in which they were excluded – for example, the ways they were routinely not listened to – in the same ways as adults. They spoke about their feelings when being asked to leave their own reviews, and the conflict between their wishes and feelings and the adult perception of their 'best interests'.

Sociological theories on childhood also contribute to a critical understanding of the role of social workers in youth offending or youth justice and the controversies between the punitive-justice and welfare models of social policy. The youth justice system provides a 'good practice' example of how contradictions between the need to punish and the need to provide support and protection of children, operate in reality. The welfare imperative is the idea that the welfare of the child takes paramount importance over any consequences of any offences they may have committed. This is an alternative to the punitive-justice model, which argues that age must not be used as a sufficient indicator of responsibility and that the punishment should fit the crime. The welfare and punitive-justice models have vied for predominance within the youth justice organizations around the globe for the past 150 years. This has resulted in tensions in youth justice policy where it has been pulled in competing and contradictory directions.

The welfare imperative argues that primacy should be given to a child's welfare over the need for justice and control. Unfortunately this has compounded the controversy between the welfare and social justice approaches owing to the fact the age of criminal responsibility (the legal age a person can be held accountable for a crime) varies in different European countries. For example, in the Irish Republic it is 7, in Scotland 8, in England and Wales 10, France 13, Germany 14, Spain 16, the Netherlands and Belgium 18. Thus, the ways in which 'childhood' is socially constructed in these countries is not universally agreed upon, but rather it is a socially and historically specific concept.

Despite the UN Convention on the Rights of the Child, inaugurated in 1989 and signed by over 191 nations, the global violations of children's rights abound. This is reflected in the form of child slavery, prostitution, child rape, murder, sexual and physical abuse (Healy, 2001; Cemlyn and Briskman, 2003). Different sociological perspectives inform an understanding of the debate about children's rights and hence help the development of anti-oppressive practice strategies. These perspectives prompt practitioners to reflect on the ways children's autonomy and agency are often ignored in legislation or social and political processes. A number of social work academics within the new 'sociology of childhood' perspective such as Fox Harding (1996) and Munroe (2001), question whether the adult-centred emphasis on the international rights of the child actually undermines children's agency. Fox Harding notes that advocacy has become increasingly professionalized and this has led to little global progress on children's rights. This has affected children's rights not just to autonomy, but to safety, welfare and protection.

The debate over children's rights appears to be inextricably linked to the controversy over children's competence. This complexity leads to controversy as to what rights children should be entitled to. For example, David (2002) argues that one of the six barriers to children's rights around the globe is the failure of the UN to monitor and regulate the extent they are engaged in labour. Paradoxically however, Liebel's (2002) research has identified the growth of independent children's labour organizations, run by and for working children themselves in Latin America, Africa and India (Liebel, 2002, p. 266). These have come together on a regular bases in the form of international conference meetings on working children's rights around the globe.

The development of these groups demonstrates that children are capable of rational decision making and able to mobilize as autonomous agents for their own interests. Liebel asserts therefore that children should be afforded the status of 'subject' as citizens in law (on a parity with adults), and not as subjects in the sense of subjects of welfare and protectionist interventions. As a result of the agency demonstrated by international organizations of working children he argues that the relationship between children's rights and child labour is far more complex than most welfare debates suggest. He notes that elements of the UN Convention on the Rights of the Child are in contradiction. For instance, Article 12 includes the right of children to 'be taught a trade' and 'the right to security when working' (Liebel, 2002, p. 265). He suggests therefore that whilst not leaving children open to adult exploitation, it is difficult for governments to steer the right balance and avoid their oppression and exploitation. Governments must try on the one hand to avoid children's exploitation, yet on the other, to support their children's autonomy, development and independence, through work (Liebel, 2002, p. 265).

The main criticism of the children's rights perspective, however, is the over-emphasis on children's agency and the lack of clarification as to how to generate children's autonomy when they lack competence. Punch (2002) argues that children do lack the same degree of autonomy and competence for independent thought as adults, simply because they are younger and have had less life experience. Cooper (1999) asserts that there is a danger that children could be exposed to increased exploitation by giving them the same rights as adults. Nonetheless, this children's rights perspective helps social workers deconstruct the discourses underpinning traditional sociological and psychological child development theories. It does this by identifying the adult-centred assumptions behind them and it highlights power imbalances between adult practitioners and children as clients/service users.

# Older People

Social work involvement in the lives of older people is likely to increase over the next fifty years if we consider the global demographics of ageing (OECD, 2004; Hill, 2006). Hill (2006) notes that this global trend is characterized by falling birth rates, premature deaths (due to war or AIDS pandemics) and paradoxically, a higher proportion of people living over the age of 65. For example, Biswas et al. (2006) note that in Bangladesh the proportion of the population over 65 will have doubled from 7 million to 14 million by 2017. Hill (2006) suggests that much of the official literature on this trend focuses upon the 'economic burden' of older people in the context of the costs their pension and care charges represent for the 'economically active'. He points out how the term makes assumptions about older people and ignores the fact that many of them are economically active well after the official retirement age.

A number of sociologists, Yu (2007) on China, Cebulla et al. (2007) on the UK, and Kaseke (2005) on sub-Saharan Africa, refer to the 'pension crisis' and how a global ageing population represents a potential tax and welfare burden on younger citizens. Consequently, Kaseke questions whether it is accurate to categorise this demographic trend in this way and notes the range of capital assets many older people have in the form of savings, investments and home ownership. He argues that this idea of a global pension crisis makes assumptions about a homogeneous experience of retirement and ignores the extent of labour market participation of many people over 65 around the world.

Phillipson (1993) also questions whether 'older age' represents a financial burden and he points out that the idea that older people are unproductive is based upon a set of assumptions: first, that poverty for older people is now confined to a minority; secondly, that the incomes of retired people are on a pary with those of non-waged persons; thirdly, that the global rates of labour shortages have now undermined the legitimacy of retirement. Furthermore, the 'worker-versus-pensioner' perspective (implicit in the 'ageing-as-a-tax-burden' argument), adopts a limited view of productivity as entailing only waged labour. There are varieties of non-waged productivity such as voluntary work, grandparents assuming parental roles and support for grandchildren, and befriending activities.

Similarly, Grimley-Evans (2007) exposes the fallacy of 'pensioners-as-an-economic-burden', in his rebuttal of the 'moral' argument for resource rationing in health and welfare services. He critiques this argument for the way it is used to legitimate resource rationing. He rebuts this idea on the following grounds. Ethics are not value free but based on ideologies and are highly discursive entities. They provide a rationale for rationing, but not a moral justification (which is not the same thing), and ethics, i.e. what is right/wrong, are not self-evident nor can they be scientifically proven. He points out that those advocating ethical rationing fail to see that their ethical position is underpinned by a specific ideology and by certain assumptions. First, an ecological fallacy – that is, the idea that age is a clear and direct factor in the unequal distribution of disability. This is not the case because age is not a major cause of disability. Secondly, the idea that older people represent a tax burden is inaccurate as it ignores the fact that many older people save and hence invest in the economy. At the same time they pay taxes and have done so for longer periods than the young, thus their cumulative contribution to the state-funded health services is proportionately greater. Thirdly, the incremental pattern of age presented in most global demographic studies concerning the average population statistics, do not match the life span trajectory of most individuals. Many older people maintain functionality until the onset of terminal decline (Grimley-Evans, 2007, p. 309). Moreover, this moral rationing argument fails to address a key question as to whether the national health services of a nation are seen as part of the public health system, aimed at maximizing the productivity of the state, or as a service to enable individuals to achieve self-defined life goals. In using these arguments Grimley-Evans is not suggesting that poverty is not related to the process of ageing, but rather that it is not experienced homogeneously by older people.

## Reframing Ageing as a 'Burden'

The concept of a 'burden', along with a common experience of poverty amongst older people, tends to result in assumptions about their autonomy and capacity for self-determination. It also adopts Western and ethnocentric assumptions about intergenerational relationships. For example, studies in Malaysian, Singaporean and Aboriginal Australian cultures identify that there is a reciprocal relationship in relation to care giving and receiving. The traditional Western model of older age being a period of decline, lack of resources and increased dependence ignores the diversity of informal kinship networks in which many older people engage, and the reciprocal arrangements where they are both providers and recipients of informal care services (Vebrugge and Chan, 2008; Yi and Nauk, 2006). The global pattern is both diverse and contradictory. For example, Biswas et al. (2006) identify that there is a formal welfare system in Bangladesh. However, this system is means tested and better organized in cities than in many rural districts and this leads to a very uneven pattern of informal family support for older people. In rural areas the welfare system is under-utilized, with older people relying on children, and the cost of health care often prohibiting its use. In contrast, Verbrugge and Chan (2008) and Mendes (2006) found that Singaporean families and communities show strong kinship bonds, which act as effective informal welfare support systems where children provide support in the form of cash, payment of household expenses, and being companions for activities away from home. In return, many older Singaporeans reciprocate by offering baby-sitting services, doing household chores and advising on family matters (Warburton and Chambers, 2007). However, this experience is contradicted by Bos and Bos (2007) research of older age in Brazil. This study examined the correlation between marital status, income and health in a group of older people and found that widows had poorer health than single or married older people. This global diversity in older people's informal care networks is mirrored in their experience of social isolation, poverty and social exclusion.

Scharf et al. (2002) use the concept of 'social exclusion' to examine the extent of poverty. They regard this term as discursive and argue that this discourse emphasizes the dynamic nature of social exclusion. This can be used to explain people's differing experiences of poverty but at the same time it can mask the material nature of inequalities. For example, the term 'social exclusion' to describe unemployment may be accurate with regard to younger people, who will eventually get out of poverty, but minimizes the difficulties for older people. Older people, in contrast, experience multiple forms of poverty and social exclusion. This is due to their exclusion from employment, political activity and social networks, and lack of adequate material resources. In addition, this situation may be more static and fixed for older people. Many of them in this situation will be unlikely to get out of poverty without considerable financial support from the state. Also, in many industrial nations poverty and social exclusion are linked to waged labour. This makes it very difficult to gauge the full extent of poverty and social exclusion amongst older people.

Phillipson (2007) examines the extent of social exclusion amongst older people within the context of globalization and highlights its class-based nature. He compares those older people who are financially more affluent and can migrate abroad, with those who are poor, in receipt of benefits and living in socially excluded and deprived neighbourhoods (Byrne, 2002). There are those older people in the UK who are affluent enough to migrate from metropolitan districts to rural areas like the Cotswolds in England, or parts of Wales, or those who go to Spain. Similarly he identifies affluent Swedes who migrate to France, or 'better off' Canadians who go to Florida for the sun. These migrants have a different sense of community belonging. This is identified in the migrant community itself rather than in the location and these older people's perceptions of social exclusion are very different from older people who lack the same financial resources. This group of older people, who are able to control the extent of their social exclusion, is relatively new, reflecting factors like the emergence of positive attitudes to retirement, the impact of globalization and changing forms of consumption (Phillipson, 1998). This is in stark contrast, however, to the vast majority of older people, who have far less financial and other resources to influence the physical and social environments in which they live.

## Loneliness in Later Life

Though the issue of loneliness is personal and dependent upon emotional as well as social factors, it can be examined in terms of the extent of a person's social engagement and participation. There are key dimensions in defining and enhancing the quality of life in older age. In defining loneliness, sociologists examine the lack of close intense personal relationships. This is in contrast to social loneliness, which is conceptualized in terms of a lack of overall social engagement and a limited social network. A significant factor in assessing loneliness is the demographic change in the number of people living alone. Research undertaken by the European Commission (2004) estimate that in some European countries the number of older people over 80 years of age living alone ranges from between 32 and 51% (European Commission, 2004: 180).

As Hill (2006) points out, demographics on residential placements for older people do not give a full picture of European patterns of loneliness and family care. This is because they do not provide information about the extent of care given outside the home, or the extent of informal patterns of family support. In addition, precise figures for residential locations of older people are unavailable for many Asian-Pacific countries, sub-Saharan Africa, parts of North America, Eastern Europe, South Asia, China and the former Soviet Union. However, this chapter has identified a range of informal support networks and family reciprocal support amongst older people and their families in Bangladesh, Singapore and parts of Europe, North America and Latin America (Biswas et al., 2006; Mendes, 2006; Phillipson, 2007; Vebrugge and Chan, 2008). These reciprocal kinship networks may provide a means for assuaging feelings of loneliness amongst older people (however it is culturally constructed).

## Sexuality in Later Life

A further aspect precipitating social exclusion could be the way society constructs older people's sexuality. Biggs (1999) focuses on the ways that older people are socially constructed as a-sexual beings and their needs for sexual fulfilment are ignored via traditional Western cultural taboos on older sexuality. He identifies one training video in residential social work where male sexuality in particular is socially constructed as a nuisance to staff. He points out that some of the most cutting ageist stereotypes and popular catch phrases are reserved for sexuality in older age, such as 'mutton-dressed-up-as-lamb' or 'cradle snatcher'. He considers the impact of such ageist stereotypes for older people, which affect their quality of life in terms of sexuality. Similarly, Bytheway (1995) points to the number of serious attempts to raise the question of older people and sexual activity. These have sought to challenge these stereotypical images, often conveyed in birthday cards and ageist humour, of a decline in ability not matched by a decline in inclination. He asserts that the impact of ageism is such that it has the power to ensure that intimate personal relationships for older people are the ones that are most tightly circumscribed by age prejudice. This occurs both within public life and in health and social care settings.

Challenging oppressive ageist assumptions and practices is hampered by the dearth of effective critical theories. Baars et al. (2006) note the lack of a developed theoretical knowledge base to modern social gerontology. Consequently, they seek to develop an holistic theoretical framework for social gerontology that adopts a feminist component to examine the gendered nature of poverty in later life, a social constructivist perspective to critique medical discourses of older age as a 'non-functioning' period in the life cycle. They also seek to develop a perspective that includes a critique of the anti-ageing industry and biomedical discourses on Alzheimer's disease. Traditional medical discourses on Alzheimer's disease often fail to provide an adequate appraisal of the emotional and social dimensions of the disease. In considering social dimensions, they seek to include a structural analysis using cumulative disadvantage to identify the range of inequalities older people experience. Blackie (1999) demonstrates the ways such theorizing has practical benefits for practice. He gives the example of how the discourse of geriatrics as an expert medical discourse had the effect of moving those defined as 'senile' into care homes in the early to mid-twentieth century.

The central elements of this social constructivist approach, which contribute to a critical analysis of the issue of ageing, form several strands. First, it challenges the primacy of biological explanations of ageing in which biological changes (which are part of the ageing process) are used to legitimate the exclusion of older people from decisions over their lives. Secondly, it stresses that the concept of age must be seen in its structural context and linked to factors such as ethnicity, class, gender and the employment/unemployment experiences of older people. Thirdly, social constructivism recasts 'older age' not as a period of economic burden and inactivity, but as a renewed period of the search for meaning within the contexts of work, leisure and intimate friendships. Fourthly, it highlights the ways older people are marginalized in society. It does this by focusing on the ways that older people's lives can be regarded as in tension with the socio-economic aspects of capitalism, and this tension is reflected in the extent of poverty, social exclusion, experiences of employment, and the ways older people are socially constructed as a burden on various welfare states.

## Ageism and Older People

Powell and Biggs (2004) use a social constructivist analysis to deconstruct oppressive medical discourses on ageing. For example, they identify that since the nineteenth century in Western societies, the autonomy of older people has come increasingly under medical control. The control is justified through scientific claims as to the efficacy of medical interventions to increase the quality of a person's life. However, the application of biomedicine in this process can also reinforce stereotypical assumptions of the older person as 'dysfunctional'. They cite the power of biomedical discourses and argue that sociology should critically examine such discourses and the knowledge claims made by biomedicine. This is in order to avoid 'epistemological imperialism' in the definition of illness and its relationship with ageing. Thus, statements like 'healthy old age', they argue, are not neutral because they entail assumptions that this situation is the result of prudent self-care. In contrast, becoming unhealthy approximates to 'undeserving' and these kinds of discourses are used in debates over whether to treat sick older people, obese people, or those with health problems who smoke. Biggs and Powell (2004) use Foucault's discourses on self-identity (see Chapter 1) to deconstruct the standard equation of ageing with vulnerability or sickness.

Using social constructivism, Grenier (2007) illustrates how biomedical discourses of 'frailty' are used to undermine the autonomy of older people and ration health and welfare resources. Within society the ways frailty is conceptualized will have profound implications for a person's care experience and she considers how biomedical discourses on 'frailty' can lead to oppressive practice with older people. This can occur through the ways the term 'frailty' represents and orders the contexts and 'organisational practices, social representations and lived experiences of care for older people' (Grenier, 2007, p. 425). Power over older people is secured through the separation of the 'healthy' from the 'unhealthy'. In making these distinctions, value judgements are made about what forms of experience are significant, such as functional decline, and are accepted, while others such as strengths and abilities are subjugated or dismissed (Foucault, 1988, pp. 78–108). The practice of assessing 'frailty' in the provision of services for older people can be considered as a form of this 'dividing practice' which serves to determine provision for older people, or to restrict their access to care. Thus, assessors separate frail from non-frail to facilitate or block access to services and target services to those they deem are at greatest risk.

The dominance of this discourse of frailty is reinforced by its claims to be underpinned by objective science. Clinical research on frailty focuses upon predicting risk, targeting interventions and responding to adverse outcomes in care. In clinical settings frailty is considered a syndrome, with specific frailties regarded as signs that present as functional impairments, disabilities or morbidities. This concept of frailty has been used to predict the likely use of long-term care services and to target interventions to reduce treatment costs. But as sociologists note, frailty is a social construct and it can lead to oppressive practice where the social construction of frailty transforms from a lived set of problems into a diagnosis and a subsequent treatment plan. This plan is then imbued with a set of rules and assumptions about what *ought* to be done. The danger of this approach is that it reduces the complexities and conceptions of care to a tick list of objective classifications of need. These in turn ignore the cultural and material factors that affect the experience of being frail, such as low income, low level of education, and a lack of family, religious or support networks.

The frailty discourse entails a number of limitations. First, it gives primacy to the observable and functional notions of ill-health, which tend to reduce it to a narrow medical construction of frailty. Secondly, it assumes the pre-eminence of a service-led tick box assessment of impairment. This in turn tends to overlook the social and emotional dimensions which accompany changes in the body in later life. These could include, for example, separations from partners caused by hospital admissions (which for older people who have been together for many years can be very traumatic, exacerbating their vulnerability). Moreover, the concept of frailty ignores the ways it is structured by cumulative disadvantage such as age, gender, ethnicity and sexual orientation.

A similar critique regarding the social construction of ageing is adopted by Vincent (2007) in his examination of the 'war on old age' lobby. He identifies four trends within this perspective. First those whose perspectives are characterized by the need to engage in symptom alleviation; secondly those who equate ageing with ill-health and regard it as like battling a disease; thirdly, those who seek to control the cellular process of ageing; and fourthly those who want to develop scientific techniques to achieve human immortality. However, he points out that all of these approaches, whether drawn from biomedicine, cell-science or the cosmetics industry, use war and military metaphors in their advertising literature. This can have damaging and negative consequences for perspectives on older people:

> Older people are characterised by the different elements of anti-ageing science as having lost their good looks, succumbed to disease, become overwhelmed by senility, and as surrendering to death. Constructing older people as defeated adopts another battle metaphor, denies the possibility of positive models of old age, and reinforces the fear of ageing and death.   (Vincent, 2007, pp. 957)

Social constructivism has been fruitful in terms of identifying ageism and for illustrating its various dimensions. Sociologists argue that ageism is a situation where older people are subjected to the application of negative and unwarranted stereotypes. It exists in the form of employment discrimination, a decline in personal status on retirement, and through stereotyping and dehumanizing treatment. Ageism identifies the ways that through these forms of discrimination, age is redefined and configured from simply being a stage in the life cycle into a socio-economic problem (Phillipson, 1998, p. 16).

## Social Work Practice Implications

Thompson (1993) has identified the ways ageist stereotypes lead to forms of oppressive practice. These include perceiving older people as a burden on the welfare state, and treating older people like children (infantilization), thus minimizing their competencies and capacities for agency. Alternatively, it can mean perceiving older people as different, i.e. less important, than children and this can lead to substandard service provision. Other stereotypical ageist assumptions include the idea that older people are lonely, a-sexual and unintelligent because of the (assumed) inevitable onset of senility. The perception of older people (particularly in Western culture) as lonely ignores and minimizes the positive roles and networks that older people have fostered and enjoy, while the assumption about a-sexual behaviour renders limited social work intervention. Often care plans and support services fail to recognize the need for sexuality support. By reflecting upon these ageist assumptions it is possible to identify the connections between certain beliefs and assumptions about older age and the practices of institutions.

Thompson (1996) argues that it is possible to develop anti-ageist social work practice in the following ways:

- By recognizing that ageism needs to be challenged on the social work practice level or individual level. This can be done by challenging the stereotypical notions of older people's dependency, giving older people more choices and doing more interactive and development work with individual service users. This can include focusing upon self-esteem, recognizing the existence of ageist oppression, and developing theory, which can begin with developing critiques of the medical models of ageing and disability.

- By challenging ageism at the group level by influencing and shaping the practice of other social workers.

- By challenging ageism on the organizational level. This can be achieved by influencing agency policies and procedures.

- By challenging ageism on a wider societal level by developing anti-ageist theory.

# Sociology and Disability

Social constructivism has also been useful in deconstructing medical discourses on disability. Saraga (1998) identifies the way traditional medical discourses regard the person's impairment as their defining quality and construct this as a social problem, and this approach dominates social policy. The social model of disability, on the other hand, illustrates how medical discourses on disability have been central in the construction of disability as a sickness or form of individual pathology. In doing this the social model has been able to identify how such discourses can be regarded as a form of oppression. This has occurred through the way they lead to attempts to adapt the person to fit into able-bodied society. In addition to this criticism, the social model of disability identifies how the medical model gives primacy to clinical diagnoses of the impairment. This results in the extension of the boundaries of medical expertise not only to treatment but to the determination of the lifestyle of the person with disability (Healy, 2005, p. 22).

The social model of disability highlights the complex interconnections of social constructions, health and social work interventions and policy outcomes around the contested concept of disability and the ideology of disablism. This term refers to sets of ideas which legitimate existing power relations, which results in the discrimination and oppression of disabled people. Oliver (1996) identifies that one of the key consequences of disablism is that disabled people are subject to particular forms of compounded and multiple oppressions where they are discriminated and marginalized by institutions and the able-bodied. This in turn is exacerbated by the ways welfare services create dependency amongst people with disabilities.

The social model of disability has itself, however, been criticized for its potential to lead to hierarchies and divisions within the Disability Movement. According to Bury (1996) this is manifest in the danger of giving primacy to personal experience as a form of valid knowledge, over any sociological research methodology. He notes that disabled researchers have criticized the role of able-bodied researchers in addressing issues involving the politics of disability. They have done this by arguing that these researchers are part of the oppressive able-bodied majority. The hierarchy within the Disability Movement is reflected in the fact that the complex relationship of chronic illness to disability is often not addressed in disability movement literature. Bury argues that this has led to an ageist social division whereby young people with disabilities use the social model of disability to mobilize political support, whereas the needs of those with non-chronic, relatively stable though severe forms of disability (usually older people) are largely ignored within the Disability Movement. What has occurred here is the development of what Merton (1972) calls an 'insider doctrine' amongst 'Outsiders' (a traditionally marginalized social group). This is where an outsider group (in this case the Disability Movement) has developed its own elite 'insider doctrine' in order to deal with its social exclusion by wider society. However, in doing this it ends up excluding and marginalizing other less powerful, and vulnerable, groups in society, in this case older people with disabilities. (Insider and Outsider doctrines and practices are explored in more depth in Chapter 7.)

In relation to sociological concepts of disability, the 1980s saw the development of Wolfensberger's Social Role Valorization (SRV) theory. The term 'valorization' derives from the French word 'valorise' meaning to value. SRV theory examines the ways in which various groups (but specifically learning disabled people in Wolfensberger's approach) have become devalued in society. Race (1999) argues that SRV was developed into a full-blown sociological theory by Wolfensberger in 1994. It was an attempt by Wolfensberger to address the social marginalization of all devalued groups in society and to provide a means to structure personal social services to meet their needs. Consequently, he defines devaluation as a process by which low or negative value is assigned to an entity (Wolfensberger, 1998, p. 3). A person perceived by society to be of low value tends to be treated in ways which reflect that perception and this is represented in the way they are afforded low-quality housing, poor educational provision or none at all, low pay and low-status employment (if employed at all), and health care of poor quality (Wolfensberger, 1998, p. 5). He argues that it is the second level of devaluation, the one that takes place on the level of small groups, communities or society, that is the most important. This is because it creates and maintains socially devalued classes of people who systematically receive poor treatment.

One major consequence of devalued roles is that once ascribed they seriously diminish people's access to valued ones. Major negatively devalued roles that people are likely to be cast in are 'alien' (so different they cannot be classified); sub-human, non-human or pre-human (older people or young unwanted newborns); in the role of a menace, or objects of dread; cast in the role of trivia or objects of ridicule; or as objects of pity. Therefore, because society feels sorry for them it makes few demands upon them, which affects their learning and growth. Alternatively they are perceived as a burden, in need of charity (and one consequence is that the devalued person may only be provided for on a subsistence level), or subjected to infantilization. Infantilization is where a person is cast into childhood roles like an eternal child who never matures into adulthood and whose capabilities will always remain childish. Alternatively, another form of devaluation is through reversion from adulthood back to childhood. People with a disability may also be perceived as 'sick/diseased' and thus they are exonerated from responsibility but deemed in need of various forms of therapy. Moreover, they may be subjected to death-related or death-image roles. Examples of these include older chronically ill people, or long-term prisoners who are deemed to have outlived their usefulness. These people may be related to as if they have already died.

Rejection by society often takes the form of social exclusion accompanied by the negative images to which socially devalued people are continually juxtaposed. On many occasions they are physically excluded via segregation from places that those with valued social roles inhabit. In addition, their devaluation is reinforced in the language and description of services provided for them, e.g. 'mentally retarded', 'mentally handicapped'. People with disabilities often experience *distantation*: loss of control over their lives, where other people make the decisions or they are subjected to frequent moves. This results in relationship loss or breakdown and relationship discontinuity, where people come and go endlessly. The consequence of this for many devalued people is 'boughten' relationships. This is where people are recruited and paid to do what is needed, and these therefore are artificial relationships. *De-individualization* is also a feature of their lives and this can take the form of regimentation and mass management. Often people with disabilities have to accommodate themselves to whatever is available in welfare services provision, rather than getting what they need or want. Wasting is also a feature in that many devalued people spend years where they are denied a lifetime of opportunity and their potential is wasted.

Competency in SRV theory refers to the integrity of body and mind and what is in a person's behavioural repertoire: skills, habits and whatever resources they have to participate in society. Competency is important for devalued people because the development and exercise of competency is a natural mode of growth in humans. In addition, being competent represents a higher state of the actualization of human potential. Personal competency is highly valued in Western cultures and hence Western society is more accepting of more competent devalued persons. This is because competent people can carry out more social roles. Therefore competency enhancement is a mission of human services and any programme which fails to enhance competency may actually do harm. Competency, in an SRV sense, refers to the ability to see, hear, walk, talk, think, analyse and reason. It also includes the ability to feed, dress, and groom oneself, and to apply one's abilities to specific situations and adapt one's behaviour to relate to others in a range of different contexts (Wolfensberger, 1998, p. 70).

## Social Work Practice Implications

In order that social services achieve their role of social valorizing they need to have three characteristics. These are relevance, potency and model coherency. *Relevance* means the content of the services that address the major or most significant needs of the devalued group or person. In addition, relevance means that the services address the most pressing need or problem before others. It is frequently the case that services fail or are of low quality because the fail to meet the relevance and grouping criteria, and often they fail in relevance because of an incoherent grouping. Services may fail to give their recipients what they really need because they pander to what service users like to do, or what the group founders demand, or what governments will fund.

*Potency* refers to the fact that the most efficient and effective processes should be employed in addressing a party's needs so that they make the best use of the time of recipients. Thus, services can be said to be potent only to the degree that they employ measures that are the most effective. The potency requirement is important in order that it maximizes competency (to the full potential) of a service user. For example, material support and equipment can be brought to bear that can help bring about greater competency.

*Model coherency* as defined by Wolfensberger et al. (1996; 1998), is a situation where the real, primary and urgent needs of the clients or service users are addressed by the services provided. That is, an ideal match between all of the processes and components of the services, to facilitate effective addressing of the service user or users' primary needs. In other words, the right servers should be using the exact materials, methods, resources and language that are then used in the right setting, so that the exact services are matched with the right recipients, who are grouped in the right way.

Very often social work services fail to configure in this way and hence are incoherent in their model of service. Frequently, in the field, practitioners encounter the medical model of service provision for people with disabilities, but there are other models, which affect model coherency. These are the menace–defective model (which regards people with disabilities as a menace or 'defective'), the pity–charity model (where people with disabilities are seen as the 'burden of charity'), or the commercial–industrial model (which gives primacy to technical rationality over service users' needs), and the religious reform model.

Some models may be morally or technically flawed in their essence because they build upon fundamentally false assumptions. Alternatively, they may be incoherent, because people have the same needs but the service model to address those needs may not be appropriate or relevant to each or all of them within the service user group.

One of the things that can nullify the model coherency of a service is the use of processes in service delivery that can generate new problems. For example, one way this occurs is where a service exacts an 'image cost' (creation or reinforcement of a negative image). This can occur through meeting the needs of a social services recipient but providing services in a degrading way. Thus, people may get their need for skills development addressed but in settings and via activities that reinforce childish or inferior images. Moreover, one potential sign of model incoherency is if a model does not make sense to the clients or service users. This, at the very least, will result in an image cost for the service recipients.

The principle of model coherency within SRV theory is useful in assessing the quality of service provision because it asks several pertinent questions to be applied to all elements of the service. What is the *match* between the most pressing need of the service user (or service user group) and the needs the service is addressing? What is being done to meet those perceived needs? And what is likely to be most effective in doing so? Is it being done with intense and efficient use of the resources applied? This element in the process is known as *potency*. The converse of this process is model inco-herency. Model *incoherency* occurs where efforts to provide services are either not really relevant, in that they address only secondary or even no real needs of the client/service user, or they lack potency because they only touch the surface in dealing with those needs.

SRV theory uses the sociological concept of role theory to examine how people with disabilities become devalued. Sociological theory defines 'statuses' as positions people occupy in society that are defined by society or by key groups within it. Statuses are ascribed on the basis of gender, or of ethnicity or they can be acquired, for example, marital or occupational status. Status also entails roles, and roles carry with them certain rights and privileges but equally certain expectations demanded by society. Expectations are very powerful in shaping both the person holding the role and the rest of society.

## Disability, Education and Sexuality

Cambridge (1997) undertook a literature review of research into prejudicial attitudes regarding the sexuality of people with learning disabilities and critiques the arguments for 're-criminalizing' homosexuality for people with learning disabilities in an attempt to risk manage dangers from HIV/AIDS infection. Similarly, Jacobsen's (1992) research identifies the experience of women with learning difficulties and how their narratives about their sexu-ality expressed anger and frustration over their lack of choice, autonomy and control over their own sexual relationships. This is consistent with McCarthy's (1993, 1998) research findings of women with learning disabili-ties in long stay hospitals, where very often notions of 'appropriate' sexual-ized behaviour and norms were identified for the women by staff.

Heyman and Huckle (1993) demonstrate how the perceived abnormality of sexuality amongst people with learning disabilities is reinforced through the ways social workers and other professionals and carers socially construct sexuality as an issue of risk. The research identified that risk in this context was not risk assessed in terms of sexually transmitted diseases or unwanted pregnancy, but rather risk in terms of exposure to exploitation. This tended to presume a lack of competence and capacity to give informed consent to sexual relations. The research further identified how professional and carer attempts to limit such risks led to restricted learning environments. These restrictions then exacerbated many of the difficulties experienced by the person with a learning disability in understanding the biological, psychological and cultural dimensions of their sexuality.

In the UK and Australia there has been controversy over the devaluation of the parenting skills of learning disabled adults in child protection cases on the basis of their perceived cognitive abilities. Common stereotypes that are often used in the assessment include, a 'presumption of incompetence', a 'deficiency perspective' (which is contrary to the ethos of promoting social justice) and system abuse. This is manifest in the discriminatory treatment of learning disabled parents, characterized by an 'overzealous' approach to the assessment of risk (UK Social Services Inspectorate, 2000), an underfunding of preventative resources that could support the parenting, and the fact that learning disabled parents are disproportionately represented in child care proceedings. In Australia, Swanson and Cameron (2003) identified court practices in the state of Victoria where the parents had a disability. They noted that such parents often lacked legal representation and formal court interventions seldom made recommendations for support, training or guidance in order to facilitate custody or to regain custody of children. The research concluded that the presumption of a causal link between disability and parental inability must be strongly challenged if serious attempts are to be made to generate empowering professional social work practice and valued social roles for people with disabilities.

Oliver (1990) criticizes SRV theory for its lack of structural analysis in looking for the causes of disabled people's oppression and by arguing that only through the economic and political transformation of society will devaluation of disabled people be eradicated. In contrast, Williams and Nind (1999) claim that SRV theory ignores issues of racism, classism, and sexism and sexual oppression in attempts to promote valued social roles for people with disabilities. They adopt a lesbian feminist perspective and assert that SRV theory has the potential to lead to oppressive sex education for people with disabilities (particularly women with learning disabilities) through the primacy it gives to normality couched in terms of heterosexuality.

Despite these criticisms SRV theory represents a sociological theory which provides analysis of the ways people with disabilities are devalued. In relation to the impact of devalued social roles, it seeks to identify means to establish, enhance and maintain valued social roles for devalued people. To this end, 'the good things in life', as Race (2003) terms them, represent a social work charter which attempts to enhance and maintain valued social roles for people with disabilities. The good things in life represent a series of rights and these include: the absence of threats or coercion, the right to be viewed as part of humanity and treated with respect, the right to a family and a place to call home, the right to good health, access to meaningful social networks, and the right to make a contribution and to have it recognized by society. This charter, formed through sociological analysis of services, can underpin anti-oppressive practice (AOP) in social work.

# Sociology and Mental Health

Competing sociological theories of mental health include: interpretivist approaches (Scheff, 1966; Goffman, 1968), social constructivist (Horner, 2006) and structural perspectives (Illich, 1976). Within the interpretivist school, Scheff (1966) argues that mental illness is a social construct used to describe bizarre behaviour where an organic cause such as alcohol or drug misuse cannot be identified. Most people display odd behaviour at some point in their lives but this is not always labelled as deviant and therefore usually has no consequences for the person. However, this is not the case with the 'mental illness' label.

Scheff maintains that stereotype images of mental illness are learned from childhood via socialization. Within the family, where we often hear childhood behaviour being described in clichés like 'acting like a lunatic' or 'going mad', and in wider societal socialization, our knowledge of mental illness often comes from media images in films or high-profile press coverage of crimes committed by 'mentally ill' people. These stereotypical images are the main medium by which the majority of people recognize mental illness. However, such stereotypes are also influenced by the behaviour of those labelled as mentally ill. The significance of Scheff's analysis is that it opened up some key questions on the nature of power in relation to mental illness. This was achieved by asking why some people are labelled mentally ill and others are not.

Goffman (1968) argued that people are labelled when it is in someone else's interests for them to be so labelled. His concepts of *stigma* and the *mortification of self* have been useful to our understanding of the processes by which people come to be labelled mentally ill. In terms of stigma, Goffman was more concerned with the consequences and how these impacted on the person. According to him, once somebody has been labelled 'mentally ill' other people treat them differently. Their words and actions are given less currency because they are seen within the context of this label. This results in *spurious interaction*, i.e. people no longer give any currency to what they say or do; rather (like children or older people), their words or actions are not given equal weight to those of a 'normal' person.

In his research on asylums Goffman (1968) examined the experience of 66 people who had been labelled 'mentally ill' and had been incarcerated in an asylum. In 66 per cent of these cases he claimed the legal criteria for committal had not been met, and he alleged that where there was evidence for committal people were detained as a result of the psychiatrist's fear that they might harm themselves or others. This was despite the absence of historical evidence to support this fear. Goffman provides an example of a spurious interaction where one psychiatrist terminated an interview after only eight minutes by saying:

> I don't bother asking them [schizophrenics] more questions . . . because I know what they are going to say.   (Cited in Haralambos and Holborn, 2004, p. 325)

Goffman believed the process of becoming labelled 'mentally ill' is linked to the way a person's presenting culture (i.e. the way they choose to portray themselves in the use of language, accent, dress, hairstyles etc.) is appropriated (taken possession of) once they enter a mental institution. He also pointed out that they were expected to conform to the institution's rules, as failure to do so was often deemed to be evidence of mental illness and of the need for medication. Appropriation of personal culture is achieved via *mortification of the self*. This is a process where new inmates are systematically humiliated in front of peers and staff. Mortification can occur in a number of ways, such as the removal of personal belongings on admission, having one's head shaved, being compelled to wear a uniform, the lack of privacy, the performance of menial tasks and having to seek permission before carrying out tasks (Giddens, 2001, p. 302).

In this analysis Goffman accounts for the agency and resistive capacities of inmates by identifying five possible responses to mortification. These range from complete withdrawal to outright resistance. Most inmates in his study tended to adopt a pragmatic approach and resist the pressure to relinquish their presenting culture and sense of self by protecting themselves psychologically. This was achieved by doing the minimum to get by and staying on the right side of the asylum staff.

Gove (1982) argues that the interpretivist perspective on mental health is over-simplistic and inaccurate in arguing that mental illness is simply the product of labelling by powerful groups in society. He argues that the vast majority of people who use psychiatric services have had serious mental health problems before they were labelled mentally ill. Miles's (1981) research tends to support this contention. This research demonstrated that the family and friends of the person only adopted the 'mental illness' label after an exhaustive and desperate search for other explanations for behaviour.

In contrast to these approaches, Foucault (1971, 1986) argued that any analysis of the ways society manages and responds to people with mental health problems must be explored within the socio-political context. He believed that both mental illness and the medical discourses that seek to address it are sets of social constructs that reflect the existing socio-political configurations that exist in society at any given time. In this respect, medical knowledge reflects society's increasing shift towards social control and surveillance, and the management of those labelled mentally ill is simply part of this shift. He details how the seventeenth and eighteenth centuries saw the rise of the Enlightenment in Western Europe, characterized by the dominance of scientific and medical discourses over religious ones. Scientific rationality was seen to be the driving force behind the growth of capitalism and industrialism, both of which relied upon collective rational thought and organization for their survival. As the emphasis on rationality and disciplined action came to dominate Enlightenment thinking, irrational and undisciplined behaviour came to be regarded as deviant and defined as 'madness'. People were subsequently incarcerated on a large scale in the newly established asylums.

Horner (2006) notes Foucault's (1961) description of this process as a 'great confinement occurring across Europe in the mid-seventeenth century' (p. 63), and argues that those labelled mentally ill replaced lepers in these institutions, which were purpose-built to secure their segregation from mainstream society. The sociological analysis of Pilgrim and Rogers (1999) is relevant to this assertion. When identifying the social control dimensions in examining the political economy of mental health services they cite the socio-economic factors underpinning this change. These were, first, the pharmacological revolution (which enabled the control of mentally ill patients using drugs); secondly, the shift in services from high-cost hospitals to cheaper community-based support, coupled with in-patient care for acute disorders; thirdly, there was a shift in psychiatric discourses, which resulted in a reframing of mental illness within psychiatric services.

Horner (2006) identifies some of the main barriers to the promotion of engagement and advocacy with mental health service users: for example, professional culture clashes in the multi-agency community mental health teams. Often social workers trained in the social model of disability may be struggling against the discursive dominance of the medical model in assessments (Healy, 2005). In addition, social workers in mental health settings occupy a contradictory position operating between the state's power to control what it deems inappropriate or dangerous behaviour and the rights of mental health service users.

Unlike the interpretivist perspective, social constructivism does acknowledge the existence of organic causes of mental ill-health. However, one of the biggest criticisms of social constructivism is that it fails to demarcate where the social constructions end and when social reality begins. This can have important implications for understanding mental ill-health. Also, in his analysis of asylums and the increased social control of society, Foucault concentrates on the more oppressive institutions and ignores the more egalitarian ones (which promote the participation of mental health service users in society). This means his analysis cannot account for the contradictions in the experiences of mental health services users where at times their civil rights and rights to privacy or services are upheld, using the law, by psychiatrists, social workers, and community nurses.

Sayce (1993) addresses the material dimensions and problems facing mental health clients/service users by identifying the particular forms of social exclusion and marginalization in society:

> People with a diagnosis of mental illness face specific discrimination: it is hard to obtain work, training, a mortgage, even life assurance. A record of using psychiatric services, unlike a criminal record, is with you for life. (Sayce, 1993, p. 3)

Reflecting upon the structural context of mental health service users' oppression is one way to develop strategies to engage with them. In this respect, Illich (1976) argues, many medical or pharmaceutical advances have had such serious side effects that they may actually be worse than the original condition. In contrast, Navarro (1978) concentrates his analysis on the political economy of health care in capitalist societies and in particular the link between the pharmaceutical industry and the medical profession in the social control of the capitalist labour force. This control occurs by hiding the real causes of ill-health (many of which relate to the dangerous nature of work in factories, mining industries etc.), and secondly, by developing drugs which help to control what is deemed risky behaviour. This point is particularly pertinent given what Horner points to as the 'pharmacological revolution' for mental health patients in the twentieth century (Horner, 2006, p. 65).

Other sociological–structural perspectives on mental health adopt an anti-racist, feminist, or social-class-based approach to identify the multiple inequalities that mental health service users face. This is due to the interconnections of ethnicity, gender and class. Using income as the basis of 'class', Rodgers and Pilgrim (1996) discovered that for nearly every mental illness including paranoid schizophrenia, obsessive compulsive disorders and depression, lower socio-economic groups were affected more, with more severe symptoms and for longer periods, than those from higher socio-economic groups. Similarly, a number of feminist authors point out the disproportionate numbers of women within the morbidity statistics of mental ill-health, which is a reflection of the effects of a patriarchal society.

Women who fail to conform to traditional stereotypes of the 'feminine role' are at risk of being labelled mentally ill. Chelser (1972) argues that these traditional cultural stereotypes permeate Western psychiatry.

## Social Work Practice Implications

Prior (2003) adopts a social constructivist approach to examine the ways terms such as 'mental illness', 'parent' and 'child' are socially constructed in different discourses where parents with mental health problems have sought redress in the European Court of Human Rights when their children have been compulsorily removed. She examined nine cases from the UK, Finland, Sweden, Norway, Italy and Greece. She noted that despite the differences in national law, policies and procedures and the differences in the organizational structures for dealing with child protection issues, similar courses of action were implemented. These related to the social construction of the parents' diagnoses of mental illness. The most concerning aspect of the common response (which could lead to oppressive practice) was what Prior terms the 'static model of mental health and illness' (2003, p. 181). This was where the authorities based their long-term care plans on the short-term nature of the parents' mental health problems and did not amend these plans when the parents' mental health improved.

The usefulness of sociological theories to an understanding of mental health as illustrated here, is to identify the complexities and contradictions in the socio-political and economic configurations that are involved in the management of mental health. In addition, sociologists have provided empirical evidence which refutes biomedical accounts of the nature of mental illness in Europe, by arguing instead that it is a socially created concept. However, the sociological explanations of the evolution of that construct vary (Illich, 1976; Foucault, 1986; Sayce, 1993; Horner, 2006; Prior, 2003). Most importantly, sociological perspectives have drawn attention to the context of mental ill-health and demonstrated that (whether or not there is an organic cause of their mental ill-health) those who become defined as mentally ill, and subject to health or social work interventions, tend to be drawn from the poorest and least powerful groups in society (Sayce, 1993; Horner, 2006).

# Summary of the Main Points

- The sociology of childhood provides useful theoretical frameworks to deconstruct traditional theories of child development and point to their adult-centred and oppressive dimensions.

- Sociology demonstrates that childhood is a social construct, which varies from society to society.

- From a sociological perspective ageism can be defined as the application of negative and unwarranted stereotypes of older people.

- Empirical evidence challenges the notion of a global pension crisis and the idea of older people as a financial burden.

- Structural sociological perspectives have informed an understanding of the extent of poverty, social exclusion, unemployment and ill-health that older people experience.

- Social constructivism and discourse theory have deconstructed the oppressive treatment of older people within health and social service organizations.

- The social model of disability and SRV theory, have informed the ways people with disabilities are oppressed and devalued.

- SRV theory provides a useful concept to assess whether clients/service users are getting services that address their primary needs.

- Interpretivist sociological and social constructivist theories point to the ways that many mental health assessments are based on cultural rather than biomedical knowledge, which can lead to oppressive practice.

- Illich and Horner point to the social-control dimensions of drug treatments for people with mental health problems.

# Conclusion

This chapter has demonstrated how different types of sociological theories can inform the theorizing of social work interventions with different client/service users groups such as older people, people with learning or physical disabilities, mental health service users, and children, young people and their families. Sociology can inform social work practice with service users, using interpretivist, social constructivist and structural theories. Particular sociological concepts and theories that inform social work practice with particular service user groups are Social Role Valorization (SRV) theory and the principle of model coherency, the social model of disability and the sociology of childhood. In addition, Goffman's (1968) concepts of stigma and mortification of the self, various labelling theories and sociological theories of social exclusion also identify forms of social control and oppression that different care groups are exposed to in society. Through these different perspectives and forms of analysis, sociology has identified a number of contradictions, and different forms of oppression, which act as barriers to empowering practice with clients/service users. In Chapter 6 the complexities of those contradictions will be evaluated in more depth as the focus will be on three specific forms of oppression based upon ethnicity, sexuality and religion.

## Case Study

Mary is a social work lecturer teaching social work theories to first-year social work students. In a lecture she wants to try to demonstrate the ways sociological perspectives can inform the assessment of the quality of social service provision. Therefore she has decided to use SRV theory and to locate it within case examples relating to children, older people and people with mental health problems.

She begins by outlining the fact that SRV theory has three concepts that can facilitate critical evaluation of social work services. These are 'relevance', 'potency' and 'model coherency'. Relevance occurs in a service only if the contents of the services provided address the most significant need or problem for the service user. In addition, those services must address the most pressing need or problem first, before all other needs/problems. Mary cites the case of working children in the child labour organizations in Africa, Latin America and South Asia, and she suggests that they could argue that social workers and welfare professionals often provide an incoherent or irrelevant service. This is because by providing services in accordance with the UN Convention on the Rights of the Child 1989, and by adhering to national policies prohibiting child working and enforcing the statutory duties for protection, they are failing to address what these children see is their primary need. This need is the opportunity to work and earn a living.

With regard to the issue of the potency of a service, this means that the most efficient and effective means must be employed in addressing the service user's needs. Therefore, the services should make the best use of the recipients' time, skills and resources. Mary cites the work of Grenier (2007), who identifies how the frailty discourse and other biomedical discourses can lead to services for older people that lack both potency and relevance because of the ways older age is conflated with vulnerability or dysfunction.

For people with mental health problems she notes that the dangers of social workers failing to match services with the most pressing need of the service user is high. She gives the example of Sayce (1993), who identifies how the increase in drug treatments coincided with the de-institutionalization of millions of people with mental health problems around the globe. This may have addressed one need, i.e., to remove them from oppressive, institutional structures like asylums, and at the same time provide governments with a form of treatment which is cheaper and acts as a form of social control. However, this approach did not address other key primary needs such as accommodation, training or employment.

# Further Reading

Grenier, A. (2007) 'Constructions of Frailty in the English Language: Care Practice and Lived Experience', *Ageing & Society*, vol. 27, pp. 425–55.
This article provides clear social work practice examples of how medical discourses on frailty permeate health and social work departments and become rationales for rationing services.

Prior, P. M. (2003) 'Removing Children from the Care of Adults with Diagnosed Mental Illness – a Clash of Human Rights?' *European Journal of Social Work*, vol. 6(2), pp. 179–90.
Prior demonstrates the oppressive practice dimension of treating mental ill-health as a static entity.

Race, D. (2003) *Leadership and Change in Human Services: Selected Readings from Wolf Wolfensberger* (London: Routledge).
This book is particularly good for the ways it simplifies the concepts of potency, relevance and model coherency and for illustrating the ways they can inform the evaluation of services.

# 6

# Valuing Diversity and Difference

## Introduction

The theme of valuing diversity and differences relates to the underlying principle of Valorization, or the 'valuing' aspect of SRV theory discussed in Chapter 5. This chapter will explore the various ways clients/service users are devalued, stigmatized, de-individualized, on the basis of their ethnicity, sexuality or religion. It is relevant to devote a full chapter to these particular forms of discrimination and oppression because, despite the ethnic diversity and cultural plurality of contemporary societies, the rates of racist, homophobic and sectarian violence are increasing. As a result, sections of society are becoming more polarized. The forms of this polarization are beginning to permeate the social organization of social work practice despite the existence of an internationally recognized value base, which stresses the duty to counter all forms of discrimination and promote social justice. Therefore, this chapter will evaluate critically the potential of different sociological theories to see how well they account for these developments and provide strategies to challenge these forms of oppression.

> ## Key Words
>
> prejudice, discrimination, oppression, ethnicity, homophobia, institutional racism

## The Sociological Dimensions of Oppression and Discrimination

The word 'prejudice' comes from the Latin word *praejare* meaning to prejudge. The *Oxford English Dictionary* refers to this as 'biased opinion, based on insufficient knowledge' or 'unthinking hostility towards a particular religious or racial group' (1989, pp. 970–1). In the *Dictionary of Race and Ethnic Relations* (1984), Cashmore defines prejudice as learned beliefs and values that lead an individual or group to be biased for or against members of particular groups. *Discrimination* refers to the 'unfavourable' treatment of all individuals assigned to a particular category. Solomos (1986, 1993) defines racism as embodying a particular form of prejudice and discrimination:

> those ideologies and social processes which discriminate against others on the basis of their putatively different racial membership. (Solomos, cited in Haralambos and Holborn, 2004, p. 183)

The terms 'prejudice' and 'discrimination' can be applied to many forms of social exclusion and marginalization that exist in society. The most noticeable ones that social workers have to try to address include racism, sexism, disablism, homophobia and sectarianism. *Oppression*, as defined in the *Chambers Combined Dictionary and Thesaurus* (1997), is 'a state of cruelty and injustice'. It also means the 'suppression, maltreatment and hardship imposed on others' (p. 871).

# The Meaning of 'Race' and the Myth of 'Race'

Many years ago, I and a host of other sociology undergraduates were taught that one of the best ways to understand racism was to break it up and separate the 'meaning of race' and the 'myth of race'. That is, to deconstruct racism, by distinguishing between the meaning of race (the social constructs attached to skin colour) and the myth of race (the fact that there is no genetic or biological evidence to support the myth or notion of different races). For example, Banton (1997) examines different theories that have tried to distinguish between races and has identified three types of race theory: *race as lineage* theory, *race as type* and *race as sub-species*.

The idea of race as 'type' began to emerge in the nineteenth century. This was predicated upon a *polygenetic view*: that is, the idea that the human race has several origins, not just one. Theories in this approach developed in different Western societies (especially in North America and Europe) and should be seen in the context of the Western colonial and imperial expansion that was occurring during the latter half of the nineteenth century. For example, Morton (1839) used skull measurements (craniometry) as an indication of intelligence and on this basis argued that races could be categorized in a hierarchy. At the top of the hierarchy were Caucasians (people from Europe, India, parts of North Africa and the Middle East), then Mongolians (Chinese and Eskimos), next Malaysian people (from Malaysia and the Polynesian Islands), then Americans (that is, Native Americans from North and South America) and lastly, Ethiopians (from sub-Saharan Africa), suggesting the latter were a form of 'sub-species'.

The idea of 'race' as a sub-species combines elements of the idea of race-as-lineage and race-as-type. These ideas are to be found in the work of the Scottish biologist Charles Darwin (1887). Darwin saw evolution as a slow process resulting from *natural selection*. This is the idea that only those members that were best adapted to their environments were most likely to survive and therefore pass on their genetic characteristics to future generations. Darwin's ideas were further developed by the English sociologist Herbert Spencer (1889), who developed some very influential ideas on the relationship between 'race' and human social development. Spencer argued that the mixing of races could result in some societies becoming unstable, and he cited modern Mexico, South American republics and Spain as having this potential. He maintained that 'superior societies' tended to be more stable ones where the 'races' were not inter-related, and hence these societies developed further.

Nineteenth-century 'race' theories were based upon the claim that physical differences between 'races' were caused by genetic differences. However, nineteenth-century scientists lacked the scientific knowledge or technology to examine these differences, as genetic technology only developed after the Second World War. Jones (1991; 1994) is a geneticist who has examined nineteenth century 'race' theories using genetic science. He argues that there are over 50,000 genes in the human body and fewer than 10 per cent of these determine skin, eye and hair colour. Consequently, Jones argues that genetics has very little to do with race, as about 85 per cent of variations in genes result from differences *within* individual groups within the same country. A further 5 to 10 per cent of genetic diversity comes from differences between countries on the same continent (such as the differences between the English and the Spanish or between Nigerians and Kenyans).

Jones (1994) asserts that thinking about 'race' has shifted from mere classification to making value-judgements entailing racial stereotypes and prejudice. Therefore, the issue about 'race' is a moral and ideological one, not a scientific one because there is no biological evidence for the idea of different 'races'. This is because the genes that result in different physical characteristics are not sufficiently significant to allow different races to be identified.

Richards and Lambert (1985) criticize the idea of 'pure races' as dangerous and extremely misleading. They outline several problems with the doctrine of racial superiority. First, there is no clear connection between biological differences and cultural and behavioural differences between humans. Secondly, social explanations of behaviour have proved far more convincing than biologically determinist ones. Thirdly, people of the same 'race' have produced different behaviours in different historical contexts; the authors compare Afrikaners and the apartheid regime in South Africa with the more liberal regimes of their Dutch ancestors in the Netherlands. Fourthly, there is no objective measure to establish the 'superiority' or 'inferiority' of 'races'; and fifthly, Victorian notions of racial superiority were based on measurements and assumptions of technical and cultural achievements. However, the Ancient Egyptian, Ashanti and Zimbabwean societies were highly developed civilizations when Europeans were living in huts.

## The Social Construction of Race and Ethnicity

Many sociologists argue that 'race' is a social construct that has no objective biological reality. How people come to define race depends on the dominant value system of that society and the extent to which people are shaped by or resist the ideas of that dominant value system. In addition, beliefs about 'race' are also the product of a specific historical and cultural context. In the most extreme form the impact of the 'myth' of racial superiority has led to the genocide of Jewish people during the holocaust in the Second World War, ethnic cleansing of white Muslims and Albanians in the former Yugoslavia and the atrocities committed on black people in Rwanda in the 1990s. In other forms, Jewish people (no matter what their nationality), black and Asian people (no matter what their nationality), within Europe and North America in particular, have historically met with racism, hostility and discrimination over the centuries. It is interesting to note, in the cases of all non-white ethnic groups and Jewish people, and later in the case of Muslims, how the concepts of 'skin colour' and 'religion' have been used in different ways to exclude and oppress them. In addition, both have been conflated in different historical periods to legitimate their marginalization and exclusion form decent incomes, jobs, housing, educational opportunities, government and political activity, and used to justify human rights violations. In extreme cases this has included genocide.

Ethnicity is usually seen in terms of a group's culture. Eriksen (2002) argues that 'ethnicity' is a better term than 'race' for understanding all the dimensions of racism for the following reasons: because it helps contextualise the relationship between groups who regard themselves as different and are regarded as culturally different, while the beliefs of ethnic groups tend to represent a common origin and common ancestry. Eriksen identifies how some ethnic groups have become racialized as a result of slavery, such as black people, or as a result of religion, such as Jewish people. He argues that 'ethnicity' is a better term than 'race' to explain human interaction in a multi-cultural context. This is because ethnicity refers to the relationship between groups who see themselves as 'different' and as a consequence may be ranked hierarchically in society.

'Black' is a term that is often used in UK society to refer to all the disadvantaged ethnic minorities, but 'black' is not appropriate because some disadvantaged ethnic minorities include Greeks, Cypriots and Turkish people, people from the Middle East. In addition, many Asian people do not consider themselves black. The black/white dichotomy results in the homogenizing of the experiences of racism and oppression of all black and non-white groups. For example, in research into the experiences of ethnic minority children in the UK public care system, various researchers (Jackson, 1998; Ince, 1999; Comfort, 2001) talk about the needs of 'black, ethnic minority children'. However, they fail to make distinctions between these groups of children

Anthias and Yuval-Davis (1992) in their analysis of the relationship between patriarchy and ethnicity in the UK, warn against the 'lumping together' of all white groups as an 'ethnic majority' and all 'non-white' groups as 'black' or 'non-Caucasian'. Such a crude black/white dichotomy assumes a homogeneous experience of racism and oppression, which is in fact highly diversified both between and *within* ethnic groups. The failure to recognize this can have damaging and possibly fatal effects (see Lord Laming's report on the death of Victoria Climbie, 2003). Such a framework that presumes a homogeneity of experience on the basis of colour rather than ethnicity is, as Dominelli argues (1997), inherently racist.

Hall (1990) identifies the fact that in an earlier period of civil rights resistance to oppression in Britain, particularly in the 1970s and 1980s, the term 'black' was used to refer to people of Asian, African-Caribbean and African origin. It was used as a way of referring to their common experience of racism and marginalization and became the by-word for a *new politics of resistance*. The cultural politics that evolved from this process involved challenging the negative stereotypes and representations of all black people that were common within white British culture at the time. However, Hall points out the fact that by 1989 a new era in black cultural politics had emerged. Despite the fact that the old struggle against discrimination and oppression existed and had been far from won, new struggles were emerging involving a re-conceptualization of what he terms the 'black subject'. This recognized the differences between various groups based upon religion, class, gender and sexuality, which resulted in ethnic *pluralities*. Consequently (according to Hall), the 'black perspective' is represented increasingly from a particular ethnic group perspective. The ethnic and cultural diversity and different nationalities that now constitute modern nation states all contribute to this confusion. Many people have a number of identities simultaneously and may think and act in terms of belonging to a whole variety of groups.

The weakness of Hall's analysis is that he fails to explain the new ways people make absolute distinctions between different groups and not all such distinctions can be attributed to a revival of nationalism. Often, far from liberating societies, the development of new ethnic identities might encourage people to reassert their prejudices. Batt (1997) argues that intolerant or fundamentalist beliefs develop sometimes because people fear that their cultural distinctiveness will disappear as elements of other cultures become incorporated into their own. They may act to defend their culture in ways that might seem to others to be threatening and intolerant.

Eriksen (2002) argues that in order to understand the impact of globalization and global mobility on the issue of multi-cultural societies we need to see that ethnicity is a dynamic entity. It is not fixed and unchanging and there are always cultural differences within ethnic groups. In addition, ethnic groups can be mobilized, and he cites the way that they were mobilized into conflict in Bosnia. Furthermore, ethnic groups can also become racialized as a response to racism; for example, black people in the US who came from various different African countries, with different cultures, languages and religions. They developed a common identity as black people as a result of their treatment as slaves. It is important to recognize that ethnicity is also shaped by cultural processes, through which people learn their cultural attachment to a particular group. Equally, ethnicity is often ascribed (particularly in a racist society), and often people cannot choose which ethnic group they belong to.

Pilkington (2002) traces the historical development of national identity and argues that it is a social construction. For example, prior to the eighteenth century British nationality did not exist. It came about through two reluctant (as far as many Scots and Irish were concerned) Acts of Union in 1707 and 1801 and it developed through a social process known as 'othering' (i.e. by constructing others who were not British, particularly the French and members of the Catholic faith, as different). This was because British identity was perceived as Protestant. Using this process and by developing a series of stories, symbols and rituals, the British identity developed. It was based upon stories of British heroes who defeated the French and forged a global empire, while the rituals included the pageantry of the British monarchy, even though, after the 1720s, most monarchs were predominantly of German descent. However, British national identity never overwhelmed ethnic identities such as the English, Scottish, Welsh or Irish. Pilkington asserts that the impact of globalization and progressive EU integration is resulting in polarities in the expression of ethnic identities. This is manifest on one side by what is termed 'Little Englanders', such as the Conservative MP John Redwood, whom Pilkington describes as a 'cultural racist', because Redwood believes in the superiority of a white, English culture. On the other hand, there are people who consider themselves to have multiple identities, such as the UK Prime Minister Gordon Brown, who describes himself simultaneously as Scottish, British and European.

## Global Ethnic Conflict

Brown (1997) tries to define ethnicity and believes that six criteria must be met for a group of people to qualify as an ethnic group. First, they must have a name that qualifies them as a group. Secondly, they must believe in a common ancestry (it is irrelevant whether this common ancestry is real; what matters is that they believe it exists). Thirdly, they need to have shared beliefs about their collective past, and these beliefs sometimes take on the form of myths. Fourthly, they must have a sense of shared culture, which is passed on through language, religion, laws, customs, institutions, music and food. Fifthly, the group has to have an attachment to a specific territory; and lastly, members of the group must believe they constitute an ethnic group.

He argues that the likelihood for conflict to occur is contingent upon 'systematic requirements' and 'domestic and national perceptions'. 'Systematic requirements' refers to situations where different ethnic groups live in close proximity. He suggests that out of the 180 nation states around the globe, fewer than 20 are ethnically homogeneous and this makes for a volatile situation where ethnic conflict can occur. However, he points out that such conflict is not always inevitable. It is only likely to occur where national governments or regional authorities are relatively weak and unable to mediate and control conflicting ethnic groups. This is what happened in the 1990s. Following the break-up of the Soviet Union a power vacuum was created in Eastern Europe, particularly in the former Yugoslavia, which witnessed high levels of ethnic conflict due to this power vacuum.

'Domestic and national perceptions' refers to a situation where nationalistic sentiments are aroused when people feel they lack a strong state to protect them. In former Yugoslavia some groups have felt particularly vulnerable because the state has been weak or they have found themselves in a state dominated by other possibly hostile ethnic groups. At the same time, other ethnic minority groups have been blamed by the majority populations and have responded by seeking independence. In addition, Brown suggests that the trend towards democratization can produce problems for multi-ethnic societies. Where old regimes collapse and new regimes are being developed there can be major tensions between competing ethnic groups, especially in situations where it is perceived by some ethnic groups that they have been persecuted or discriminated against. Problems are particularly acute if a powerful majority negates or ignores the civil rights of a less powerful smaller ethnic group. Perceptual explanations relate to the ways different ethnic groups perceive one another. Hostility can be intensified by myths and false histories, which distort and demonize other ethnic groups.

Ethnic conflicts may take violent or non-violent forms. Non-violent ethnic conflicts are manifest in the campaigns of some French Canadians to win autonomy for Quebec, or the campaigns of Welsh and Scottish Nationalists, which have led to some forms of devolved government in Scotland and Wales. Peaceful separation has occurred between the Czech Republic and Slovakia, while in Australia and New Zealand, campaigns continue on the part of the South Island Secessionists and Queensland Secessionists, the latter of whom want independence from the rest of Australia. Though there is ongoing controversy in Australia as to the causes and extent of material inequalities experienced by indigenous Australians (Swanson and Cameron, 2003), this has not exploded into open ethnic conflict.

Sadly, violent ethnic conflicts outnumber the non-violent ones globally. In 1990 after the end of communist rule, former Yugoslavia erupted in violent ethnic conflict between Serbs, Croats and white Muslims. In parts of Bosnia whole ethnic groups were either exterminated or driven out of an area so that it might be occupied by another group. This process was known as *ethnic cleansing*. In the late 1990s Serbia engaged in ethnic cleansing on a massive scale in Kosovo, forcing thousands of Albanian refugees to flee to neighbouring countries. In Northern Ireland conflicts between Protestants and Catholics are now reaching a peaceful, political ending with the formation of a Northern Ireland Assembly. In Spain, after years of conflict and insurgency, there have been moves towards reconciliation between Catalan and Spanish groups. In Sri Lanka, Tamils fight Sinhalese, and in East Timor, guerrilla leaders seek independence from Indonesia. The end of the 1990s and the beginning of the twenty-first century witnessed ethnic cleansing on a horrific scale in Rwanda, where Tutsis were slaughtered by Hutus. In Kenya at the beginning of 2008 there was civil strife which threatened to turn into civil war and ethnic genocide as the dominant tribe in government, the Kikuyu, fought with Kalenjin, Lou, Kisii, Meru, Embu, Kamba, Luhya and Mljikenda tribes and the Somali minority (Channel 4 News, 29 January 2008). On the eve of the Beijing Olympics, China is being accused of heavy-handed treatment of Tibetans who object to its occupation of Tibet (which China has claimed sovereignty over since 1910), while there is growing support for the Tibetan Independence Movement (CNN News, 11 April 2008).

## Institutional Racism

Though equally insidious, *institutional* racism is different from the individualized racism that occurs between people. Institutional racism can be defined as the prevalence within any institutions, government or state bodies, universities or schools, of systematic policies, practices or laws that have the effect of disadvantaging certain ethnic groups. Institutional racism can take the form of racial profiling by security or law enforcement agencies, and housing, immigration or bank lending policies which impose certain conditions on specific ethnic groups. Other forms of institutional racism include the under-representation or misrepresentation of certain ethnic groups in the media, the use of stereotyped racial caricatures by institutions, and barriers to employment or professional advancement based upon ethnicity. Similarly, what Williams (1995; 2003) terms 'assimilationist policies' in education and welfare pursued by the British welfare state in the twentieth century (which expected black and Asian citizens to assimilate into British culture as opposed to integrating) could be regarded as a form of institutional racism.

The term 'institutional racism' was first invoked in the US by the African American leader of the Black Panther Party, Stokley Carmichael, in the 1960s. He defined it as 'a collective failure of an organisation to provide an appropriate and professional service to people because of their skin colour, culture, or ethnic origin' (Race, 2003, p. 79). In the UK the term was used by Sir William MacPherson in the inquiry into the murder of the teenager Stephen Lawrence. The inquiry cited institutional racism within the Metropolitan Police as one of the main causes of the failure to apprehend and secure the convictions of the murderers. In referring to the Metropolitan Police the Inquiry Report stated that there was a collective organizational failure to provide appropriate and professional services to people because of their culture, colour, or ethnic origin and it accused the Metropolitan Police Force of behaviour and attitudes which were tantamount to discrimination. It also cited unwitting racism, discrimination and racist stereotyping which disadvantages minority ethnic people.

In other countries institutional racism has taken other forms. For example, in the US the 1935 Social Security Act made provision for retirement pensions applied to all forms of employment with the exception of domestic and agricultural workers. This had the effect of excluding mainly African Americans, Chinese Americans and Mexican Americans. Similarly in 1956, the Sri Lankan government passed the Sinhala Only Act, which made Sinhalese the country's official language and excluded Tamil. In addition, it introduced university quotas to restrict the number of Tamils entering higher education.

## Gypsies

Gypsies are another ethnic minority who experience racism and discrimination around the globe, and who, with global diaspora and migration, are subjected to increasing marginalization, spatial control, and exclusion from health, welfare, educational and civic rights in many countries, particularly Europe and North America (Bancroft, 2001; Holloway, 2005). The common themes in all of these pieces of research around the globe are reflected in Bhopal's (2006) study of gypsies in the UK.

Bhopal's (2006) research identifies the racism and marginalization gypsies experience particularly with regard to education and accessing services. Her study of a small rural community in the UK describes how racial harassment went unnoticed because 'racism' was conflated with skin colour and some staff failed to take on board or take seriously the issues of racist harassment and name-calling gypsy children experienced. There was also evidence of institutionalized racism, manifest in failure to acknowledge the nomadic lifestyle of gypsies so that they had difficulties obtaining places in schools. Also within schools, there was a lack of awareness or reference to gypsy culture and there were no books and literature celebrating gypsy culture or festivals. Within one school, though it claimed to integrate all pupils, the onus was on gypsy children to integrate or rather, assimilate into the main-stream culture (Bhopal, 2006, p. 208).

In order to develop good practice with gypsy traveller children, Bhopal argues, school culture needs to change and have an anti-racist strategy which monitors racial abuse towards gypsies, a strong Travellers' Education Service (TES) presence within the school, and a culturally affirmative curriculum which includes literature celebrating and displaying knowledge of gypsy lifestyles and cultures and awareness that, for many gypsy traveller children, English may be a second language.

## Refugees and Displaced People

The term 'refugee' has a legal definition incorporated into the Geneva Convention in 1951 and the 1967 Bellagio Protocol, both of which were signed by over 190 countries worldwide. It refers to the need for any nation to afford protection to people outwith their country of nationality because of a well founded fear of persecution or genocide due to race, religion, nationality, political opinion or membership of a political or social group (Cohen and Kennedy, 2007, p. 249). Unfortunately this legal definition gives nation states considerable latitude in determining which groups of people constitute refugees, and the global trend has been increasingly to narrow the criteria for the status of 'refugee'.

During the 1990s there were considerable numbers of refugees in Africa and Asia, where those continents were affected by war, famine, and ethnic conflict which triggered forced migration. In addition, the collapse of the Soviet Union in Eastern Europe led to civil war all over the Eastern bloc, especially the former Yugoslavia, where ethnic cleansing became the order of the day. In 1999 half a million refugees fled Kosovo to Macedonia and Albania.

While the causes of refugee flows continue, increased entry restrictions into stable countries has resulted in the phenomenon known as 'internally displaced persons' (IDP). It is estimated that there are about 22 million IDPs around the globe and most have been displaced by war or ethnic conflict, or civil war. There are 4 million in Sudan, 1.45 million in Afghanistan and 1.2 million in Angola. The number of IDPs has also risen because of environmental changes; for example, in China over I million people were displaced by the Three Gorges Dam Project on the Yangtze River, while in India dam construction has caused the displacement of 16.4 million people (Mishra, 1999). Thus, in 2004 the number of refugees around the globe stood at 9,236,600. Of these, 839,000 were asylum seekers and 1,494,500 were internally displaced people (Cohen and Kennedy, 2007).

### Social Work Practice Implications

Given the global empirical evidence on the consequences of racism in the form of inequalities, the lack of civil and political rights, violations of human rights and risks of ethnic cleansing and genocide, it is important to have sociological theories which identify the various ways these forms of racism and discrimination occur. First, the 'meaning- and myth-of-race' concepts deconstruct the oppressive discourses about racial differences used to legitimate many discriminatory and racist policies. These include those of extreme eugenic groups such as Hitler's Nazi Party; apartheid in South Africa prior to the 1990s; social research on educational attainment, IQ testing, crime and deviance, which uses skin colour in an explanation of behaviour. Secondly, concepts of ethnicity enable us to avoid conflating skin colour with ethnicity and culture so as to identify the varieties of racist conflict that occur globally, and to begin to recognize the levels and diversity in different forms of racism. Thirdly, the concept of institutional racism informs practitioners of the way racist ideologies become inculcated in policies and procedures, and social workers need to be aware of these in order to avoid racist caricaturing and stereotyping in practice. They also need to determine the adequacy of practice interventions to ameliorate discriminatory effects of racist policies.

# Sectarianism

The historical treatment of Jews all over the world throughout history has been one of an open practice of sectarianism. The Egyptians kept Jewish slaves, while in Europe they have been subject to laws as 'aliens' since medieval times. The English playwright Shakespeare's portrayal of Shylock the Jew in *The Merchant of Venice* is steeped in anti-Semitism (prejudice against Semites or Jews). In the UK the 1905 'Aliens' Act was introduced specifically to stop the immigration of Jews (whatever their nationality) from Eastern Europe. In the 1930s the Chancellor of Germany Adolph Hitler adopted a strong racialized policy against the Jews in Europe culminating in the 'final solution' when over six million Jews were murdered in what became known as the Holocaust of the twentieth century. All over the world today, the number of anti-Semitic attacks on Jewish people and Jewish property, and the desecration of Jewish graves and religious sites, are on the increase (UK Commission for Racial Equality, 2006).

Like anti-Semitism, Islamophobia conflates ethnicity with religion. Research has shown that since the 1990s Muslims in the West, particularly Asian or Arab Muslims (more than Eastern European Muslims), have begun to experience new forms of racism and racial harassment. These have worsened since 11 September 2001 (Cohen and Kennedy, 2007). They have been regarded by many in the Western media as a problem and the principal focus of racist antagonism. The Runnymede Trust (1997) defines 'Islamophobia' as an unfounded hostility towards Islam, which could lead to unfair discrimination against Muslims. The Report produced by the Trust identified eight differences between an open and closed view of Islam. A closed view of Islam sees it as a single, unchanging, inflexible religion, with several negative traits the constructions of which, conflate religion, ethnicity and nationality. For example, a closed view regards Islam as a completely independent separate religion, as inferior, uncivilized, violent, irrational and repressive. In contrast, an open view does not see the Muslim religion as inferior and acknowledges that sexism, intolerance and literal interpretation of scriptures or religious texts are features of all religions. In addition, the closed view perceives it as a violent and aggressive enemy, as a religion manipulated by political leaders to gain political or military advantage and it assumes that all Muslims reject out of hand all criticisms made by Westerners. In contrast, an open view would not conflate religion and ethnicity in this racialized way. Similarly, the closed view of Islam argues that discrimination against Muslims can be justified and sees it as natural and normal that Westerners should be hostile to Islam. However, an open view of Islam would argue that religious intolerance of any kind (and especially one with racist overtones) is unacceptable in any society which regards itself as civilized and democratic. It would recognize the importance of religious plurality, the dangers of sectarianism, and how this can easily be used to legitimize ethnic and sectarian oppression. In addition, it would reflect upon the fact that amongst many Eastern and Western Muslims (including many British Muslims) there is intense reflexive and critical non-violent debate about Islam's relationship with the contemporary world, just as there is amongst all religions (for example, the controversy within the

Catholic Church in England over gay and lesbian adoption). Moreover, the open view recognizes that many Muslims are opposed to the actions of terrorists who claim to be Islamic, and of regimes in Islamic countries which are aggressive and oppressive. In addition, an open view acknowledges that there are numerous presentations of Islam depending upon differences in generations, different interpretations of the Qu'ran, and differences between those who are critical of human rights abuses in some Muslim countries and others who adopt more traditional views.

Said (1997, 2003) points out that the term 'Orientialism' is part of Western discourse, and argues that this term is an integral part of the way Westerners see themselves and that through a process of 'othering', the Orient discourses of Western superiority and Eastern inferiority are perpetuated. He cites evidence to show that Western media coverage is littered with racist images and stereotypes of Islam. In *Covering Islam*, Second Edition (1997) he argues that such images are imbued with stereotypes and exaggeration and in many cases outright hostility. Moreover, he points out that racism is manifest in the way that the denigration of the teachings or ideologies of Islam goes almost unchallenged, whereas such forms of denigration would be unacceptable with other religions. He explores the rise of Islamaphobia in the Western world within the context of US global foreign and military policy. He refers to its alliances with Israel and the fact that many Islamic countries have spoken out against what they see as the racism and imperialism of the US. This is in order to provide an explanation for the development of this phenomenon.

For many European Muslims their experience is one of a combination of racism and sectarianism on the basis of their ethnicity and religion. Historically in Britain this has been a feature of the experience of Irish Catholics (Lewis, 1998; Garrett, 2006) Jews (Lewis, 1998) and more recently Muslims (Said, 1997). As with the need to separate the meaning of race from the myth of race: in order to practise in an anti-oppressive manner, it is important to begin to 'de-couple' religion from ethnicity or nationality in a similar way. Equally it is necessary to separate ethnicity from race, the latter, being a very dangerous social construct. This is because the way these things are conflated or lumped together leads to oppression. I illustrate the findings of the Runnymede Trust in particular because in one sense it demonstrates some unwitting discourses that are embodied in the closed view of Islam and the dangerous dichotomies they embody. For example, these dichotomies include Muslim/Christian, East/West, tyranny/democracy, religious intolerance/religious tolerance. They are crude and out of date and in no way account for the cultural diversity and religious plurality of contemporary societies around the globe. However, for social workers it is important to reflect on why these dichotomies are being used now and why they are gaining currency in public debate. It is also interesting to note how the term 'religious fundamentalism' has been reconstructed within certain media and governmental discourses to mean 'radical' and 'fanatical' (particularly in relation to Islam) rather than implying a strict adherence to original religious doctrine. Giddens (2001) argues that the term 'fundamentalism' can be applied in a range of contexts to describe strict adherence to a set of principles or religious beliefs. Speaking as a lapsed Catholic myself, I know of a number of Catholics (my mother included) who could be described as a 'fundamentalist' in the sense that they adhere to strict doctrines and teachings of old Catholicism. However, these religious practices are not thought of as constituting a 'fundamentalism' with connotations of radicalism or extremism that is perceived as threatening to the British state, because Catholics are no longer socially constructed as a threat to the British identity, as they were from the sixteenth to the nineteenth centuries.

To understand the development of Islamaphobia it is necessary not only to de-couple religion from ethnicity, but also to recognize the political ways in which religion is manipulated and how these are linked to foreign and domestic policy. It is also imperative that social workers locate debates about religious pluralism within the realm of contemporary international politics, as Said (1997; 2003) does. The process is important with respect to another group of socially marginalized people, that of gay, lesbian and transgendered people.

# Homophobia

The word 'homophobia' literally means 'fear of the same' and is used to mean an irrational fear or disgust towards lesbians and gay men. Research, including that of Wilton (2000), identifies that homophobia is common among those involved in the health and social work professions. Wilton (2000) points out that such research into violence and discrimination against gay, lesbian and transgendered people lacks any sense of the emotional impact that homophobic incidents have. She notes that it is important for social workers to understand the socio-cultural sources of homophobic stereotypes – whether it be pub humour or newspaper editorials – and to take seriously the consequences of political debates around such issues as equalizing the age of consent or permitting lesbians and gay men to serve in the armed forces. It is not difficult to see how many factors, from government legislation to the banter of canteen culture, may contribute to the 'sense of virtue' that one researcher found amongst violently homophobic individuals (Comstock, 1991). Wilton (2000) argues that homophobia is not taken seriously in medical, allied health and social work professions in the same ways that racism or sexism are. Similarly, *heterosexism* refers to a situation where people regard heterosexuality as being better, more normal and natural, and more morally right than homosexuality. Heterosexism can lead to oppressive practice in the form of the invisibility of care issues and in the provision of services. Researchers have found a clear association between homophobic attitudes and strong religious beliefs (Pharr, 1988; Sears, 1991). Sometimes, homophobic individuals opportunistically make use of what they assume to be religious doctrine in order to justify their own prejudices.

The British charity War on Want reports that homosexuality remains illegal in many parts of the world including Singapore, Jamaica, Zimbabwe, Bangladesh, Malaysia, India, Pakistan, Algeria and Chile. The situation is particularly dangerous in countries under Islamic law, such as Iran (where punishment for being accused of homosexual acts includes whipping, cutting off hands or feet, or stoning to death), or Pakistan (where life imprisonment and/or a beating of up to 100 lashes are the common penalty). In China, homosexuality has been racialized and is considered to be a 'foreigner's disease' and there have been attempts to 'cure' gay men with electric shock treatment, while in Ecuador men have been killed by death squads (Wilton, 2000).

The English and Scottish legal systems have been amongst the last in Europe to introduce the equalization of the age of consent on parity with heterosexuals and there continue to be prohibitions on lesbian and gay men serving in the armed forces. In the United Kingdom Mason and Palmer's (1996) study found that one in three gay men and one in four lesbians has experienced at least one violent assault in the last five years.

For over fifty years the medicalization of homosexuality and the claim to have discovered a genetic or biological cause, have also led to attempts at 'curing' homosexuality. Despite the fact that many of the studies on genetics and biological studies are now being discredited because of flawed methodology and the failure to reproduce findings when applied to a wider population, or due to heteronormative bias (Terry, 1997) contained in the research, these ideas have great sway with the general population. This is because they are believed to be sanctioned by objective medical science. But as Wilton (2000) points out, social scientists and social historians regard both religion and science as – among other things – important instruments of social control. Since Foucault (1973), historians have recognized that sexuality is a key element in the process of social control. In addition, it must also be acknowledged that the disease model of homosexuality has been put to catastrophic uses, such as on homosexual inmates in the death camps during the Second World War, who were used as living experimental subjects by Nazi doctors. Since the 1940s various 'cures' for homosexuality have included chemical castration, electro-convulsive therapy, surgical removal of the hypothalamus, pre-frontal lobotomy, hormone injections and clitoridectomies, while some lesbians have been subjected to forcible heterosexual intercourse and various forms of aversion therapy. Such abuses have now been discredited and attempts to cure homosexuality have been largely abandoned. The disease model of homosexuality has lost credibility with the noticeable exception of the evangelical 'ex-gay' movement (Hicks, 2005).

What biomedical theories of sexual orientation have in common is *essentialism* – a belief that sexuality is an essential or innate component of our biological makeup. Critics, however, point to the inherent weaknesses of the traditional approach to essentialism. Racism, sexism, disablism are all based on assumptions and arguments about supposedly innate biological characteristics over which individuals have no control. These arguments have for centuries legitimated these groups' oppression, marginalization and social exclusion and there is no reason to suppose that essentialist explanations of homosexuality would have any different outcomes.

Foucault (1976) noted that the concept of the 'homosexual' was a nineteenth-century development. He identified the ways different forms of socio-political power were mobilized in the construction of sexuality. The significance of Foucault's analysis is that he moved 'sex' beyond something that was simply exploited in the interests of powerful groups to something that was actually *produced* by powerful groups via discourse. This meant that different discourses, from pop songs to medical textbooks, manufacture a wider social construction of sexuality in terms of what is considered both 'normal' and 'abnormal'.

The implications of social constructivism, are that it moves the analysis of homosexuality beyond simple essentialism and biological reductionism by providing a critical perspective on such approaches and by deconstructing the cultural and political bias and vested political interests that are bound up in them. In developing such perspectives, social constructivists are not suggesting that sexuality as a social role is unreal; rather, that both heterosexuality and homosexuality are identities that change and vary in different historical and cultural contexts. Social constructivism is useful because it enables us to deconstruct social norms and identify which groups in society benefit from such normalizing processes, as Wilton states:

> If a 'gay' man is a social construct so, too, is a 'heterosexual man'. This may actually strengthen the demand for lesbian and gay human and civil rights since it enables us to deconstruct *all* sexualities and see *why* some are accorded higher social value than others . . .   (Wilton, 2000, p. 78)

## Legal Discourses and Homosexuality

The law has played a crucial role in the construction of homosexuality. One of the many difficulties for social workers in promoting the civil and political rights of lesbian and gay service users is that in many countries there are strict laws prohibiting homosexual relations. Moreover, it is difficult to assess accurately a country's views on the issue because the laws are not necessarily indicative of social attitudes. A number of nations have laws prohibiting homosexuality and have had them for years, but in practice these countries may be far less oppressive than their laws suggest. These laws may be a residue of an earlier more oppressive period. Equally, however, countries that have laws prohibiting discrimination against gays and lesbians may yet have a hostile culture towards homosexuality and persecute gays and lesbians in other ways. In a number of countries the laws on homosexuality stem from Judaic, Christian and Islamic teaching and are sometimes used to legitimate sanctions against gay and lesbian relationships even when there is no legal prohibition. Such countries include the Vatican City and Egypt. A further complication is that in many countries in Africa, Asia, Oceania and Central America there are laws prohibiting gay relationships but not lesbian relationships. There are also different degrees of punishment for breaches of the law. For instance, 25 African nations, 14 Asian, 13 Oceanic, 5 Central American and 1 South American country prohibit homosexuality. Of these, in Mauritania, Sudan, Iran, Saudi Arabia, United Arab Emirates and Yemen, a maximum conviction carries the death penalty, while in India, Bangladesh, Guyana, Sierra Leone, Tanzania, Myanmar, Singapore and Barbados the maximum sentence is life imprisonment. Paradoxically, however, 28 countries legally recognize civil or registered partnerships between same sex couples, while Canada, some states in the US, Belgium, Spain, and the Netherlands all legally recognize same sex marriages (Kitzinger and Wilkinson, 2004). In a number of countries including the UK, Canada, US and Sweden the adoption laws have changed to allow gay and lesbian people to adopt and foster.

However, in all these areas – discrimination, civil partnerships, marriage and adoption – the situation is complex and contested and the relaxation of legal codes in any one country does not readily translate into civil and political rights for gay and lesbian service users. A number of sociologists (Weeks, 2004; Clarke and Finlay, 2004) identify the ongoing discrimination and violation of civil and legal rights that gays and lesbians continue to experience in areas such as immigration, civil partnerships, pension and inheritance rights and marriage. These violations of civil and legal rights have occurred in what are often stereotyped as some of the more 'liberal' Western democracies such as the UK, Canada, the US, Australia and the Netherlands. Similarly, Hicks (2005) has researched extensively on the effect Christian fundamentalism in both the US and UK has had upon the debate within social work regarding the issues of gay adoption and fostering and how this has led to the marginalization of gay and lesbian adopters.

## Social Work Practice Implications

Manthorpe (2002) argues that in terms of the treatment of older people the issue of caring within gay and lesbian relationships has been wholly neglected by health and social work professionals, who still only conceive of caring relationships in a heterosexual context. Green's (2005) research identifies how, in the last forty years, child sexual abuse inquiries ignored the issue of sexuality and embodied a host of heteronormative assumptions in the management of child protection. She cites Berridge and Brodie (1993), in which the researchers conflate child sexual abuse with 'homosexual abuse' and recommend that residential staff in children's homes should be vetted in terms of their sexuality to identify gay and lesbian staff and prevent them working with children. Here homosexuality is conflated with a predilection for paedophilia and it is suggested that gay and lesbian staff are more likely to engage in child sexual abuse than heterosexual staff. Similarly, McMullen's (1991) research illustrates how the punitive staff responses in residential care have disempowered and disadvantaged young lesbian and gay people within the public care system and made them reluctant to disclose their sexuality.

A study by Ben-Ari (2001) showed the extent of 'low-grade' homophobia (which he defined as a desire to avoid homosexuals) amongst social work academics and trainers in an Israeli university. He identified the practice implications such an approach has by illustrating how professionals who maintain negative attitudes towards gay and lesbians are less effective, if not harmful, in their dealings with homosexual clients. Commenting on the extent of homophobia amongst health and social care professionals, which she claims is one of the main reasons many homosexual service users prefer to remain 'in the closet', Wilton states:

> Personal anxiety, unease, or disgust about some aspects of human sexuality are not acceptable reasons to remain ill-informed about something which may have implications for professional practice. We would expect someone who routinely faints at the sight of blood to choose a career other than midwifery: it is equally reasonable to expect that anyone who is unwilling to provide respectful care to lesbian, gay and bisexual service users should not work in health and social care. (Wilton, 2000, p. 3)

In relation to the practice implications of Wilton's comments, various strategies have been used with social work students and other students in the US. Both DuBose-Brunner (1997) and Mager and Sulek (1997) have used narrative techniques and social constructivism to get their students to reflect on stereotypical and homophobic assumptions that might affect their social work practice. For example, DuBose-Brunner got her social work students to compare, analyse and reflect upon the experiences of racism and homophobia using personal stories.

# New Social Movements

New Social Movement (NSM) theory can be defined as theories which refer to an analysis of new social movements such as the Women's Movement, the Black Civil Rights Movement, the Gay Liberation Movement and the Disabilities Rights Movements that sprang up in North American and European liberal democracies in the 1960s and 1970s. These are movements which are regarded as posing new challenges to the established cultural, economic and political orders of modern and advanced capitalist societies. The term is not usually used to apply to more traditional movements supporting more traditional or conservative values, such as the anti-abortion groups, or more long-established movements such as the trade unions. NSMs are seen by some sociologists as a key change in the nature of socio-political participation in contemporary society. Sociologists such as Touraine (1977) and Melluci (1980) see NSMs as having certain key or defining features. First, they tend to have an issue basis and are concerned with political, civil, natural or ecological issues. Secondly, they have a commitment to furthering the civil and political rights of specific socially marginalized groups. Thirdly, NSMs extend the definition of the political to include issues such as individual prejudice, housework, and domestic violence.

NSM theory is concerned to explain what the development of these movements tells us about contemporary cultural and structural changes. Touraine (1977) identifies a new central conflict in society, which replaces the old class struggle. At the centre of this struggle is a battle between technocrats and a multiple range of adversaries (which include NSM). Similarly, Melluci (1980) argued that the major structural changes occurring in society at the end of the twentieth century created a major realignment between society, the state and the economy. This has in turn created new forms of social conflict. The late 1960s and early 1970s represented a period of intense accelerated social and cultural change, especially within the sphere of identity politics around the issues of sexuality, nuclear disarmament, and civil rights and 'race' equality, and the development of self-help groups. These were all issues which by the 1990s had become part of mainstream politics in many societies. However the second most important 'moment' in theorizing NSMs is the context of the 1990s–2000s, which Melluci claims is a period with a far more reactionary political climate around the globe where such forms of opposition by NSMs were suppressed. At the beginning of the twenty-first century we are seeing other forms of NSM in the form of the anti-capitalist movement, which campaigns against the inequalities, unemployment and forms of oppression generated by global capitalism.

Throughout Western Europe in the 1980s and 1990s there were considerable attacks made on the gains achieved by the working class and the popular women's, gay and lesbian, anti-racist and disabilities movements. This has led to a fragmentation of the European working class by income, occupation and status. In addition, there have been developments of different forms of oppression and thus sociologists now pay much greater attention to other social divisions, such as those based upon disablism or homophobia. In contrast, Shakespeare (1993) argues that there is very little difference between the Old Social Movements (OSMs) that developed in the 1960s and the new ones (NSMs) of the 1990s. He argues that social movements are concerned with the relationship between the market and the welfare state and are about groups trying to secure an equitable distribution of material resources. As such, they represent the interests of some very traditional socially marginalized groups such as the poor. The so-called NSMs are often building upon a core of old community users' groups of the 1960s and 1970s. A common theme of many of them is that they are vigorously opposed to certain forms of what they see as professional control over their lives. These movements pose many questions to professional welfare workers about 'whose side' they are on, and challenge the residual prejudices about 'old', 'gay', 'mentally ill' and 'poor people'. They are not uniform and take a variety of forms. However, these groups all share a basic concern with down-to-earth questions about empowerment, rights, representation and ensuring quality in the services they require.

NSM theory enables social workers to conceptualize the agency and resistance of different groups of service users and to examine how exactly such agency has taken political form as different groups have sought to gain recognition of their civil and welfare rights. In the US and later in Western Europe, the Black Civil Rights Movement of the 1950s and 1960s campaigned for and was successful in gaining legislation in terms of civil rights in relation to voting, the de-segregation of buses, schools and universities, and improved work conditions, pay, pensions and housing conditions on parity with white people. In Britain a number of sociologists and social work academics (Dominelli, 1997; Gilroy, 1987; Williams, 1995) identify how the political agency and mobilization of the Black Civil Rights Movement in the US (particularly the political mobilization and agency shown by campaigners such as Rosa Parks or Martin Luther King, Junior) influenced the anti-racist and radical critiques of the welfare state in Europe. This in turn placed on the agenda the inequalities and different forms of oppression that black people and Asian people faced. As a result, people were compelled to mobilize political action to challenge their oppression.

Similarly, the development of the Gay Liberation Movement around the globe has resulted in the growth of pressure groups such as Stone Wall, and various gay, lesbian, bisexual and transgendered (GLBTG) groups have continually campaigned against homophobic hate crimes, laws on the age of consent, lack of recognition of gay relationships, marriage laws, pensions and employment rights, inheritance laws, adoption laws and so forth. As a result they have won some hard-fought but major campaigns in relation to their civil rights. Most notable has been the introduction of civil partnership and marriage legislation in some countries, giving gay and lesbian people pension, inheritance and property rights on a parity with heterosexuals. In addition, in some countries they now have the right to adopt.

The significant aspect of New Social Movement (NSM) theory, for social work practice, is that it enables us to analyse the agency, political mobilization and organization of the socially oppressed and marginalized in society and trace the history of those developments and the contributions they have made to key legislative changes in terms of civil and political rights. These developments have influenced the development of anti-oppressive practice and of radical social work theory and practice. At the same time, NSM theory offers a framework to identify the ways these groups have both contributed to and adapted to the changes in forms of political activity that occurred at the end of the twentieth century as a result of socio-economic and political changes in welfare states. In doing so, these New Social Movements (particularly the ones that focus on self-help approaches rather than alternative service provision) compel welfare professionals to conceive of the reconstruction of the discourse of rights. To quote Fagan and Lee (1999):

> NSMs construct a discourse of alternative rights which can only be met by radical change in the existing structure of society and which involve the construction of new political and social institutions.   (Fagan and Lee, 1999, p. 153)

However, many of these NSM theories can be criticized for their failure to give adequate attention to oppressive and fascist-oriented NSMs like the British National Party in the UK or the Ku Klux Klan in the US, or extreme religious groups – all of whom advocate violence or promote ethnic or religious hatred as a means of achieving their political ends. Thus, we need to have a conceptual framework to analyse the practices of such NSMs and their implications for social work practice. Many radical NSM groups such as these claim that they work within the operations of democratic institutions, observe the law, and use the law to advocate for their member's interests; and argue that they are as much an oppressed minority as black people, gay and lesbian people, or people with disabilities. Cooper (2004), in her analysis of equality and diversity, provides a useful conceptual framework to challenge these kinds of oppressive discourse. First she asks the question: How should equality politics respond to controversial constituencies such as smokers or sports hunters, when they position themselves as disadvantaged? Cooper (2004) uses these examples to warn against the homogenization of equality or equal access to civil and political rights by differently marginalized groups. Indiscriminate access of all groups claiming to be oppressed minorities undermines and undervalues the different forms, levels, and degrees of socio-economic, political, civil and psychological oppression experienced by women, ethnic minorities, gays and lesbians and people with disabilities. In addition, to put the situation into context she cites Weeks' (1995) definition of harm as: 'that human interaction where free choice impinges on the freedom of choice of others' (p. 33). When fascist groups, or extreme religious groups (of either the Christian Right or Islamic 'Right' or extreme Jewish groups) demand freedom which then results in the incitement of religious or racial hatred, or when they are putting forward ideologies calling for the death of gays and lesbian people, black people or people with disabilities, they are encroaching on the freedom of choice of others. In addition, Cooper (2004) notes that harm is also manifest in hate speeches of various groups, which in turn makes the issue of 'freedom of speech' very complex. She cites the work of Matsuda (1993), who asserts that hate speeches are more than simply a form of verbal abuse, which has no significant impact, and she argues that:

> The negative effects of hate messages are real and immediate for the victims. . . . As much as one may try to resist pieces of hate propaganda, the effects on one's self esteem and sense of personal security is devastating.   (Matsuda, 1993, pp. 24–5)

## Summary of the Main Points

- Separating out the 'meaning of race' from the 'myth' of race can assist in identifying and deconstructing the implicit racist nature underpinning many nineteenth- and twentieth-century theories on race.

- Sociological theories of ethnicity are useful in identifying the complex ways in which racism operates in any society and in order to critique the crude black/white dichotomy of racism and help avoid dangerous and oppressive practices as a result.

- Sociological theories on anti-Semitism and Islamophobia identify the ways that religion and ethnicity can become conflated in the production of racism.

- Social constructivism is useful for deconstructing medical discourses on homosexuality and for identifying how these have been used to legitimate medical control over homosexuality and hence homosexuals.

- New Social Movement theory informs empowering social work practice strategies by illustrating and analysing the agency and self-advocacy power of various historically marginalized social groups; while Cohen and Kennedy (2007) and Copper (2004) provide frameworks to critically examine the claims made by NSMs like the BNP or radical religious groups as they are representing the interests of marginalized minorities.

## Conclusion

This chapter has sought to examine three specific forms of oppression that affect clients/service users around the globe, namely racism, sectarianism and homophobia. This is not to suggest that there is a hierarchy of oppressions. Dalrymple and Burke (1995) point to the dangers of setting up a hierarchy of oppressions because of how it mitigates against anti-oppressive practice (by asserting, for example, that racism is more damaging than homophobia). Rather, the emphasis on these three forms of oppression was for three reasons. First, on the issue of racism, to prompt consideration of the differences and interconnections between ethnicity and racism and the way the mythical entity of 'race' is used to legitimate institutionalized racist and oppressive practices, and to illustrate the danger of adopting a simplistic black/white dichotomy in an analysis of racism. Secondly, to examine the ways religion has been conflated with concepts of ethnicity or nationality to legitimate sectarianism. Thirdly, the focus on homophobia is not so much because of the ways it interconnects with racism or sectarianism (the connections are easier to make in terms of the other two forms of oppression) but to identify the ways the needs of lesbians, gay and transgendered people have consistently been ignored by welfare professionals (and this is reflected in the lack of attention given within much social work literature on anti-oppressive practice). Fourthly, the aim has been to raise awareness of the negative ways homophobia is legitimated within religious beliefs. Such examples inform our awareness that discrimination and prejudice are dynamic and multifaceted entities and that they require continual reflection upon them, to examine how they affect practice. Such vigilance on reflexivity is important to help clients/service users in the promotion of social inclusion and citizenship. It is also pertinent to any evaluation of services. This will be considered in more depth in Chapter 7, which examines assessment and care planning in social work.

## Case Study

Lawrence is a youth worker who runs a youth club for 14–17-year-olds. Last week an argument broke out between Ronnie, a white English youth member, and the rest of the group, who are Irish, Scots, Bangladeshi and Jamaican. The youth made racist remarks to Moneer who is a Bangladeshi youth in the group. The incident occurred after Moneer asked Ronnie to put his cigarette out, as there is a smoking ban at the club. When spoken to by Lawrence, Ronnie said he was both a victim of racism by the other members (as he is the only English person in the group) and being picked upon and oppressed for being the only smoker. To try and sort the problem out, Lawrence has decided to have a discussion group to promote awareness of diversity and equality amongst the group.

When trying to get the young people to understand the damage caused by racism, sexism, homophobia or religious intolerance, Lawrence could employ Cooper's (2004) perspective on the issue of 'harm' in an assessment of promoting equality and diversity, and examine the ways the forms of political expression that negative NSMs use in the exercise of their civil rights affect other socially marginalized groups. This is important because usually the two are connected. In addition, Cooper warns against getting into the 'equivalence trap' when considering forms of oppression. Readers are advised to reflect critically upon the extent to which different groups experience disadvantage. This argument could be used to explain to Ronnie the relevance of his claims of being 'victimized' for smoking, or to compare his claims of racism and what he was doing to Moneer. Cooper argues that it is very dangerous to equate the forms of oppression and disadvantage that tobacco smokers or Christian activists experience, for example, with that of women, gay or lesbian people, and people with disabilities or non-white ethnic minority groups.

# Further Reading

Cooper, D. (2004) *Challenging Diversity: Rethinking Equality and the Value of Difference* (Cambridge: Cambridge University Press).
A particular strength of this book is the way without generating a 'hierarchy of oppressions', it shows how to differentiate the claims of competing oppressed groups and generate empowering practice.

# 7

# Social Theory, Assessment, Care Planning and Evaluation

## Introduction

There is broad consensus amongst social work academics and practitioners (Lewis. 1988; MacDonald, 1995; Shaw, 1996; Parker and Bradley, 2004; Tsang, 2000; Pawar, 2004) that assessment is a key social work task. Moreover, Parker and Bradley (2004) identify two crucial strands of the assessment: first, that social workers should know what makes for a good assessment, and secondly, they should recognize the key elements of the assessment, which include ethics (which were discussed in Chapter 1), power, professionalism and anti-oppressive practice. This chapter examines the different sociological theories and research approaches that inform an understanding of all of these elements. In addition, it shows how they can contribute to the deconstruction of the complex relationship between assessment and evaluation within the context of social work practice.

> ### Key Words
>
> systems theory, focused interview, power, professionalism

## Assessment and Evaluation

In reality evaluation should be central to the assessment process. This is because of the complexity and diversity of social work roles, with a wide variety of care groups using a host of different intervention methods. Evaluation is an integral part of effective working to protect vulnerable service users. As mentioned in Chapter 1, Caney (1983) asserted that being a safe and competent practitioner means recognizing and acting upon significant cues in a case. Evaluation enables us to reflect upon what is significant. In addition, Cheetham et al. (1992) identify that evaluation is even more important in contemporary social work. This is because demands for it have been triggered by external pressures (such as the need for social work practice to be accountable and cost effective) and internal pressures, so that social work can defend its professional standing.

Evaluation is also important because social workers are not just technical rationalists who operate in accordance with agency policies and procedures. They are also required to exercise professional judgement, critical thinking skills and reflection on the ways social work develops and progresses. This requires them to be conversant on the ways research can inform practice, the use of the service user's perspective and the importance of pluralistic evaluation. That is recognizing the competing interests of the various participants to the assessment process, which all entail different notions of successful outcomes.

The contemporary quality of assessments in social work practice is often poor ('Messages from Research', 1995; Shaw, 1996; Calder, 2003). This is due in part to a culture of management by outcomes, an overemphasis on accountability to the detriment of critical reflection on quality, and the preoccupation with Evidence Based Practice (EBP). 'Evidence Based Practice' refers to social work interventions based on research, carried out in practice on 'what works'. Within European and North American social work it has been used extensively. For example, it has been developed by Sheldon and Chilvers (2000) at the Centre for Evidence Based Social Services, promoted by the Social Care Institute for Excellence (SCIE, 2003) and employed by the charity Barnardos in a series of social work studies entitled 'What Works' (2002). In the US it has been used by Howard and Jenson (1996) to develop practice guidelines (Thyer and Kazi, 2004), while Faul et al. (2001) use it to underpin social work research.

Sociological perspectives can help identify the limitations of EBP. Goding and Edwards (2003) question the relevance of EBP in complex care cases where service users' life choices or the needs of vulnerable service users (such as those with mental health problems) are being assessed. Moreover, they argue that EBP research can be used to generate oppressive practice under the guise that it is underpinned by objective science (Goding and Edwards, 2003, p. 55). Smith (2000) also criticizes EBP approaches by contending that they are obsessed with outcomes and ignore social processes and structural constraints. Consequently, they fail to consider the complexity and the contradictory nature of the social work practice context and the fact that social work interventions may vary in different circumstances. This has implications for what Payne (2002) argues is one of the hallmarks of reflexivity: being able to discern which interventions will work in which practice contexts.

These problems have been exacerbated by some of the practice problems in generating partnership working with clients/service users. First, there seems to be a tacit assumption on the part of the social worker that being involved in a client's/service user's life entails their agreement. 'It's part of the professional thinking to assume the work is based on negotiation and consent' (Fisher, 1983; p. 48). In reality, agreements with service users tends to be verbal, non-specific, based on a nebulous concept of 'an understanding' between worker and service user. Secondly, there is also often a reluctance to allow the client's/service user's definitions of their problems to gain primacy in the assessment process. This reluctance is due to fears that this will lead to the deskilling of the worker. Thirdly, resource constraints act as a constant barrier to partnership, as often social workers are fearful that any engagement with clients/service users on decision-making will lead to false expectations. This is due to the belief that expectations will be raised on the part of the client/service user which resource-strapped services will then fail to meet. This problem is compounded in countries were case work adopts a communal approach involving clients/service users, family, wider community members, and community leaders or elders. This is because this can lead to competing interests and agendas, and difficulties as to whose needs/interests should be given priority.

Poor quality assessments are also the product of an over-reliance on narrow routine ways of learning about client/service users and the mechanistic and technical way the assessment process has been perceived. It has often been regarded as a series of discrete phases, which incorporate assessment, care planning, intervention, review and evaluation. In reality these processes overlap or vary in length. Frequently, social work practitioners ignore the fact that evaluation is an integral part of the whole assessment process, not something that is 'tacked-on' at the review stage. The problem with doing this is that the evaluation is then in danger of being assimilated into a formal review process instead of forming an integral part of the assessment involving the client/service user. In this respect, interpretive sociology is useful to inform this process because it concerns trying to interpret the clients'/service users' meanings and understandings of their situations.

Both crisis intervention and task-centred social work entail elements of the interpretive sociological approach in that they lay emphasis on how service users give meanings to their social situations. In addition, both methods try to gain insights into clients'/service users' definitions of reality. In crisis intervention it is the client's/service user's definition of the 'precipitating hazardous event' (Payne, 2005; p. 103) which gives rise to the crisis that the social worker seeks to solve. In the case of the task-centred method, it is the service user's definition of the priority issues, which needs addressing. A different form of interpretive sociological approach is adopted by Shaw (1996) and Hall (2001). They identify the benefits of using ethnography in social work research. Ethnography is 'a research method in which the researcher immerses him- or herself in a social setting . . . observing behaviour and listening to what is said in conversation . . .' (Bryman, 2004, p. 539).

In 1967 Harold Garfinkel first coined the term 'ethnomethodology', which roughly translated means 'ethno' or 'folk' and methodology, in other words 'folk-methodology', i.e. the methods everyday folk use to make sense of the world. Thus, ethnomethodology is concerned with the methods used by society's members to construct, account for and give meaning to the world around them. Garfinkel (1967) argues that members of society employ the 'documentary method' to make sense of social reality and to bring order to their lives. This method entails picking out specific features from a complex social context and defining them in a particular way.

Ethnomethodology is a branch of interpretive sociology based on ethnography. It uses the concept of 'indexicality', the belief that the sense or meaning of any object or activity is derived from its context, i.e. where it is 'indexed' in a particular situation. Society members' sense of what is happening in a situation is determined by the way they interpret the context of the activity concerned. In this respect their understandings and accounts are indexical: they make sense of action or behaviour in terms of particular settings.

Garfinkel (1968) believed that in using indexicality, people are skilled members of society who are constantly applying indexical qualities to situations, giving them meaning, making them knowable and communicating such knowledge to others. This in turn communicates sense and the appearance of order in the situation. In this way members of society construct and accomplish their own social world rather than simply being shaped by it.

In terms of social work practice De Montigny (2007) asserts that using ethnography with clients/service users can prove to be an invaluable form of collaborative practice, because ethnography is a useful method for getting people to reflect on the ways they make sense and bring order to their everyday interactions. It can also inform the reflexive capacity of the social work practitioner in separating out the discrepancies between people's descriptions of what they do and what they do in reality. This is a useful approach in child protection social work. In addition, De Montigny (2007) argues that ethnography represents an excellent methodology to enable social workers to integrate theories into practice reality, and for unpacking the taken for granted in everyday routines that clients/service users use to structure their interactions.

Both Shaw (2001) and Hall (2001) stress the importance of using ethnography in social work. Shaw emphasizes the uniqueness of culture and context in any given research case study, which is also what any good social work assessment should elucidate. Hall examines the way ethnography is used for capturing the contradictions and discrepancies between people's interpretations about their social work practice and what they actually do. He found this method useful in his research on residential practices in a young homeless persons' hostel. He used it to differentiate the staff group's views of good practice and their actual practice with the young people.

A good evaluation means subjecting both descriptions of practice and analysis of practice to rigorous measures of their strengths and weaknesses. It requires a good methodology underpinning it. In this respect, Shaw (1996) advocates using sociological ethnography incorporating participant observation, the focus group method, or life course or life history work with clients/service users. These methods are invaluable to help the assessment process and to avoid it becoming 'culture-bound', or an end in itself, or to avoid the 'after-the-event' justifications that social workers sometimes use in defence of their practice decisions (Shaw, 1996; p. 143). To be competent in developing evaluation it is necessary to know the difference between *formative evaluations* (which explore social work's delivery of services and their quality) and *summative evaluations* (which examine the impact of social work interventions, the social work intervention process itself and the outputs and outcomes).

Ethnography has been popular in social work practice and social work research and is predicated on the idea that service users are expert in themselves and their situations. For instance, White (2001) used auto-ethnography to deconstruct the discourses of social workers who negatively labelled certain types of child rearing practices amongst some mothers in child protection cases. In contrast, Scourfield (2001) used ethnography to focus on the construction of gender in the occupational structure of child protection work. This research examined female carers, being both the focus of social work intervention and the main source of social work monitoring and assessment. This occurred even in cases where the perpetrators of the harm were male partners. Scourfield suggests that research has the potential to highlight the lack of evidence based for decisions taken by social workers with regard to assessments of parenting. Similarly, Trotter (1999) found auto-ethnography a useful methodology to engage social work educators and students in training on working with gay and lesbian clients/service users.

In terms of the interview method this ethnography is not without its problems, and practitioners need to consider some of the difficulties that they may encounter. People often recollect their past decisions as more rational than they actually were in practice. Moreover, there are several difficulties when interviewing clients/service users. First, people overestimate connections between events, and secondly, there is a tendency to match events to stereotype images of situations. Thirdly, humans tend to downplay socially undesirable behaviours and overemphasize socially acceptable ones, and both constructions of events suffer from the fact that they are cultural constructions of what is desirable or undesirable behaviour. As a result of these tendencies, social workers interpreting the information may be tempted to oversimplify the cause-and-effect relationships in their analysis of the case. This can lead to a misdiagnosis of the service user's situation and to poorly informed and evaluated service interventions being implemented.

Evaluation also entails three strands. The first strand is generating meaning out of the life histories of service users. This is a skill, because in reality social workers are only interested in those aspects that can be codified or contextualized in terms of social work functions and social work interventions. The danger here is that in the pursuit of these, social workers are sometimes guilty of reductionism. This means that the skills and techniques used in the assessment process obscure the reality of the service user's experience. The second strand in the evaluation is to recognize that the evaluation of practice is also an evaluation of social work competence. To generate this in an informative and empowering way the evaluation process must facilitate various things. First, an open space or forum is needed that welcomes such professional evaluation, learning and development. Secondly, a good evaluation requires skills and techniques to enable the worker to assess their practice. Thirdly, the worker needs to find ways in which the new knowledge learned from the evaluation can be disseminated. Consequently, social workers need to be proactive in supervision to ascertain what, if any, of these resources are available. The third strand in the evaluation must involve the service user. Life histories can be useful here because they have the potential to empower the service users by giving them a voice in the whole assessment process.

# The Practice Context

The context in which we reflect and exchange information is also important and this is where the 'sociology of professions' is useful. This is to help us understand the influences on the exchange of information. In Chapter 2 the stress was placed on the contextual nature of social work as part of the wider welfare state and its contradictory role in terms both of the promotion of citizen's rights and as an agent of social control. Equally, an understanding of how professions operate in society is necessary to evaluate how professionalism creates contradictions and tensions in the social work role. These are relevant because they have implications for service user empowerment. For example, Noel and Jose Parry (1979) define professionalism as a strategy for controlling an occupation, in order that its members can self-govern.

Thus the profession is controlled primarily in the members' interests. Control of an occupation is achieved by setting entry restrictions and having a controlling association that regulates conduct, and by claiming the right to discipline members. Macdonald (1999) calls this process the 'professional project', and for members of any given occupation this represents a continuous, contested and contradictory process. The professional project can have considerable practice implications for clients/service users. Dominelli (2005) adopts a Marxist feminist perspective to criticize situations where the professional project overrides meeting service users' needs. She criticizes the global neo-liberal agenda and professional project being put forward by international organizations such as the World Bank and the IMF as well as a number of Western international relief organizations. They seek to control the operations of social workers in local or international NGOs and set the agenda of these organizations, which often run counter to the civil and welfare rights of many indigenous populations. This then results in an unequal and three-tier global welfare system.

Approaches to the contexts of social work assessments have also been influenced by external pressures and developments in sociology, namely the impact of the sociology of risk. Douglas (1992) proposes a cultural theory of risk in order to explain how the ideology of blame develops in a society when humans are confronted by and seek to make sense of risk. In high modernity (which is how Douglas sees contemporary society), 'risk' equates to a sense of danger and the feeling of anxiety created by uncertainty. She argues that risk is a social mechanism that enables cultures to determine accountability, and it represents a form of social control. Risks are in essence social constructions. In analysing risk-consciousness in any given society, she argues that two questions need to be asked concerning the sociology of risk. First, how safe is safe enough? Secondly, why do people seek to avoid risk? Douglas maintains that the public response to risk has become personalized and individualized in high modernity, where people are expected to be proactive in looking after themselves, and should not to expect the state to 'rescue' them.

Societal perceptions of risk coupled with the blame culture reinforce already existing social divisions in society. For example, there becomes a tendency to ascribe risk or danger to already socially marginalized groups in society such as refugees or asylum seekers, lone parents, or gay and lesbian people (Douglas, 1992, p. 40). One interpretation of the link between the individualization of risk and blame strategies is that, in neo-liberal market societies, this leads to two types of responses to perceptions of risk. At the societal level there will be the 'scapegoating' and blame of already vulnerable individuals and groups. On a personal level the more affluent individuals will buy themselves out of dangerous, natural or social environments. The main way the rich do this is through the colonization and purchase of private space.

Beck (1992), in contrast to Douglas, believes we are living in a 'risk' society, not just a 'risk culture', and this is characterized by the fact that modern institutions have become global, while on an individual level people are breaking free of tradition, religious ideas and custom. The old industrial society is disappearing, being replaced by the risk society. Beck argues that these risks are qualitatively different from those of previous ages because they occur less from natural hazards than from the uncertainties created by developments in science and technology. In a period of risk society, reflexivity is characterized by uncertainty that science and technology can solve society's problems or address unpredictable outcomes. Risks in this risk society are reflected in the incidence of poor health. Even in rich societies with plentiful food, there are diseases such as obesity, unhealthy diets and health-related problems. In addition, a situation has arisen in which atomic energy leads to the abundance of energy supplies but also proliferates nuclear waste and increased risk of nuclear accident (like in Chernobyl), while toxins in air, water and foodstuffs produce systematic and irreversible harm. This problem is compounded by the fact that toxins are invisible, and often people are not immediately aware of the risks they create.

Parton (1996) argues that the concept of risk is a social construction and has led to important changes in the way practitioners think about and constitute their practice. In this respect, social work and other welfare professions are in a vulnerable position because, unlike in the financial and insurance professions, there is no equivalent technology for measuring risk in welfare. Unfortunately social work practice has failed to provide a systematic and methodological approach to risk assessment and has relied on an EBP approach, which is inappropriate. What is needed is a way of classifying 'high risk' in different social work contexts. One way has been to measure and improve the quality of decision-making in the hope of improving opportunities for more effective supervision and management of the social work task. However, professional judgement and decision-making are essentially concerned with the identification and assessment of 'high risk', but in relation to this, social worker skills in conceptualizing and identifying notions of harm, risk and protection and the way they interrelate, are extremely underdeveloped. This is particularly the case in the ways risk is understood and the concept is applied and operated in everyday practice. Many social work practice guidelines in all care groups fail to address what factors a risk analysis might involve and how professionals might approach the task of risk assessment. Paradoxically however, risk has become the key criterion for targeting resources, for protecting vulnerable clients/service users and for making agencies and professionals accountable. Thus, examples of risk in different care groups include: risk in relation to mentally disordered offenders, debates about concepts of risk and the need for incarceration or care, and questions of their civil rights.

Parton notes that with the decline of welfarism and the dominance of neo-liberalism concepts of risk have not only been recast but have been accorded greater significance. Within social work, neo-liberal discourses on risk have helped reconstruct the social worker–client/service user relationship. This is now reduced to a brokerage relationship between service users and the state via the social worker, for services. The implicit contract between the service user and the social worker replaces the therapeutic, enabling and supportive relationship. At the same time the service user's narrative (which used to be at the centre of the assessment) is now replaced as the service user is re-categorized as a 'welfare client' and part of a *risk group*. This distinction is crucial in securing a specific function for social work in the redefinition of 'risk'. Case management replaces the social work role, and the 'core task' of case management is risk profiling or assessing need against pre-established risk factors. This moves away from the traditional and more empowering model of social work, which included the client's/service user's rights to self-determination and to engage in a degree of risk-taking behaviour. Here Parton is referring to situations where risk taking used to be a feature of practice. For example, where an older person who was assessed as being 'frail' had the freedom to remain at home and to decide whether to live with an element of risk.

Rose (2000) argues that these changes in the technology of welfare mean that case management is now characterized by 'competition', 'quality' and 'customer demand' rather than collaboration in the social worker–client/service user relationship, in the amelioration of need. Moreover, in high modernity, risk is no longer conceptualized in terms of what might happen but as a threat, and this is linked to security; and the neo-liberal idea is one of security through market efficiency and emphasizing people's self-reliance, and the employment of their (as opposed to the state's) resources.

Sociologists like Delanty (2000) criticize Beck's analysis of risk because he fails to make clear whether the individual or global risks he refers to are real or social constructions. In addition, apart from ecological disasters he does not provide any empirical evidence on how or why this particular risk society is qualitatively different from previous eras. Scott (2000) argues that Beck's analysis entails an all-embracing, catastrophic model of risk and this does not, however, reflect on the form of risk-taking behaviours that occur when actors are making routine daily decisions as to where and how they live. In this respect it has limited practice application. The weakness in Beck's analysis is that despite his awareness of gradations of risk in society there is slippage in the analysis, in which at key points the actual existing risks – as opposed to hypothetical risks – are subsumed under ultimate catastrophe (i.e. the only empirical risks he can quantify are ultimate catastrophe ones like nuclear disaster).

Despite its weaknesses Beck's sociology of risk informs critical social work practice in two ways. It provides a critical evaluation of contemporary society by identifying how risk has been constructed within social work practice and hence curtailed the freedom of the client and social worker to collaborate on decisions as to what is an acceptable level of risk. For Adams et al. (2002b), however, the impact of Beck's risk society is that it introduced into social work practice the notion of uncertainty and an acceptance of working in the grey areas of practice where there are no clear-cut solutions. Thus, this risk society thesis encourages social workers to accept and cope with uncertainty.

## Power in Assessments

In order to engage in effective assessments, social workers need to have some sort of operational definition of 'power'. This is in order to understand the contradictory nature of the social work role between the service user, the agency and the wider welfare state and in order to have some frame of reference to analyse the competing interests that underpin these relationships. Lukes (1974) not only provides a working definition of power, but also points out the covert nature of power and the fact that it can be exercised, and people can be affected and harmed by its use, whether or not they are aware of its existence. Langan (2002) suggests this is what has happened to concepts of empowerment in social work in many Western countries under the auspices of neo-Conservative policies. This latter point has implications for any notions of empowerment adopted in social work practice. Acknowledgement of the power imbalance between social worker and client/service user and of the centrality of client/service user involvement are central features of the assessment process (Parker and Bradley, 2004). So too is the necessity of negotiation to obtain 'planning permission' for care plans. But what exactly do we mean by the term 'empowerment'? Wise (1995) states:

> empowerment . . . involves a commitment to challenging and combating injustice and oppression, which shows itself in action and in words. . . . The underlying philosophy of empowerment involves a commitment to encourage oppressed people to understand how structural oppression . . . impacts upon individuals and to enable them thereby to take back some control over their lives. (Wise, 1995, p. 108)

Fook (2001), however, asks the question 'Empowerment for whom?' Reflection on this question reminds practitioners that they need to consider all the dimensions of empowerment. That is, they need to consider to what extent they provide clients/service users with the 'means', 'knowledge', 'opportunity' or 'legal capacity' to become involved in decisions concerning their lives? Thus, reflection is necessary when pressing for empowerment of service users because of the value-laden nature the term 'assessment' embodies, which has the potential to lead to oppressive practice.

One of the *Oxford English Dictionary* (2000) definitions of 'assessment' describes it as judging the value or worth of something. Social workers do this on a daily basis by judging the value or worth of clients/services users in terms of their eligibility for services. Immediately, therefore, social workers are embroiled in tensions and contradictions in terms of empowerment. The assessment process seeks to address this by emphasizing the person-centred nature of the process. However, critics assert that there are structural and organizational barriers to its effectiveness. Lymbury (1998) argues that the care management approach in many European social services represents a 'top down' system in which professional ethics and values are secondary to administrative and managerial requirements. Postle (2001) argues that the increasingly bureaucratic nature of social work means that social workers will have less time for direct work with service users and less time to involve them in decision-making and evaluation of services and to assess their 'desert' or 'worth' for services.

In terms of empowerment, one of the key developments in social work, which should inform the assessment process, is the adoption of the 'human strengths' approach to practice, and acknowledgement that people are expert in themselves. Pawar (2004) adopts this in his community welfare programmes and Herscovitch (2001) sees it as a fundamental underpinning 'plank' to international social work in NGOs. Here again, reflection upon the *context* in which that expertise is demonstrated is important because it can have implications for the generation of AOP and the process of empowerment. Social workers need to be mindful when the situation of insider and outsider groups develops, as is often the case with various service user groups, simply because they are invariably constituted by some of the most socially marginalized people in society. But oppression can occur within the client/service user groups that the social workers are attempting to empower. This can happen when insider doctrines develop within that service user group.

Merton (1972) reflected on the development of insider and outsider doctrines and their impact on the development of critical sociology. He commented on how the rise of New Social Movements (NSMs) in terms of race, gender, class, sexuality or disability had occurred in response to the elitism of white, male insider groups (e.g. fascist or Nazi groups) in America. This focus was Merton's attempt to address different forms of discrimination and oppression and develop critical sociological frameworks to analyse them. However, owing to the historical context of the social upheavals and cultural antagonisms that were occurring in the US, he argued that both insider and outsider group doctrines were equally damaging to intellectual and political arguments within sociology and detrimental to social reform. This is because they both make claims to the truth, and the mutual distrust between them results in deterioration of intellectual argument as each group adopts a simplistic interpretation of the other's viewpoint or values. Thus, they fail to assess the merits of that viewpoint according to academic rigour or logical structures. Merton distinguishes between weak and strong insider doctrines. Weak insider doctrines claim *privileged* knowledge, i.e. access to knowledge, and are thus open to the possibility of other groups gaining access to this privileged knowledge. Strong insider doctrines, on the other hand, claim *monopolistic* access to particular kinds of knowledge and argue that it can only be accessed by group members. In an attempt to develop strategies to counter insider group oppression and discrimination, outsider groups can end up adopting extreme insider positions manifest in claims to *monopolistic* knowledge. In other words, you have to be a group member to truly understand the group, and group members then demand total allegiance to that one group status.

Merton argued that such knowledge claims represent the 'balkanization of social science' (1972, p. 17) and he maintains that, as a result, the outsider doctrine develops into a form of insider knowledge. Consequently, it becomes a form of ethnocentricism as bad as that of elite insider groups.

> Ethnocentrism, then, is not an historical constant. It becomes intensified under specific conditions of acute social conflict. When a nation, race, ethnic group, or any powerful collectivity has long extolled its own admirable qualities and, expressly or by implication, deprecates the qualities of others, it invites and provides the potential for counter ethnocentricism. (Merton, 1972, p. 17)

Merton argued that the development of insider doctrines like this within sociology was divisive and this had implications for developing collaborative efforts to address and formulate anti-oppressive sociological research practices to address social problems. The sub-text of Merton's analysis on insider and outsider doctrines, points to the dangers of oppressive practice when outsider groups obtain some degree of representation and develop insider doctrines. This was the criticism Merton was levelling at the US Women's Movement and Black Civil Rights Movement. For if, as they suggest, only women can understand women's history, sociology and experiences of oppression and only black people can understand black history, sociology and experiences of oppression this has implications for generating truly empowering social reform. Under such circumstances (Merton asks), how do white, middle-class and heterosexual men like himself, who are members of the US elite, ever gain access to the *monopolistic knowledge* that they need, to reflect upon their own ethnocentricism and racism and challenge these forms of oppression? In addition, the problem with both insider and outsider doctrines is that they ignore the fact that we all have multiple status sets and can be either insiders or outsiders at different times and in different contexts.

Sociology, therefore, informs an understanding of the key elements of the assessment process by highlighting their complex, dynamic, contested and contradictory nature. In addition, deconstructing these elements helps identify the practice dilemmas in attempting to work in ethical and empowering ways with service users. Moreover, identifying how sociology informs evaluation skills, and highlighting the centrality of evaluation to the assessment process, assists social workers in knowing what makes for a good assessment. It is to this issue that the chapter now turns.

Shaw (1996; Shaw and Gould, 2001) argues that developments of sociological methods such as ethnography, in the form of the focus group and life history methods, are crucial in the development of good evaluation skills. Sociology has contributed to the assessment process through life history or 'life course sociology' as it is sometimes termed. This development was due in large part to the work done by ethnomethodologists in the Chicago School of Sociology in the 1930s (Becker 1971). More recent sociological developments in this method include Morgan (1985), Clapham et al. (1993) and Clifford (1994). This type of life history method is useful for the way it moves the story backwards and forwards from the individual biography to the social system (Clifford, 1994).

Life course sociology or life history contributes to the evaluation process by bringing the client/service user and social worker together by combining observation with interviewing. Also, it analyses change and development in the service user's circumstances and it is useful for examining the time dimension in people's experience of events. Similarly, Clapham et al. (1993) used life history with older service users looking at their housing provision and to identify their housing needs. These life histories were then used to help the service users make decisions about housing and accommodation issues. This social constructivist approach seeks to understand the narratives of vulnerable clients/service users. It has been used by the social work academic Kasuma (2007) to support young refugees re-settling in Canada. Similarly, Sands and Bourjolly (2007) used this method in face-to-face interviews with African American women who had converted to Islam.

A particular strength of this type of housing life-history in the Clapham study was the way it focused both the clients'/service users' and social workers' attention on how people come to be in their present accommodation situation and the choices they were able to make. It also considered why certain options were chosen and others rejected. Clifford (1994) reminds us that it is important in life-history work to develop a critical reflexive dimension, which incorporates anti-oppressive practice when listening to people's narratives.

# Groupwork

Groupwork is another method for engaging clients/service users in the assessment process. One key approach is the *remedial approach*, which seeks to provide a context for a group of service users to address their deviant behaviour. In contrast, the *reciprocal approach* tries to promote mutual support and goal setting by the group members with the social worker acting as a facilitator. Another form of groupwork is the *social goals approach*, which is mainly used in youth and community, and education projects. Brown (1992) has added the *mediating model* of groupwork, which seeks to enable group members to role build in a safe, supportive but challenging environment. More recent attempts at groupwork have incorporated task-centred methods of intervention, or feminist or therapeutic approaches: for example, Sharry (2001) has identified solution-focused therapy groups.

Brown (1987) suggests that in terms of groupwork the size of the group can vary from 3 to 12 persons and that 'groupwork' is manifest in the notion that the group exists for some purpose, however ill-defined. He also argues that the aims of groupwork vary but they usually include individual assessment, support, maintenance or individual change, educational aims or information giving. Alternatively they cover mediation work, group support or change and social or environmental change. However, Brown's (1992) account of groupwork theories includes reference to groupwork models where the worker acts as a facilitator, but social change is not the primary aim. Instead, there is an assumption that the group members with shared circumstances or problems would be mutually beneficial and supportive of one another. Such self-help and mutual support groups do not seek to promote therapeutic change.

Groupwork evolved out of the focus group method in market research and developmental work undertaken by the American sociologist Robert K. Merton (1946) on the focused interview. In terms of understanding how services users behave and are influenced in groups it is worth considering Kitzinger's (1994) sociological analysis of focus groups. She argues that the focus group represents a useful method to determine people's views and attitudes in a particular social context, because it focuses upon how meanings are constructed, negotiated, changed and experienced within the group interaction. She used the focus group method in her sociological research on people's views about HIV and the AIDS virus. She observed that group behaviour is characterized by joking, teasing and various forms of acting out in front of and between peers and she gives the example of the group members acting out what they perceived as the 'look' of an 'AIDS carrier'. Kitzinger's use of the focus group method might be useful to social workers when working with clients/service users diagnosed with HIV/AIDS. It could also be useful in developing strategies for a group casework context which addresses culturally sensitive issues like domestic abuse or child sexual abuse. This is because in such group contexts confidentiality and privacy are of prime importance.

Some of the advantages of using the focus group method in social research are similar to those that can be gleaned in social work. First, it highlights group members' attitudes and priorities, via the kinds of language and frames of reference used to understand issues. Secondly, it encourages a greater variety of communication and hence taps into a range of understandings. Thirdly, it helps identify the group's norms; and fourthly, it provides some insight into the processes by which the group articulates knowledge and what information is censored or mooted by the group. It has the potential to encourage conversation on embarrassing subject matter and can facilitate the expression of ideas and experiences that might be far less forthcoming in a one-to-one interview. Moreover, the social worker/group facilitator's attention to detail in the group dynamics has the potential to explore the differences between the group members, and to clarify why they believe what they do. Also, it can examine the kinds of questions people ask and in doing so reveal the underlying assumptions they make and theoretical frameworks they use. It can also explore the arguments group members use against one another. Moreover, it can be useful in exploring how facts and stories operate within the group and what function these perform. In this respect it helps social workers identify what kind of forms of speech facilitate or inhibit group communication.

Focus groups are useful in contexts where there exist power differentials between the group's participants and decision makers. Secondly, they can uncover the extent of conflict or consensus that exists over an issue. Thirdly, they act as a useful medium to ensure the participants'/service users' narratives remain at the forefront of the group discussion. Fourthly, they can inform practice through the way they can make a useful contribution to the evaluation process in the assessment, planning, intervention and review of outcomes.

Focus groups (according to sociologists) should never be used where the participants know each other extremely well, or where the aim is to secure some kind of immediate action. In addition, they should never be used for therapeutic purposes because of the power imbalances that arise between the group facilitator and group members. Moreover, there are several things which have the potential to affect the validity of a focus group:

- Social desirability (where respondents mask undesirable or embarrassing information in order to engage in what Goffman (1967) terms 'impression management').

- Compliance – this is responding in a way that the respondent believes is expected by the group facilitator.

- Identification – adopting a position similar to that of someone the respondent admires, or choosing a position because they want to feel part of a group. This can lead to a 'group think' situation, which is due to the group's desire for cohesion. This can lead to a lack of critical thinking on an issue.

- Internalization – this is where a respondent's views on a situation are so deeply entrenched that it is unlikely that participation in the group will lead to critical thinking on an issue and perspective transformation. In such circumstances it will be difficult for the focus group method to obtain the 'real' or hidden opinions of group members (Kelman, 1961).

Fantasy theme is another major problem affecting communication in groups. Bormann (1972) defines 'fantasy theme' as a situation where members of the group unintentionally, but naturally, weave a story, constructing a fantasy as they build on one another's statements to collectively describe a situation, explain events or justify their verdicts or social attitudes. A classic example of fantasy theme development occurred in Putnam's research in Chicago (2001) concerning the ways in which teachers and local district representatives negotiated on pay and on health and safety issues. In the group discussions teachers and district representatives began to weave a story based upon previous individual and negative experiences of pay negotiations with management. This then developed into a discourse about common enemies and past negotiations. These two elements combined and became the basis of later negotiations about salaries.

Bormann (1972) argues that as the drama unfolds within the group the fantasy theme may often incorporate a here-and-now theme. Smith (1988) extends this idea by stating that common discourses that develop in groups and that are incorporated into the fantasy are 'the powerful-versus-the-powerless' or 'the-good'-versus-the-evil'. These themes then underlie the discourses in the developing conflict in the 'here-and-now'. The viability of using focus groups in social work is supported by Shaw (1996), who argues that the focus group method has informed social work practice by the way it has enhanced dimensions of the evaluation process. He identifies the way this method can be used effectively in social work assessments.

Bearing in mind that assessment is a value-laden process with overtly political dimensions it is worth considering the ways sociological knowledge can inform an understanding of the power dynamics that can come into play in the evaluation process. Social constructivism has been useful in enhancing an understanding of discourses that seek to lay claim to boundaries of what is worth knowing. Equally, Merton's concepts of 'social sadism' and 'sociological euphemism' are useful in examining the other oppressive dimensions of language. By the term 'social sadism' Merton (1972) was referring to the ways various social institutions are organized and the practices that are produced in those institutions which result in the exclusion, oppression and social marginalization of various groups. He stresses that often these are not calculated and deliberate practices. Nonetheless, the consequences of these 'ways of doing things' are oppression, exclusion, pain and humiliation for the individuals who are often on the receiving end. In other words, the institutionalized forms of oppression (manifest in the 'objective, socially organized and recurrent set of situations'; Merton, 1972, p. 38) continue through practices and social organisations and in turn affect service delivery. This occurs not because individuals are committed to their maintenance, but because of the social conditioning of society on what are 'normal' or 'acceptable' forms of behaviour and interaction. These practices serve to create hierarchies for insider groups, whose 'normality' other people's deviance is measured against. Thus the assumption that able-bodiedness is the norm unconsciously reinforces the abnormality of a person with a disability and hence their perceived deviance. This marginalization and exclusion occurs not simply by deliberate victimization but by the unconscious ignorance of the person's needs. For example, often welfare and social service offices lack lifts or ramps, or the corridors are not wide enough to fit wheel-chairs. This is also very often the case with public transport.

Equally damaging in terms of generating oppressive practice with service users, is the minimization of people's pain, suffering and oppression by the use of language, and this is what Merton (1972) refers to as 'sociological euphemism'.

> Sociological euphemism refers to the kind of conceptual apparatus that, once adopted requires us to ignore such intense human experiences as pain, suffering, humiliation, and so on . . . the intense feeling of pain and suffering that are the experiences of some people caught up in the social patterns under examination. By screening out these profoundly human experiences, they become sociological euphemisms.    (Merton, 1972, p. 38)

Though in anti-oppressive practice training students are taught to reflect on the oppressive nature of labelling, discourse or the use of negative language, there is very little reference to the oppressive and damaging nature of mini-mization. This can occur through the reframing of the client's/service user's circumstances. Often in the assessment process there is a danger of drifting into sociological euphemism. This occurs when we refer to someone's trau-matic experience of constant physical abuse or rape as 'domestic violence' or 'couple violence'. It occurs when social workers minimize the trauma of an older person's enforced transition to residential care as a 'change of circumstance'. This phrase bears no relation to the actual experience of their loss of home, familiar surroundings, loved ones, their separation from family members and sense of social isolation. Sociological euphemisms are manifest in the ways the terms 'asylum seeker' or 'refugee' are conflated with the term 'economic migrants', thus minimizing the traumatic experiences of exposure to violence, ethnic cleansing or genocide. The useful (though often misapplied diagnoses of post-traumatic stress disorder (PTSD) is sometimes used in child protection cases as a euphemism to describe a horrendous and often lengthy pattern of cumulative neglect, physical attacks, violence, aggression, humiliation, pain and sexual abuse that children face.

In terms of theorizing in the assessment process various types of discourse theory have proved useful. Ingamells and Westoby (2008) use discourse theory in work with adolescent asylum seekers in Australia to critically eval-uate the dominance of psychiatric approaches to trauma work. They argue that the assessment process is already complicated by two contradictory discourses. One discourse recognizes the refugee status (which embodies the humanitarian principle of supporting people's right to protection from persecution) while the other discourse embodies the stigma of 'exclusion', 'alien' or 'other' which is attached to the refugee label. The result of these competing discourses is that they tend to reinforce the homogenization of different experiences of refugees both in fleeing from persecution and in the process of resettlement in the new country.

Using discourse theory, Ingamells and Westoby (2008) identify the prac-tice implications of the dominance of medical discourses in refugee work. This particular discourse emphasizes the 'recovery from torture'. This results in mental health approaches dominating funding priorities for refugee work and setting the agenda in the multi-professional assessment process. They cite Summerfield (1999), who argues that the dangers of giving primacy to psychiatric constructions of trauma are that they result in the medicaliza-tion of both the nature of the distress and the professional responses. This undermines the significance of the emotional, social and emotional impact of loss of a person's social world (Ingamells and Westoby, 2008, p. 6). Moreover, the dominance of medical models of trauma (particularly with child refugees) means that they tend to emphasize vulnerability as a key element in the assessment process. This in turn legitimizes increased social control (2008, p. 6).

# Theory and the Assessment Process

Within social work the issue of assessment is made more complicated by the lack of consensus as to which theory, model or method of intervention should be used and in what circumstances. Trotter (1999) has tried to address this issue by developing a model of the types of theories commonly used in practice. These include ecological or systems approaches, which explore the interrelated nature of systems and how intervention in one system may affect another system. Secondly, there is the use of behaviour or cognitive behavioural theories, which consider the influence of feelings in the production of behaviours and the importance of role modelling. Thirdly, there is feminist case-work theory, which examines the way patriarchal structures disadvantage women through sexist stereotyping. Fourthly, there is radical case-work theory, which is predicated on examining structural constraints and inequalities. Fifthly, there is task-centred case work (this is not a theory, but rather a model of intervention), which is influenced by both psychodynamic and social constructivist theory; it is concerned with service users' narratives of their situation, and sets the agenda according to their definitions. Lastly, there is the solution-focused approach, which emphasizes human strengths and solutions that service users can generate in the management of their situation.

Within sociology, systems theory has been manifest in different forms in the work of early sociologists such as Comte (1798–1857) and Durkheim (1858–1917), and refined by Parsons (1902–79). In explaining the operations of society, Parsons (1937; 1969) used systems theory to identify the ways in which the family, the economy and education systems all functioned to secure social order. Similarly, the social constructivist Luhmann (1995) drew on cybernetics (the science of self-regulating systems of information) to explore the theory of autopoiesis (from 'auto' meaning self and 'poieses' meaning generating) to see how social systems were capable of regenerating themselves. Within sociology, neo-Marxists have been keen to explore how autopoiesis can be used to explain capitalism's capacity (despite its frequent socio-political crises) to self-generate.

Payne (2005) asserts that systems theory had a major impact on social work in the 1970s and exists in two forms. There is general systems theory and ecological systems theory. General systems theory, as applied to practice, is manifest in the work of Pincus and Minahan (1973). Ecological systems theory has had considerable impact in the US. Brown (1992) shows the application of the idea of 'boundary' and environment to groupwork, while Kabadaki (1995) shows how the possibility of intervening at different levels in society is particularly relevant for social development work.

Ecological systems theory seems to offer social work an approach that allows for structural constraints, which is an important determinant that psychodynamic theory ignores. It has several advantages. First, it's ability to analyse circular connections in interactions between social worker and service user; secondly, its value in the assessment process; thirdly, systems theory has a capacity to integrate other social work theories and its inclusion of social factors balances the emphasis in individual casework. However, according to Wakefield (1996) it has several weaknesses in terms of social work practice. It lacks the power to explain why things happen and why particular connections between social variables exist. It does not tell social workers what kinds of interventions to make to affect any system, because it lacks the capacity to explain *how* each part of the system will interact with others. Moreover, it incorporates everything, but not everything is relevant to the assessment. At the same time it cannot provide insight as to what is salient in a case. Deciding on boundaries in a system may be complex or impossible and often it assumes connections between parts of the system without providing empirical evidence for such connections. In *encouraging* social workers to concentrate on macro-issues it tends to neglect small scale personal issues, which might be highly significant for the quality of life of the individual client/service user. In addition, it fails to fully evaluate the nature of conflict and assumes that conflict is less desirable than cohesion and integration, which may not be true in practice. Furthermore, a common criticism made by neo-Marxists of systems theory (Lavalette and Pratt, 2001: Jones, 2002; Poulantzas, 1976) is that it does not take account of dialectics and contradictions within different parts of the social system. In capitalist societies the contradictions and tensions generated by the relations of production, class conflict and the state's role in the economy create a host of conflicts, tensions and contradictions. These result in a plethora of unpredictable and variable outcomes, which affect the process of integration and, on a more micro-level, affect the varied nature of social work outcomes with different groups of clients/service users.

Ecological theory is used in the assessment process and this is manifest in *Framework for the Assessment of Children in Need and Their Families* (DoH, 2000), which is used in UK Children's services. Calder (2003) criticizes this framework on several grounds. This claims to be an ecological model of assessment entailing three integrated sub-stems or dimensions, which are: (1) the child's developmental needs; (2) dimensions of parenting capacity; and (3) family and environmental factors. Commenting on the simplistic conflation of environment with wider society he states:

> the ecological claims of the assessment model are compromised by its conflation of community and societal considerations into one 'domain' (family and environmental factors). By failing to set the child, their carers and their family/community environment into a wider socio-political context (i.e. a fourth domain) the

model fails to prompt critical reflection on the influence of wider social trends, e.g. gender roles; perceptions of child maltreatment, poverty . . .   (Calder, 2003, pp. 30–1)

Such contradiction and complexity is often missed by social workers in the assessment process and this problem is compounded by practitioners' lack of evaluation skills. Shaw (1996) comments on the fact that social workers and social work students note that evaluation of practice is a pervasive yet difficult aspect of their work, because many believe they lack the skills to engage in evaluation. Furthermore, they believe that they are ill equipped in this on social work training courses or practice placements. Shaw argues that in order to equip students with the necessary skills to evaluate their own practice, they require the 'translation' of sociological methodologies and methods as discussed in this chapter. In addition, in a move away from the current culture of 'assessment outcomes' he argues that evaluation is more than determining whether social work is effective, it is also about evaluating the extent to which it promotes empowerment and social change (Shaw, 1996, p. 148).

## Summary of the Main Points

- The key elements in the assessment of process are ethics, power, professionalism and anti-oppressive practice (AOP).

- Each of these elements is complex and contested and they create dilemmas when attempts are made to implement them in practice.

- Sociology can inform an understanding of ethics as they apply to social work practice by analysing the nature of professionalism, ascertaining the legal context of social work, and considering how social work practice is socially constructed.

- Sociological analysis of professionalism identifies its impact on service user empowerment.

- Sociology informs an understanding of the assessment process by providing analytical concepts to understand power, professionalism, the development of insider doctrines, and AOP.

- Sociological research methods such as the focus group and life history methods contribute to the development of evaluation skills.

# Conclusion

In this chapter sociological theories have been proved useful for examining assessment as a dynamic social process and for showing the interconnections between assessment, care planning, intervention, and review. In addition, it highlighted the dangers of treating these as discrete phases and stressed the need to regard evaluation (including the client's/service user's evaluation) as an integral part of each aspect of the assessment. Moreover, different sociological theories and research methods were identified, which included life history, focus groups, the ethnographic interview method and insider doctrines: each providing insights into the complexities of power, politics and service user involvement when conducting assessments. Furthermore, sociological research methods identified ways to inform social work evaluation skills and to underpin ethical considerations. These in turn were linked to issues of reflexivity and critical practice. All these strands will be brought together in the final chapter, which explores the uses of sociology within the context of interprofessional practice and international social work.

## Case Study

Thomas Obeyu is twelve years old and fled his native Somalia when his village was caught in the crossfire between rival militia forces. His parents and three younger brothers were killed when the village was destroyed. Thomas has a young sister who lives with a paternal uncle. Thanks to help from Save the Children Fund, Thomas has been reunited with his sister and the paternal uncle and his family in South Africa. However, the social worker is having difficulty arranging for Thomas to resettle with his uncle's family owing to the fact that the Immigration Department are suspicious about his refugee status, and this is under review. Thomas has had a medical assessment and the GP suggests that Thomas is suffering from post-traumatic stress disorder and has referred him to a psychiatrist. However, Thomas has told his social worker that he does not need to see a psychiatrist, he just needs his refugee status to be sorted out so he can remain living with his sister and uncle.

Thomas's social worker might find that using Ingamells and Westoby's (2008) approach to discourse theory is useful in this assessment. This deconstructs the socio-legal discourses on refugee children's rights and medical discourses relating to diagnosis and treatment. In doing so they locate both sets of discourses within the context of multidisciplinary working and its practice implications. This informs not only a critical understanding of the contested nature of the social work assessment process but also the barriers to generating holistic and empowering assessments. This is because they identify the contradictory and competing discourse underpinning the term 'refugee', i.e. humanitarian considerations versus the stigmatizing processes of 'othering' associated with labels such as 'foreigner' or 'alien' that are linked to the term 'refugee'. This also has connotations of welfare dependency and being an economic burden.

## Case Study (*cont'd*)

Similarly, they effectively deconstruct psychiatric discourses on trauma and vulnerability and in doing so illustrate the power and practice implications of these discourses. These in turn lead to assessments of refugee needs being 'heavily weighted to mental health considerations' (Ingamells and Westoby, 2008, p. 5). This ignores the social and emotional impact of the loss of home or former lifestyle, while the conflation of the concept of trauma with vulnerability leads to a process of stereotyping of the young refugee. Both of these processes deny the individual agency and resilience of young refugees or asylum seekers and they legitimize state intervention and social control.

# Further Reading

Ingamells, A. and Westoby, P. (2008) 'Working with Young People from Refugee Backgrounds in Australia', *European Journal of Social Work*, vol. 1, pp. 1–15.
This article deconstructs oppressive discourses on refugee children and highlights how a diagnosis of 'trauma' legitimizes their social control.

Merton, R. K. (1972) 'Insiders and Outsiders: a Chapter in the Sociology of Knowledge', *American Journal of Sociology*, vol. 78, no. 1, pp. 9–47.
This is not only a classic example of critical sociology at its best, but Merton also takes complex ideas like 'monopolistic access to knowledge' and makes them easy to understand and demonstrates their practical application.

Shaw, I. F. (1996) *Evaluating in Practice* (Aldershot: Arena).
This book provides very good definitions of the term 'evaluation' as applied to social work practice. In addition it includes a host of case examples of the uses of ethnography and highlights the practice dilemmas of trying to generate service user participation in assessment.

Shaw, I. and Gould, N. (2001) *Qualitative Research in Social Work* (London: Sage).
This book outlines different types of sociological research methods and shows how they can be applied to case work to enhance critical reflexive skills.

# 8

# Sociology and International Social Work

## Introduction

This final chapter explores how sociology is linked to two developments in social work, the growth of interprofessional practice, and international social work. Both these trends can be seen in international non-governmental organizations (INGOs) and Non-governmental organizations (NGOs). Ironically, the development of the risk society and the uncertainty associated with it, has led to a crisis over the reliability of scientific knowledge. This has prompted an increase in collaboration between the natural and social scientific disciplines and the rise of interdisciplinary research (Gibbons et al., 1994). It is argued that this has fostered the view amongst governments that such an approach to knowledge is transferable to the health and social work fields. Consequently, we are witnessing the proliferation of interprofessional practice in relation to social services provision. This approach is influencing practice, not only in state-funded social services departments but also in INGOs and NGOs. Moreover, these developments are occurring in a period of major, global, social transformations, which some sociologists such as Beck (2006) term 'cosmopolitanism'. This is why cosmopolitan sociology is being used in this chapter, to analyse these social transformations and to evaluate critically their practice implications.

## Key Words

interprofessional practice, cosmopolitanism, global interdependence, international social work

# Professional Practice

'Interdisciplinary practice' is often used interchangeably with *'multi-professional* practice' but is distinctly different. Whereas multi-professional practice entails the combination of disciplinary approaches, the disciplines do not transfer, but remain located within their respective and distinctive intellectual boundaries. Interdisciplinary practice, in contrast, requires that the different insights are combined or merged in the identification and resolution of the problem at hand. *Interprofessional* practice involves members of two or more professions working together to respond more adequately to clients'/service users' needs and to improve the quality of services provided. It also seeks to optimize the use of resources by avoiding duplication. This way of working requires professionals to exchange knowledge, to combine their expertise, to plan and to provide coordinated services.

There continues, however, to be much debate about the assumption underpinning interprofessional practice: that is, whether it is necessarily a desirable objective. In many cases it may be important for both clients/service users and professionals to maintain a degree of professional distinctiveness, for example, in the area of child protection, otherwise the child's needs may be subsumed under a plethora of competing professional interests. In addition, the value for professionals of having their assumptions and practices challenged by those working with very different intellectual paradigms may be lost through interdisciplinary collaboration, as this seeks to minimize or ignore those differences. More importantly, the over-identification or collusion between different professional groups may diminish the opportunity for clients/service users who seek to use their particular services for alternative assessments or responses to their situation.

# The Context of Social Work

Despite these concerns, interprofessional practice is a reality around the globe. For instance, there are interprofessional domestic violence units in India (Orme et al., 2000), interprofessional pre-school services and services for street children in Ghana (Fadayomi, 1979; Argawal et al.,: 1997). In South Africa the treatment of HIV/AIDS occurs in an interprofessional context (Strydom and Raath, 2005). In the UK, interprofessional practice is manifest in the *Every Child Matters* (Department for Education and Skills, 2003) which heralded the end of social services departments and the introduction of Children's Services. These integrate professionals from education, health, youth offending teams and youth services. Moreover, interprofessional practice is being developed further within adult services in the types of collaboration occurring in the Care Trusts and the development of the

Single Assessment Process (SAP). Similarly, in countries like Nigeria and New Zealand, interprofessional practice is being developed in NGOs (Herscovitch, 2001; Lucas, 2001).

Calder (2003) identifies a number of obstacles to interprofessional practice in child care social work and child protection which could leave many children 'falling through the net' in terms of services. First, child protection is not the exclusive province of any one profession or agency. This problem is compounded by the fact that different agencies are guided by different legislation and government guidance, and these at times cause contradictions and dialectical tensions. Secondly, professional stereotypes and prejudices persist and these have the potential to damage trust and create stress and confusion about what skills and responsibilities each profession has in relation to the interprofessional professional task. Thirdly, each professional will have been socialized into their particular role and will have a value system and language unique to that particular profession. These professional value systems are a constant source of potential conflict and interfere with how professionals view each other, and more importantly, affect their perceptions as to the level of risk that is acceptable to service users. Fourthly, there are differences in status and degrees of power, and differences in contracts of employment both between and within different professional groups. All these things can contribute to the real and felt power differentials within interprofessional practice working. Moreover, one major problem affecting interprofessional practice is that different professionals define and explain child abuse in different and sometimes conflicting ways. This approach to problem definition affects the ability to provide problem resolution, which is also hampered by the problem of communication. This is because information is power, and sharing it symbolizes the relinquishing of autonomy. This realization creates anxiety and limits information flows between professionals.

Bailey (2002) suggests that one way to address some of the barriers to interprofessional practice is to adopt the bio-psychosocial model (which is predicated on an interdisciplinary approach). This is increasingly being used in mental health settings, as a framework for understanding the factors contributing to the onset of mental distress (Kingdon, 2000). This model incorporates social factors as an integral part of a holistic approach that seeks to provide increased insight into the relapses and individual coping strategies used by mental health service users. The model is influenced by sociology in that it adopts a social constructivist stance. It does this by placing the service user's narratives as a central feature in the way the bio-psychosocial model is interpreted in the assessments. This is to avoid the discursive dominance of the medical model in the process. The model entails three interactive spheres that are considered to affect the service user. These are:

- the bio sphere (which relates to the biomedical level of functioning);

- the psycho sphere (which examines patterns of thinking, feeling and reality testing);

- the social sphere (which emphasizes personal relationships and experiences of oppression, discrimination and disadvantage in wider society).

Bailey (2002) argues that the individual understands their distress with a particular emphasis on one or more aspects of this model, so this does not preclude interventions that are based on different parts of the model. Indeed, if a holistic approach to mental health care is to be developed, then a combination approach should be followed. A particular strength of this model is that it identifies how critical reflexivity on respective elements of the bio-psychosocial framework can feature in an understanding of an individual's mental distress. Furthermore, the model prompts reflection on how a combination of interventions from one or more disciplines may meet a person's care needs.

## Strategies for Interprofessional Practice

There are several factors which contribute to the development of good interprofessional practice. First, social workers must recognize that good interprofessional practice is based upon effective networks. To achieve this they should use the teamwork process, developed because of these networks, to discuss openly and honestly the different professional and disciplinary views. Unless this process can be undertaken, interprofessional practice will suffer. Social workers should prepare in advance for this practice situation and be clear about both their role and remit and what they bring to the interprofessional context. Moreover, using supervision they should critically reflect on the boundaries of their professional role but always be prepared to be flexible about moving these boundaries in negotiation with other professional colleagues. Furthermore, they should regard networking as an ongoing exercise, engaging proactively with this and cultivating professional networks as much as possible (Payne, 2002).

These prescriptions for interprofessional practice have practice relevance for almost all forms of social work practice. Of particular importance are the emphasis on developing networks, team-building, and an interprofessional consensus on methods of working. These three facets are relevant to social workers involved in community development projects in Asian-Pacific countries (as identified by Pawar, 2004), in multi-professional NGOs (Herscovitch, 2001), working with street children in Australia (Zuffery and Kerr, 2005), working with refugees, providing educational and welfare services to isolated communities in Israel or Alaska (Berman, 2006), providing services to those affected by war or famine (Harding 2007), or working with HIV/AIDS sufferers in Africa (Steinitz, 2007).

Healy's (2001) analysis of the global nature of social work practice identifies various trends relating to interprofessional practice. Two key features are global interdependence and social work's common response to that interdependence, in the form of international social work organizations and NGOs. Citing Midgley (1997), she refers to global interdependence as

> a process of global integration in which diverse peoples, economies, cultures and political processes are increasingly subjected to international influences. (Midgley, 1997, p. 21)

Because of global interdependence, nations are becoming increasingly aware of how many ways they are connected. They are connected in terms of environmental interdependence (through the global impact of pesticides) and the growing shortages of water, mineral resources and land, and the impact of global warming. In addition, there is increased cultural interdependence due to the impact of IT technologies. This has made possible the mass exportation of almost any product around the globe, while there is increased economic interdependence due to the inroads of global capitalism. This form of interdependence has particular significance for social workers, manifest in the long-term global unemployment trends, the lack of job security, falling wages or low wages, and the cutbacks in global welfare expenditure, which are affecting human welfare around the world (Healy, 2001, p. 110).

Two particular forms of global interdependence that Healy focuses upon are global migration and the HIV/AIDS pandemic. She explores these because she argues that they are accompanied by a host of socio-economic problems that are repeated around the globe. These socio-economic problems have practice implications in terms of addressing issues of poverty, women's status and rights, the rights of street children and the issue of social policy implementation. A reflection of this sense of global interdependence and the common dimensions of international social work practice is the increase in the number of international social work qualifications around the globe focusing specifically on the international context of social work. These include different types of specialisms, such as refugee studies or disaster relief or work with earthquake or tsunami victims (Aghabakhshi and Gregor, 2007).

Herscovitch (2001) points out that though many international NGOs would not define themselves as welfare or social work organizations (Herscovitch, 2001, p. 126), they share common principles and objectives with social work. These include a concern with human rights and welfare, organizing projects and programmes to secure the protection of children and refugees, education and health projects and projects to promote economic self-sufficiency. Healy (2001) identifies the key role that the UN performs in the funding and promotion of international NGOs in the form of the UN Children's Fund (UNICEF) and the United Nations Development Programme (UNDP). UNICEF funded 160 projects for children worldwide in 1995, totalling 804 million dollars. This was in order to achieve its aim to improve the lives of children. This was achieved by ensuring community health and social services provision, safe water supplies, education and nutrition, as well as protection of children from hazardous labour and sexual and economic exploitation. With regard to UNDP, this funds socio-economic development in some of the poorest countries in the world, in developing agriculture, communication and transportation systems. In 1986, UNDP set up the Division of Women in Development, and it has funded projects for low-income women in poor countries (Healy, 2001, p. 131).

As well as international social work expanding its global remit through the work of the UN and international charities like the Red Cross, or Red Crescent, social work education is assuming an international dimension as many universities are becoming increasingly aware of their 'global interdependence'. For example, citing Healy's 'continuum' approach in the development of international social work programmes, Johnson (2004) demonstrates how the Local International Connections Committee at Western Reserve University in the US developed a curriculum for international social work. She defines international social work as having taking three forms:

- International organizations using social work methods or personnel.

- Social work cooperation between countries.

- The transfer of methods or social work knowledge between nations (Johnson, 2004, p. 7).

Using Healy's continuum she identifies how the impetus developed for an international social work curriculum in the form of the Local International Konnections (LINK) scheme. Within the faculty, sentiments went from one extreme of Healy's continuum (tolerance of the unsolicited presence of foreign students) to the other (manifest in a well articulated programme of study) (Johnson, 2004, p. 8). Thus, by the time it was set up, the programme involved over twenty countries and a variety of international exchanges and placements.

# Cosmopolitanism and International Social Work

I have chosen to devote a section on the social transformations known as cosmopolitanism for several reasons. First, I would argue that cosmopolitanism is having a bigger impact on societies and international social work than globalization. My reasons for arguing this are because there is controversy within sociology over whether the world has experienced globalization or simply new forms of global capitalism (Callinicos, 2003; Delanty, 2006). Furthermore, globalization only really focuses upon the economic dimensions of these social transformations and the loss of autonomy of nation states. Moreover, the concept of cosmopolitanism, unlike globalization, covers a host of socio-political factors that have an impact on the organization of social work. It is argued, therefore, that this represents a better framework for identifying and analysing the contemporary global social transformations that are occurring.

Beck (2006) defines 'cosmopolitanism' in three ways. The positive dimensions of it include international cultural commodities such as media, films, art and sport, dual citizenship, plurality of political representations such as global social movements and civil rights movements, multilingual societies, international communications and socio-economic and political collaboration. The negative side of cosmopolitanism is reflected in the growth of global diaspora, a global refugee crisis, global terrorism, transnational criminal activity and increased global imperialism (manifest in the extension of superpower nation-state sovereignty on the part of the US, China and Russia). In addition, Beck refers to a new kind of sociology called 'cosmopolitanism'. Thus, for him 'cosmopolitanism' represents both the social transformations that are occurring around the globe and the development of a new sociology to describe and analyse those transformations.

One key feature of the positive dimensions of cosmopolitanism identified by Delanty (2006) is the attempts by societies to develop a sense of world openness. This is by becoming more reflexive about the existence of forms of racism and ethnocentrism in society and by trying to develop a democratic dialogue with ordinary citizens, not just other governments. However, both Beck and Delanty argue that, at present, the world is a long way off from developing this positive dimension. This is because the negative dimensions of cosmopolitanism predominate.

What Beck (2006) terms the 'negative dimensions' of cosmopolitanism are manifest in the conduct of many nation states in the 'War on Terror' following 11 September 2001 and the bombing of the World Trade Center in the US. There is some degree of consensus amongst Eastern and Western sociologists, economists and political scientists (Anjum, 2006; Kaseke, 2005; Landman, 2006) that this has eroded global human rights and civil liberties. This contention has practice implications for social workers who are employees of welfare states and NGOs in terms of having the legal and financial resources to support clients where civil liberty violations have occurred. For instance, Landman (2006) conducted a study of 39 self-described 'democracies' including the US, the UK and Australia and noted that they have responded to the perceived threat of terrorism by passing anti-terrorist legislation. Much of this legislation is causing grave concern amongst international human rights groups for both citizens of these countries and the defenders of human rights (Landman, 2006, p. 124). A practice example of this trend is evident in Jones's (2001) study of unaccompanied asylum-seeking children in the UK. Her study highlighted how the power of the discourse of 'bogus asylum seekers' was acting as a barrier to civil rights. Often, social workers bowed to the Immigration Department's pressure to give primacy to the 'bogus status' and check the legitimacy of children's application for asylum, rather than giving primacy to their statutory duties to secure children's protection, welfare and civil rights in accordance with the UN Convention in the Rights of the Child.

The concerns over the global war on terror highlight the ways the political, economic and ideological pressures of foreign and domestic policy actually have an impact on the organization of welfare and constrain the advocacy dimensions of social work practice, whether such advocacy takes the form of supporting clients accused of breaches of anti-terrorism legislation, or trying to support clients suffering the ravages of war or foreign occupation as part of the 'war on terror'. It is worth noting Lind's (2007) point that Iraq has witnessed the withdrawal of a host of internationally funded NGOs due to the current instability of the country and accusations of human rights violations under Saddam Hussein. However, such accusations of civil rights violations have not prevented a host of other countries with similar problems gaining US funding for NGOs. Such countries include: Israel, Turkey, Egypt, Russia, Jordan, Pakistan, Bolivia, Peru, Democratic Republic of Congo, Ethiopia, Mexico, Columbia and Turkey (Landman, 2006, p. 134). Consequently, in the absence of international welfare funding, these external pressures will make it extremely hard for Iraqi social workers to develop any practical welfare and advocacy services on a parity with many of these nations.

The benefits of sociology in the form of cosmopolitanism in informing interprofessional and international social work practice are evident when examining the sociological processes it identifies for understanding the nature of global changes. This type of sociology also helps avoid the pitfalls of ethnocentric Western analysis. Beck (2000; 2006) makes the case for the development of a new type of social science to analyse the profound social transformations that could be described as 'cosmopolitanism'. He also criticizes the nation-state model for being too limited in analysing these transformations. This is because of the way it attributes all these changes to globalization. The danger of this (according to Beck) is that 'globalization' suggests that this is something external to human control. This in turn disguises what is going on in terms of Western superpower oppression of 'Third World' nations. He uses this contention to criticize the presumptions made within traditional Western sociology about the link between the nation state, democracy and welfare systems.

In his collaboration with Sznaider (Beck and Sznaider, 2006) he argues for the re-conceptualization of social science in the twenty-first century by adopting a cosmopolitan paradigm. Beck and Sznaider's definition of a cosmopolitan social science is a multidisciplinary definition incorporating sociology, law, anthropology, geography and politics. They reflect on the weaknesses of adopting a nation-state model of society, which Beck terms 'methodological nationalism'. This model is not helpful for understanding the cosmopolitan transformations and hence this is contemporary sociology's weakness. It fails to deconstruct the right-wing discourses on cosmopolitanism presented by the advocates of Western neo-liberalism and global capitalism.

In contrast, Delanty's (2006) form of cosmopolitan sociology shifts the focus of analysis from international relations to internal processes within a particular society. Thus, he regards the causes of cosmopolitanism as internal (i.e., caused by society's self-reflection on its racism and ethnocentrism, and its internal developmental processes) as opposed to external (caused by globalization). He talks about the development of a *cosmopolitan imagination*, which refers to the ways a society's culture understands and conceptualizes the wider world and how it is constituted. Thus, as a form of sociology, for Delanty cosmopolitanism has a specific task. This task is to make sense of the current global, social transformations that are occurring.

These sociological perspectives on the development of cosmopolitanism are crucial to promote critical reflexivity on the global context. Increasingly, social work is developing an international dimension in various forms via INGOs and through awareness of the culture clashes between Western and Eastern social work traditions (Silavwe, 1995; Dominelli, 2005; Kaseke, 2005) as nations have greater contact with one another. This contact is increasing as professional social workers come together from both areas of the globe to address the common humanitarian problems of global conflict, genocide, refugee crises, and manufactured and natural disasters. In addition, the impact of global capitalism is prompting increasing awareness of the international dimensions of social work. Hence, sociology in the form of cosmopolitanism is crucial in understanding the global context of practice.

For this reason, McRobbie's (2006) sociological analysis is important to the critical reflexive dimension of social work practice. The negative aspects of cosmopolitanism have resulted in an extension of the global resurgence of US sovereign state power. This (McRobbie argues) is manifest in military violence, which is reinforced by US neo-liberal hegemony and which stifles any real critical appraisal of US foreign policy in both the US and Europe. Consequently, she criticizes those sociologists like Beck who do not adequately address these negative aspects of the twenty-first-century developments known as cosmopolitanism and thus fail to incorporate them into the development of any critical sociology.

A contrasting interpretation is presented by Vogel (2006), who argues that those who emphasize the negative dimensions of American imperialism within cosmopolitanism ignore the positive dimensions. These are what she describes as the 'role of American philanthropy in the contemporary transformations of world society' (Vogel, 2006, p. 635). She asserts that those who claim that US foreign policy is simply the embodiment of US economic and military neo-liberal self-interest are guilty of economic reductionism. This is because they fail to acknowledge the increasing role of US philanthropy around the globe. This, she believes, is having a positive impact on the extension of democracy. This view is partly supported by Herscovitch's (2001) analysis of NGOs around the world, in which she cites the ways they offer a range of humanitarian aid and services. These vary from community programmes, after-school activities, literacy classes, health promotion on HIV/AIDS, work with street children and children who are at risk of sexual exploitation and abuse, work on famine relief, earthquake and other natural disasters, as well as supporting refugees (Herscovitch, 2001, p. 174). Many of these NGOs, as well as being funded by the UN and other international charities, receive large donations from US charities and philanthropic organizations. These donations totalled over 6.2 billion US dollars in 2004 (Vogel 2006, p. 644).

Social work academics like Roff (2004) argue that NGOs are a vital mechanism in the promotion of humanitarian cooperation and aid against the global problems of poverty, war and social injustice. She maintains they can still promote a sense of empowerment amongst marginalized groups of people around the globe provided that social workers and other professionals involved in such projects adopt a 'strengths perspective' (Roff, 2004, p. 203). By this term she refers to the potential of local communities to harness their strengths, resources and networks in their environments and work on a communal level to develop their own solutions. This generates community- led (with NGO support) programmes for social change.

However, the role of many international NGOs is criticized for being dominated by Western cultural values and for promoting a Western neo-liberal economic agenda. Dominelli (2005) is highly critical of this form of community development as it tends to take the form of Western-funded and/or Western-led NGOs. These, she argues, result in the promotion of Western solutions, which are inappropriate to the political, regional or cultural context of many non-Western countries, or worse, tend to promote the agenda of Western capitalism and thus result in exploitive relationships. These exploitive relationships take various forms. There are Western consultants imported at exorbitant rates to help with community development solutions that are often irrelevant to local community needs. Alternatively they take the form of opportunist investment in non-Western economies, which is of short duration and leaves the local economies short of funds and employment in the long term. Another form of this exploitation is what Dominelli terms 'opportunistic globalization'. This is where large transnational corporations or intergovernmental organizations like the World Bank, or the IMF, invest in the economies of countries with the promise of a cheap labour supply and tax breaks. Then, in return for this investment, these organizations insist on neo-liberal policies being pursued, in the form of structural adjustment programmes (SAPs) which reduce state expenditure on welfare and increase poverty and need.

Wool (2007) illustrates some of these negative dimensions of cosmopolitanism within welfare by exploring US economic policy in Iraq. She shows how, following the war in 2003, the impact of neo-liberal economic policy goes beyond the organization of welfare to affect people's civil and human rights. The pursuit by US and UK business interests of neo-liberal economic policies has tended to divorce Iraq's economic problems from the impact of the war and to ignore the fact that Iraq's infrastructure was destroyed. As a result, there exists virtually no state-funded health, welfare or social service provision. Wool argues that this neo-liberal discourse masks the economic problems created by the war as well as the ensuing poverty and deprivation, which she believes have been caused by the invasion and occupation of Iraq. For instance, the *US Defense Quarterly Report on Iraq* notes that unemployment is running at 28 per cent, but fails to link this rate to the impact of the war or the ongoing insurgency. In addition, these neo-liberal discourses fail to recognize that Iraq's economic problems can only be alleviated once the country's socio-economic and political infrastructure has been rebuilt to enable Iraq to compete on an equal footing in the international market.

Similarly, Harding (2007) is critical not only of US military and economic policy in Iraq but also of the lack of a critical voice within international social work on the subject. He laments the fact that there appears little attention to the need to develop welfare provision even in the form of NGOs to help Iraqi citizens. He argues that the continued military occupation by the US, and the neo-liberal economic investment by US multinational corporations, are jeopardizing any chance of stability and economic development. Yet, in the wake of this, he argues there is a lack of international social work debate and discussion about developing social work services in Iraq by rebuilding the country's economic infrastructure.

In contrast, Lind's (2007) project in Iraq suggests that this is not the case. Many Iraqi social workers are attempting to provide both practical and therapeutic services to street children, orphans and older people, to people with drug abuse problems and to those who are traumatized by the ongoing violence and insurgency. These social workers face further barriers as the scarcity of resources is exacerbated by the withdrawal of support from international organizations due to the political instability in Iraq. Lind argues that the project he was involved in with 140 social workers and 3 Iraqi NGOs to develop capacity-building training for these social workers (funded by the Iraqi Ministry of Social Affairs and UNICEF) was successful using Freire's (1972) model of consciousness raising. This facilitated the development of localized community welfare projects. However, social workers were unable to take these developments further, owing to the withdrawal of international funding.

Whether the impact of cosmopolitanism is positive or negative, the significance of cosmopolitan sociology for social work practice becomes clear when examining the international context of social work. The dimensions of cosmopolitanism as presented by Delanty (2006) and Beck (2000; 2006) are relevant to a critical understanding of the contemporary international social work terrain for several reasons. First, cosmopolitanism represents a form of interdisciplinary social science, which like social work, adopts perspectives from a range of disciplines such as sociology, politics, law, anthropology and geography. This is in order to account for the social transformations known as 'cosmopolitanism'. Secondly, it is a dialectical approach, which examines these social transformations but at the same time (unlike globalization theory) acknowledges and reflects critically upon the persistence of old socio-economic and political structures. Thirdly, cosmopolitan sociology identifies the key dynamics of this social transformation, which are: global migration and diaspora, changes to unemployment and labour patterns, transnational job sharing, and the monopoly by transnational corporations. It also focuses upon national identity questions and the global ecological crisis. Fourthly, it provides a conceptual framework to identify the extent to which nation states reflect upon their own ethnocentrisms and commitment to world openness. This aspect prompts critical reflection on a nation state's foreign and domestic policies and how they affect international social work.

## Summary of the Main Points

- Interdisciplinary research collaboration between the natural and social sciences has stimulated the move towards collaborative research in health and social work fields. This has led to further developments in interprofessional practice.

- Sociological approaches have also contributed to the development of the bio-psychosocial model in social work, which seeks to generate holistic approaches.

- Bailey (2002) and Payne (2002) identify some ways to generate inter-professional practice. These include adoption of the bio-psychosocial model, effective networking and development of a shared concept of interprofessional practice, greater interprofessional working, and discussing professional conflict in an open and honest manner.

- Cosmopolitan sociology can enhance critical reflexive practice by providing a framework to:

  (a) Assess a nation's commitment to challenging ethnocentrism and promoting world openness.
  (b) Understand the global forms of interdependence that exist and their implications for social work practice.
  (c) Deconstruct the Western discourses on cosmopolitanism which mask the inequalities generated by neo-liberal global capitalism and welfare management programmes.

# Conclusion

In focusing upon interprofessional practice and international social work, this final chapter draws the themes and strands of the book together. The themes were reflexivity, praxis and critical reflexive practice and how they were interconnected. By illustrating how they were interconnected the book achieved its aim of demonstrating the importance of sociology to social work. For example, the chapter highlighted Healy's (2001) observation that international social work is characterized by the increasing awareness of global interdependence. Once again, sociology's practice relevance in the development of critical practice skills was illustrated. This was achieved by using cosmopolitan sociology to deconstruct the social transformations underpinning that global interdependence. This in turn required the consolidation of the sociological theories and concepts outlined in Chapters 1–7. This was in order to fully evaluate the practice implications of the contemporary international social work terrain. For instance, Chapter 1 focused upon the relationship between theory and critical practice by exploring the concepts of reflexivity and praxis. Chapter 2 considered the practice importance of these concepts by locating them within the contexts of society, class and the family. In Chapter 3, this analysis was extended to incorporate grand sociological theory by exploring global welfare states, while in Chapter 4 the emphasis shifted by evaluating the contradictory nature of the legal context of social work. The theories of social construc-tivism and discourse were revisited in Chapter 5 when examining work with service users. The work with service users was then located within a specific context in Chapter 6, by exploring issues of poverty, social exclusion and citizenship. Then in Chapter 7 the focus once again shifted to illustrate how sociological research methods inform the social work assessment process.

The scope of sociological material in the book has been broad. It has covered a range of sociological theory (grand, middle-range and micro), dialectics, ideology, discourse and concepts of power. It has examined the debate over structure-versus-agency, explored issues of class and status, considered competing perspectives on the law, welfare states, globalization, cosmopolitanism, the international refugee crisis and the impact of international social work. It has compared social work on both national and international levels and explored the legal implications of practice.

However, despite the 'kaleidoscope' of sociological material presented, two features have helped retain the structure and continuity of the book, making it accessible and easy to read: first, through the ways it highlighted the interconnections between reflexivity, praxis and critical reflexive practice; secondly and perhaps most importantly, through its recognition that all the material under review has been characterized by the same recurring issues. These have been the issues of power and powerlessness and how they have affected the advocacy role of social work and acted as a barrier to the development of anti-oppressive practice (AOP). In combining all these elements in this way, the book has provided both empirical evidence and substantive argument for the importance of sociology to social work. Above all, it has reflected on the dynamic and contested nature of social work practice around the globe and considered how those contestations affect both clients/service users and social workers.

## Further Reading

Delanty, G. (2006) 'The Cosmopolitan Imagination: Critical Cosmopolitanism and Social Theory', *British Journal of Sociology*, vol. 57(1), pp. 24–45.
This simplifies the complex debates about cosmopolitanism and provides practical examples of how (using cosmopolitan sociology) social workers can challenge racism and ethnocentricism.

Dominelli, L. (2005) 'Community Development across Borders: Avoiding Dangerous Practices in a Globalizing World', *International Social Work*, vol. 48(3), pp. 702–13.
This article prompts critical reflection on the impact of global neo-liberal economic policies on welfare.

Vogel, A. (2006) 'Who's Making Global Civil Society: Philanthropy and US Empire in World Society', *British Journal of Sociology*, vol. 57(4), pp. 636–65.
This article provides an alternative perspective on the role of philanthropy in INGOs and suggests ways it can lead to the extension of democracy.

# References

Abbot, A. (1988) *The System of Professions: An Essay on the Division of Expert Labor* (Chicago: University of Chicago).

Abbott, P. and Wallace, C. (1997) *An Introduction to Social Policy: Feminist Perspectives* (London: Routledge).

Adams, R. (2002a) 'Social Work Processes', in R. Adams, L. Dominelli and M. Payne (eds), *Social Work: Themes, Issues and Critical Debates*, 2nd edn (Basingstoke: Palgrave Macmillan).

Adams, R. (2002b) 'Developing Critical Practice in Social Work', in R. Adams, L. Dominelli and M. Payne (eds), *Critical Practice in Social Work* (Basingstoke: Palgrave Macmillan).

Aghabakhshi, H. and Gregor, C. (2007) 'Learning the Lessons of Bam: the Role of Social Capital', *International Social Work* **50**(3): 347–56.

Alavi, H. (1972) 'The State Structure in Post-colonial Pakistan and Bangladesh', *New Left Review* **74**: 59–81.

Algunick, P., Burchardt, T. and Evans, M. (2002) 'Response and Prevention in the British Welfare State', in J. Hills, J. Le Grand and D. Piachaud (eds), *Understanding Social Exclusion* (Oxford: Oxford University Press).

Aliyev, F. B. (2007) 'Problems of Interaction between the State and Economy under the Post-communist Transition: The Perspective of Islamic Political Economy', *Humanomics* **23**: 73–82.

Allen, N. (2003) *Making Sense of the New Adoption Law: A Guide for Social and Welfare Services* (Lyme Regis: Russell House).

Amir, S. (1974) *Accumulation on a World Scale* (New York: Monthly Review Press).

Anjum, M. I. (2006) 'Globalization at the Crossroads – Warfare, Revolution, and Universalization: The Islamic Panacea, Stratagem and Policy Arrangements', *Humanomics* **22**: 162–77.

Anthias, F. and Yuval-Davies, N. (1992) *Race, Nation, Gender, Colour and the Anti-Racist Struggle* (London: Routledge).

Anthias, F. (2001) 'The Material and the Symbolic in Theorizing Social Stratification: Issues of Gender, Ethnicity and Class', *British Journal of Sociology* **52**(3): 367–90.

Archard, D. (1993) *Children's Rights in Childhood* (London: Routledge).

Argawal, S., Attah, M., Apt, N., Grieco, M., Kwakye, E. A. and Turner, J. (1997) 'Bearing the Weight: the Kayayoo, Ghana's Working Girl Child', *International Social Work Journal* **40**: 245–63.

Atkinson, W. (2007) 'Beck, Individualization and the Death of Class: a Critique', *British Journal of Sociology* **58**(3): 349–66.

Baars, J., Dannefer, D., Phillipson, C. and Walker, A. (eds) (2006) *Ageing, Globalization and Inequality: The New Critical Gerontology* (New York: Baywood, Amityville).

Bahramitash, R. (2007) 'Iranian Women during the Reform Era (1994–2004): a Focus on Employment', *Journal of Middle East Women's Studies* **3**(2): 86–109.

Bailey, D. (2002) 'Mental Health', in R. Adams, L. Dominelli and M. Payne (eds), *Critical Practice in Social Work* (Basingstoke: Palgrave Macmillan).

Bancroft, A. (2001) 'Closed Spaces, Restricted Places: Marginalization of Roma in Europe', *Space and Polity* **5**(2): 145–57.

Banerjee, M. and Gillespie, D. (1994) 'Linking Disaster Preparedness and Organizational Response Effectiveness', *Journal of Community Practice* **1**(3): 129–42.

Banks, S. (2002) 'Professional Values and Accountabilities', in R. Adams, L. Dominelli and M. Payne (eds), *Critical Reflective Practice in Social Work* (Basingstoke: Palgrave Macmillan).

Banton, M. (1996) 'International Action against Racial Discrimination', *International Sociology* **7**(1): 69–84.

Barnardo's (2000) *What Works? Making Connections: Linking Research to Practice* (London: Barnardo's).

Batt, C. (1997) *Liberation and Purity: Race, New Religious Movements and the Ethics of Postmodernity* (London: University College London Press).

Beck, U. (1992) *The Risk Society: Towards a New Modernity* (London: Sage).

Beck, U. (1996) *The Re-invention of Politics: Re-Thinking Modernity in the Global Social Order* (Oxford: Polity).

Beck, U. (2000) *The Risk Society and Beyond: Critical Issues for Social Theory* (London: Sage).

Beck, U. (2006) *The Cosmopolitan Vision* (Cambridge: Polity Press).

Beck, U. (2007) 'Individualization and the Death of Class: a Critique', *British Journal of Sociology* **58**(3): 349–63.

Beck, U. and Sznaider, N. (2006) 'Unpacking Cosmopolitanism for the Social Sciences: a Research Agenda', *British Journal of Sociology* **57**(1): 3–23.

Becker, H. (1971) *Sociological Work: Method and Substance* (London: Allen Lane).

Bello, W. (2001) *The Future in the Balance: Essays on Globalization and Resistance* (Oakland, CA: Food First Books).

Bello, W. (2002) *Deglobalization: Ideas for a New World Economy* (London: Zed Books).

Ben-Ari, A. T. (2001) 'Homosexuality and Heterosexism: Views from Academics in the Helping Professions', *British Journal of Social Work* **31**: 119–31.

Berger, M. (2001) 'Public Policy and Islamic Law: The Modern DHIMMI in Contemporary Egyptian Family Law', *Islamic Law and Society* **8**(1): 88–120.

Berger, P. and Luckman, T. (1967) *The Social Construction of Reality: A Treatise in the Sociology of Knowledge* (New York: Anchor).

Berman, G. (2006) 'Social Services and Indigenous Populations in Remote Areas: Alaskan Natives and Negev Bedouins', *International Social Work Journal* **49**(1): 97–106.

Berridge, D. and Brodie, I. (1993) 'Residential Care in England and Wales: The Inquiries and After', in M. Hill and J. Aldgate (eds), *Child Welfare: Developments in Law, Policy, Practice and Research* (London: Jessica Kingsley).

Bessis, C. (1995) 'From Social Exclusion to Social Cohesion: a Policy Agenda'. MOST Policy paper no. 2. http://www.unesco.org/most/bessing.htm (accessed 28 January 2008).

Bhopal, K. (2006) 'Issues of Rurality and Good Practice: Gypsy Traveller Pupils in Schools', in S. Neal and J. Ageyman (eds), *The New Countryside? Ethnicity, Nation and Exclusion in Contemporary Britain* (Bristol: Policy Press).

Biggs, S. (1999) *The Mature Imagination* (Buckingham: Open University Press).

Billig, M. (1995) *Banal Nationalism* (London: Sage).

Birke, L. (1992) 'In Pursuit of Difference: Scientific Studies of Women and Men', in G. Kirkup and L. Smith-Keller, *Inventing Women: Science, Technology and Gender* (Cambridge: Polity in association with The Open University).

Birke, L. (1996) 'Transforming Biology', in H. Crowley and S. Himmelweit (eds), *Knowing Women: Feminism and Knowledge* (Cambridge: Polity Press and Open University Press).

Biswas, P., Kabir, N. Z., Nilsson, J. and Zadman, S. (2006) 'Dynamics of Health Care Seeking Behaviour of Elderly People in Rural Bangladesh', *International Journal of Ageing and Later Life*, 1(1): pp. 69–89.

Blackburn, R. M., Browne, J., Brooks, B. and Jarman, J. (2002) 'Explaining Gender Segregation', *British Journal of Sociology* 53(4): 513–36.

Blackie, A. (1999) *Ageing and Popular Culture* (Cambridge: Cambridge University Press).

Bormann, E. G. (1972) 'Fantasy and Rhetorical Vision: the Rhetorical Criticism of Social Reality', *Quarterly Journal of Speech* 58: 396–407.

Bos, A. M. and Bos, A. J. (2007) 'The Socio-economic Determinants of Older People's Health in Brazil: the Importance of Marital Status and Income', *Ageing and Society* 23(3): 385–406.

Bosanquet, H. (1902) *The Strength of the People: A Study of Social Economics* (London: Macmillan).

Boud, D. and Knight, S. (1996) 'Course Design for Reflective Practice', in N. Gould and I. Taylor (eds), *Reflective Learning for Social Work* (Aldershot: Arena).

Bourdieu, P. (1993) *The Field of Critical Production* (Cambridge: Polity Press).

Bourdieu, P. (1996) 'Towards a Reflexive Sociology', in S. Turner (ed.), *Social Theory and Sociology: The Classics and Beyond* (Oxford: Blackwell).

Brown, A. (1992) *Groupwork*, 3rd edn (Aldershot: Ashgate).

Brown, M. E. (1997) 'Causes and Implications of Ethnic Conflict', in M. Guiberneau and J. Rex (eds), *Ethnicity: A Reader* (Cambridge: Polity Press).

Bryan, B., Dadzi, S. and Scafe, S. (1985) *The Heart of Race: Black Women's Lives in Britain* (London: Virago).

Bryman, A. (2004) *Social Research*, 2nd edn (Oxford: Oxford University Press).

Burkhardt, T., Le Grand, J. and Piachaud, D. (2002) 'Introduction', in J. Hills, J. Le Grand and D. Piachaud (eds), *Understanding Social Exclusion* (Oxford: Oxford University Press).

Bury, M. (1996) 'Disability and the Myth of the Independent Researcher: a Reply', *Disability & Society* 10(1): 111–15.

Byrne, D. (2002) *Social Exclusion* (Buckingham: Open University Press).

Bytheway, B. (1995) *Ageism* (Buckingham: Open University Press).

Calder, M. C. (2003) 'The Assessment Framework: a Critique and Reformulation', in M. C. Calder and S. Hackett, *Assessment in Child Care: Using and Developing Frameworks for Practice* (Lyme Regis: Russell House Publishing).

Calder, M. (ed.) (2004) *Child Sexual Abuse and the Internet: Tackling a New Frontier* (Lyme Regis: Russell House Publishing).

Callinicos, A. (2003) *New Mandarins of American Power: The Bush Administration's Plans for the World* (Cambridge: Polity Press).

Cambridge, P. (1997) 'How Far to be Gay? The Politics of HIV in Learning Disability', *Disability & Society* **12**(3): 427–53.

Caney. D. (1983) 'Competence – Can it be Assessed?', *Physiotherapy* **69**(3): 302–4.

Carroll, L. (2001) 'The Pakistan Federal Shariat Court: Section 4 of the Muslim Family Laws Ordinance and the Orphaned Grandchild', *Islamic Law and Society* **9**(1): 71–82.

Cashmore, E. (1984) *No Future: Youth and Society* (London: Heinemann).

Castles, S. and Miller, M. (2003) *The Age of Migration: International Population Movements in the Modern World*, 3rd edn (Basingstoke: Palgrave Macmillan).

Cebulla, A., Butt, S. and Lyon, N. (2007) 'Working Beyond the State Pension Age in the United Kingdom: the Role of Working Time Flexibility and the Effects on Home', *Ageing and Society* **27**: 849–67.

Cemlyn, S. and Briskman, L. (2003) 'Asylum, Children's Rights and Social Work', *Child and Family Social Work* **8**: 163–78.

*Chambers Combined English Dictionary Thesaurus* (1997) (Edinburgh: Chambers–Harrap).

Cheetham, J., Fuller, R., McIvor, G. and Petch, A (1992) *Evaluating Social Work Effectiveness* (Buckingham: Open University Press).

Chelser P. (1972) *Women and Madness* (New York: Doubleday).

Chou, Y. C (2003) 'Social Workers' Involvement in Taiwan's 1999 Earthquake Disaster Aid: Implications for Social Work Education', *Social Work and Society* **1**(1). Available on line at: www.socwork.net/2003/1/articles/395/SW_earthquaketaiwan_Chou 2003_.pdf (accessed 27 September 2007).

Choudhury, A. M. (1999) 'Resource Allocation, Investment Decision and Economic Welfare: Capitalism, Socialism and Islam', *Managerial Finance* **25**(5): 34–51.

Clapham, D., Means, R. and Munro, M. (1993) 'Housing, the Life Course and Older People', in S. Arber and M. Evandrou (eds), *Ageing, Independence and the Life Course* (London: Jessica Kingsley).

Clarke, C. (2000) *Social Work Ethics: Politics, Principles and Practice* (Basingstoke: Macmillan).

Clarke, J. (1996) 'After Social Work?', in N. Parton (ed.), *Social Theory, Social Change and Social Work* (London: Routledge).

Clarke, J. and Newman, J. (1997) *The Managerial State* (London: Sage).

Clarke, V. and Finlay, S. J. (2004) 'For Better or Worse? Lesbian and Gay Marriage', *Feminism and Psychology* **14**(1): 17–23.

Clifford, D. (1994) 'Critical Life Histories: Key Anti-oppressive Research Methods and Processes', in B. Humphries and C. Truman (eds), *Rethinking Social Research: Anti-Discriminatory Approaches in Research Methodology* (Aldershot: Avebury).

Cohen, R. (1987) *The New Helots: Migrants in the International Division of Labour* (Aldershot: Ashgate).

Cohen, R. and Kennedy, P. (2000) *Global Sociology*, 1st edn (Basingstoke: Macmillan).

Cohen, R. and Kennedy, P. (2007) *Global Sociology*, 2nd edn (Basingstoke: Palgrave Macmillan).

Comfort, R. L. (2001) 'The Education of Black and Ethnic Minority Children in Care', in S. Jackson (ed.), *'Nobody Ever Told Us that School Mattered': Raising the Educational Attainment of Children in Care* (London: BAAF).

Commission for Racial Equality (2006) *Safe Communities Initiative: Defeating Organised Racial Hatred – An Information Pack*. http://www.gos.gos.gov.uk/497666/docs/ 262145/525396 (accessed 29 September 2007).

Comstock, G. (1991) *Violence against Lesbians and Gay Men* (New York: Columbia University Press).

Connell, R. W. (1997) 'Why is Classical Theory Classical?', *American Journal of Sociology* **102** (6): 1511–57.

Cooper, D. (1999) 'More Law and More Rights: Will Children Benefit?', *Child and Family Social Work* **3**: 77–86.

Cooper, D. (2004) *Challenging Diversity: Rethinking Equality and the Value of Difference* (Cambridge: Cambridge University Press).

Corrigan, P. and Leonard, P. (1978) *Social Work Practice under Capitalism* (London: Macmillan).

Coulshed, V. (1991) *Social Work Practice* (Basingstoke: Macmillan).

Cree, V. (2002) 'The Changing Nature of Social Work', in R. Adams, L. Dominelli and M. Payne (eds), *Social Work: Themes, Issues and Critical Debates* (Basingstoke: Palgrave Macmillan).

Crowley, H. and Himmelweit, S. (eds) (1996) *Knowing Women: Feminism and Knowledge* (Cambridge: Polity Press and The Open University).

Dalley, G. (1988) *Ideologies of Caring* (London: Macmillan).

Dalrymple, J. and Burke, B. (1995) *Anti-Discriminatory Practice: Social Care and the Law* (Buckingham: Open University Press).

Danchev, A. (2006) 'Accomplicity: Britain, Torture and Terror', *British Journal of Politics and International Relations* **8**: 587–601.

Darwin, C. (1887) *The Life and Letters of Charles Darwin* (London; John Murray).

David, P. (2002) 'Implementing the Rights of the Child: Six Reasons why the Human Rights of Children Remain a Constant Challenge', *International Review of Education* **48**(3–4): 259–63.

Davies, C. (2000) 'Care and Transformation of Professionalism', in C. Davies, L. Finlay and A. Bullman (eds), *Changing Practice in Health and Social Care* (London: Sage).

Davies, M. (1985) *The Essential Social Worker: A Guide to Positive Practice*, 2nd edn (Aldershot: Gower).

D'Cruz, H., Gillingham, P. and Melenedes, S. (2007) 'Reflexivity: its Meanings and Relevance for Social Work: a Critical Review of the Literature', *British Journal of Social Work* **27**(1): 73–90.

De Montigny, G. (2007) 'Ethnomethodology for Social Work', *Qualitative Social Work* **6**: 95–119.

Delanty, G. (2000) *Social Science: Beyond Constructivism and Realism* (Buckingham: Open University Press).

Delanty, G. (2006) 'The Cosmopolitan Imagination: Critical Cosmopolitanism and Social Theory', *British Journal of Sociology* **57**(1): 24–45.

Department for Education and Skills (2003) *Every Child Matters: Change for Children in Social Care* (London: The Stationery Office).

Dobash, R. and Dobash, R. (1992) *Violence against Wives* (London: Open Books).

Department of Health (1995) *Child Protection: Messages from Research* (London: HMSO).

Department of Health (2000) *The Framework for the Assessment of Children in Need and Their Families* (London: HMSO).

Department of Health Social Services Inspectorate (2000) *Ninth Annual Report of the Chief Inspector of Social Services 1999–2000* (London: HMSO).

Dominelli, L. (1997) *Sociology for Social Workers* (London: Macmillan).

Dominelli, L. (2002) 'Values in Social Work: Contested Ethics with Enduring Qualities', in R. Adams, L. Dominelli, and M. Payne (eds), *Critical Practice in Social Work* (Basingstoke: Palgrave Macmillan).

Dominelli, L. (2005) 'Community Development across Borders: Avoiding Dangerous Practices in a Globalizing World', *International Journal of Social Work* **48**(6): 702–13.

Dominelli, L. and Cowburn, M. (2001) 'Masking Hegemonic Masculinity: Reconstructing the Paedophile as the Dangerous Stranger', *British Journal of Social Work* **31**(3): 399–416.

Douglas, M. (1992) *Risk and Blame Essays in Cultural Theory* (London: Routledge).

Doyal, L. (1996) *What Makes Women Sick? Gender and the Political Economy of Health* (Basingstoke: Macmillan).

Doyal, L. and Pennell, I. (1979) *The Political Economy of Health* (London: Pluto).

DuBose Brunner, D. (1997) 'Challenging Representations of Sexuality through Story and Performance', in J. T. Sears and W. I. Williams (eds), *Overcoming Homophobia: Strategies that Work* (New York: Columbia).

Dufka, C. (1988) 'The Mexico City Earthquake Disaster and Social Casework', *Journal of Contemporary Social Work* **69**(3): 162–70.

Dupret, B. (2001) 'Sexual Morality at the Egyptian Bar: Female Circumcision, Sex Change Operations, and Motives for Suing', *Islamic Law and Society* **9**(1): 42–69.

EBDR (2000) 'Annual Report: Annual Review and Financial Report', http://www.ebdr.com/pubs/general.ar00.pdf (accessed 10 October 2007).

Edwards, R. and Aldred, P. (1999) 'Children and Young People's Views of School Research: the Case of Home-School Relations', *Childhood* **6**(2): 262–81.

Eriksen, T. H. (2002) *Ethnicity and Nationalism: Anthropological Perspectives*, 2nd edn (London: Pluto Books).

Esping-Anderson, G. (1990) *The Three Worlds of Welfare Capitalism* (Cambridge: Polity).

Esping-Anderson, G. (1996) *Welfare States in Transition* (London: UNRISD/Sage).

Evans, S. (2005) 'Beyond Gender, Class, Poverty and Domestic Violence', *Australian Social Work* **58**(1): 36–43.

Fadayomi, T. O. (1979) 'The Demand for Pre-School Care: an Aspect of the Problems of the Nigerian Working Mother', *International Social Work* **22**(1): 45–57.

Fagan, T. and Lee, P. (1999) 'New Social Movements and Social Policy: a Case Study of the Disability Movement', in M. Lavalette and A. Pratt (eds), *Social Policy: A Conceptual and Theoretical Introduction*, 2nd edn (London: Sage).

Faul, A., McMurty, S. L. and Hudson, W. W. (2001) 'Can Empirical Practice Techniques Improve Social Work Outcomes?', *Research on Social Work Practice* **11**(3): 277–99.

Ferguson, I. and Lavalette, M. (2006) 'Globalization and Global Justice: Towards a Social Work of Resistance', *International Social Work Journal* **49**(3): 209–318.

Ferguson, I. and Lavalette, M. (2007) 'Democratic Language and Neo-liberal Practice: The Problem with Civil Society', *International Social Work Journal* **50**(4): 447–59.

Finch, J. (1988) 'Whose Responsibility? Women and the Future of Family Care', in I. Allen, M. Wicks, J. Finch and D. Leat (eds), *Informal Care Tomorrow* (London: Social Policy Institute).

Fook, J. (2001) 'Identifying the Expert Social Worker: Qualitative Practitioner Research', in I. Shaw and N. Gould (eds), *Qualitative Research in Social Work* (London: Sage).

Foucault, M. (1961) *Folie De Deraison: Histoire De la Folie a L'age Classique* (Paris: Plon).

Foucault, M. (1972) *The Archaeology of Knowledge* (London; Tavistock).

Foucault, M. (1973) *Birth of the Clinic* (London: Routledge).

Foucault, M. (1976) *The History of Sexuality: An Introduction* (Harmondsworth: Penguin).

Foucault, M. (1980) *The History of Sexuality*, vol. 1 (London: Penguin).

Foucault, M. (1987) *Mental Illness and Psychology* (Berkley, CA: University of California).

Foucault, M. (1988) 'Technologies of the Self', in L. H. Martin et al. (eds), *Technologies of the Self* (London: Tavistock).

Fowler, F. G. and Fowler, H. W. (eds) (1984) *The Pocket Oxford English Dictionary*, 7th edn (Oxford: Clarendon Press).

Fox-Harding. L. (1996) *Family, State and Social Policy* (Basingstoke: Macmillan).

Freire, P. (1972) *The Pedagogy of the Oppressed* (Harmondsworth: Penguin).

Freire, P. (1998) *The Pedagogy of the Heart* (New York: Continuum).

Freud, S. (1933) *New Introductory Lectures on Psychoanalysis: Standard Edition of the Complete Works of Sigmund Freud*, vol. 22 (London: Allen and Unwin).

Friend, A. and Metcalf, A. (1981) *Slump City: The Politics of Mass Unemployment* (London: Pluto).

Garfinkel, H. (1967) *Studies in Ethnomethodology* (Englewood Cliffs, NJ: Prentice Hall).

Garrett, P. M. (2006) *Social Work and Irish People in Britain* (Bristol: Policy Press).

Gerhard, U. (2004) 'Illegitimate Daughters: the Relationship between Feminism and Sociology', in B. Marshall and A. Witz (eds), *Engendering the Social: Feminist Encounters with Sociological Theory* (Maidenhead: Open University).

Ghai, Y. (1994) 'Human Rights and Governance: the Asia Debate', *Australian Year Book of International Law* **15**: 1–34.

Gibbons, M. C., Limoges, C., Nowotny, H., Schwartzman, S., Scott, P. and Trow, M. (eds) (1994) *The Production of New Knowledge: The Dynamics of Science and Reason in Contemporary Society* (London: Sage).

Giddens, A. (1992) *The Transformations of Intimacy: Sexuality, Love and Eroticism in Modern Societies* (Cambridge: Polity Press).

Giddens, A. (1996) *In Defence of Sociology* (Cambridge: Polity Press).

Giddens, A. (2000) *The Third Way and its Critics* (Cambridge: Polity Press).

Giddens, A. (2001) *Sociology*, 4th edn (Cambridge: Polity Press).

Gilbert, A. and Gugler, J. (1992) *Cities, Poverty and Development: Urbanization in the Third World* (Oxford: Oxford University Press).

Gilligan, C. (1982) *In a Different Voice: Psychological Theory and Women's Development* (Cambridge MA: Harvard University Press).

Gilroy, P. (1987) *There Ain't No Black in the Union Jack* (London: Hutchinson).

Goding, L. and Edwards, K. (2003) 'Evidence-Based Social Research', *Nursing Research* **9**(4): 45–57.

Goffman, E. (1967) *International Ritual: Essays in Face-to-Face Behavior* (Chicago: Aldine).

Goffman E. (1968) *Asylums* (Harmondsworth: Penguin).

Gough, I. and Woods, G. (eds) (2004) *Insecurity and Welfare Regimes in Asia, Africa and Latin America: Social Policy in Development Contexts* (Cambridge: Cambridge University Press).

Gould, N. and Taylor, I. (1996) (eds) *Reflective Learning for Social Work* (Aldershot: Arena).

Gove, W. (1982) 'The Current Status of Labelling Theory in Mental Health', *American Journal of Sociology* **78**: 812–35.

Gramsci, A. (1988[1936]) *Gramsci's Prison Letters [Lettere dal Carcere]* (London: Zwain in association with The Edinburgh Review, 1988).

Grande, E. (2006) 'Cosmopolitan Political Science', *British Journal of Sociology* **57**(1): 87–111.

Green, L. (2005) 'Theorizing Sexuality, Sexual Abuse and Residential Children's Homes: Adding Gender to the Equation', *British Journal of Social Work* **35**: 453–81.

Grenier, A. (2007) 'Constructions of Frailty in the English Language, Care Practice and Lived Experience', *Ageing and Society* **27**: 425–55.

Grimley-Evans, J. (2007) 'Eric Matthews and Elizabeth Russell', *Rationalizing Medical Care on the Basis Old Age: The Moral Dimensions, Ageing and Society* **27**(2): 308–9.

Habermas, J. (1993) *Justifications and Applications: Remarks on Discourse Ethics* (Cambridge, MA: MIT Press).

Habermas, J. (1996) *Between Facts and Norms: Contributions to a Discourse Theory of Law and Democracy* (Cambridge: Polity Press).

Hall, S. (1990) 'Old and New Identities and New Ethnicities', in D. A. King (ed.), *Culture, Globalization and the World System* (Basingstoke: Macmillan).

Hall, S., Held, D. and McGrew, T. (eds) (1992) *Modernity and its Futures* (Cambridge: Polity Press).

Hallett, C. (1995) *Women and Social Policy* (London: Prentice-Hall in association with the Policy Association, Women's Social Policy Group).

Halliday, E. (1996) *Islam and the Myth of Confrontation* (London: I. B. Tauris).

Halliday, F. (1994) 'The Politics of Islamic Fundamentalism: Iran, Tunisia and the Challenge to the Secular State', in A. Ahmed and H. Donnan (eds), *Islam, Globalization and Post-modernity* (London: Routledge).

Hamilton, P. and Thompson, P. (eds) (2002) *The Uses of Sociology* (Oxford: Blackwell).

Haralambos, M. and Holborn, M. (eds) (2004) *Sociology Themes and Perspectives*, 6th edn (London: HarperCollins).

Harding, S. (1991) *Whose Science, Whose Knowledge? Thinking from Women's Lives* (Milton Keynes: Open University Press).

Harding, S, (2007) 'Man-made Disaster and Development: the Case of Iraq', *International Social Work Journal* **50**(2): 295–306.

Harrison. P. (1981) *Inside the Third World* (Harmondsworth: Penguin).

Harrison, P. (1982) *Inside the Inner City* (Harmondsworth: Penguin).

Hasso, F. S. (2005) 'Problems and Promise in Middle East and North Africa Gender Research', *Feminist Studies* **31**(3): 653–79.

Healy, K. (2000) *Social Work Practice: Contemporary Perspectives on Change* (London: Sage).

Healy, K. (2005) *Social Work Theories in Context: Creating Frameworks for Practice* (Basingstoke: Palgrave Macmillan).

Healy, L. M. (ed.) (2001) *International Social Work: Professional Action in an Interdependent World* (New York: Oxford University Press).

Held, D. (1995) *Democracy in the Global Order: From Modern State to Cosmopolitan Governance* (Cambridge: Polity Press).

Herscovitch, L. (2001) 'International Relief and Development Practice', in L. M. Healy (ed.) (2001) *International Social Work: Professional Action in an Interdependent World* (New York: Oxford University Press).

Heyman, B. and Huckle, S. (1993) 'Normal Life in a Hazardous World: How Adults with Moderate Learning Difficulties and their Carers Cope with Risks and Dangers', *Disability & Society* 8(2): 142–60.

Hicks, S. (2005) 'Is Gay Parenting Bad for Kids? Responding to the "Very Idea of Difference" in Research on Lesbian and Gay Parents', *Sexualities* 8(2): 153–68.

Hicks, S. and McDermott, J. (1999) *Lesbian and Gay Fostering and Adoption: Extraordinary Yet Ordinary* (London: Jessica Kingsley).

Hill, O. (1893) 'Trained Workers for the Poor', *Nineteenth Century*, pp. 36–43.

Hill, M. J. (2006) *Social Policy in the Modern World: A Comparative Text* (Oxford: Blackwell Publishing).

Hiroshi, I. (2001) 'Industrialization, the Class Structure, and Social Mobility in Postwar Japan', *British Journal of Sociology* 52(4): 579–604.

Holloway, S. (2005) 'Articulating Otherness? White Rural Residents Talk about Gypsy-Travellers', *Transactions of the Institute of British Geographers* 30(3): 351–67.

Holt, M. (2004) 'Marriage-like or Married? Lesbian and Gay Marriage, Partnership and Migration', *Feminism and Psychology* 14(1): 30–5.

Horne, M. (1999) *Values in Social Work*, 2nd edn (Aldershot: Arena).

Horner, N. (2004) *What is Social Work? Context and Perspectives* (Exeter: Learning Matters).

Horner, N. (2006) *What is Social Work? Context and Perspectives*, 2nd edn (Exeter: Learning Matters).

Howard, M. O. and Jenson, J. M. (1996) 'Barriers to Development, Utilization and Evaluation of Social Work Practice Research Guidelines: Towards an Action Plan for Social Work', *Research on Social Work Practice* 9(3): 347–64.

Howe, D. (1991) 'The Family and the Therapist: Towards Sociology of Social Work', in M. Davies (ed.), *The Sociology of Social Work* (London: Routledge).

Howe, D. (1996) 'Surface and Depth in Social-work Practice', in N. Parton (ed.), *Social Change, Social Theory and Social Work* (London: Routledge).

Hughes, G. and Lewis, G. (eds) (1998) *Unsettling Welfare: The Reconstruction of Social Policy* (Buckingham: The Open University Press and Routledge).

Hugman, R. and Smith, D. (eds) (1995) *Ethical Issues in Social Work* (London: Routledge).

Illich, I. (1976) *Limits to Medicine* (London: Marion Boyars).

Ince, L. (1999) 'Preparing Young Black People for Leaving Care', in N. Barn (ed.), *Working with Black Children and Adolescents* (London: BAAF).

Ingamells, A. and Westoby, P. (2008) 'Working with Young People from Refugee Backgrounds in Australia', *European Journal of Social Work* 1: 1–15.

International Federation of Social Work (IFSW) (2000) 'Definition of Social Work', adopted by the IFSW General Meeting, Canada, July 2000. http://www.ifsw.org/gen/p38000208/html (accessed 20 September 2005).

International Labour Organization (ILO) (2000) 'Your Voice at Work', online March 2000, http://www.ilo.org/public/libdoc/ilo/P/200009382 (2000)88.pdf (accessed 12 November 2007).

Ishida, H. (2001) 'Industrialization, Class Structure, and Social Mobility in Postwar Japan', *British Journal of Sociology* **52**(4): 579–604.

Jackson, S. (1998) 'Looking after Children: A New Approach or Just an Exercise in Form Filling? A Response to Knight and Caveney', *British Journal of Social Work* **28**: 45–56.

Jacobsen, Y. (1992) 'National Conference for Women with Learning Difficulties', Conference Report: *Trouble and Strife* **24**: 36–40.

Jaggar, A. M. (1995) 'Human Biology in Feminist Theory: Sexual Equality Reconsidered', in H. Crowley and S. Himmelweit (eds), *Knowing Women: Feminism and Knowledge* (Cambridge: Polity Press, in association with The Open University).

James, A. (1993) *Childhood Identities: Self and Social Relationships in the Experiences of the Child* (Edinburgh: Edinburgh University Press).

James, A., Jenks, C. and Prout, A. (1999) *Theorizing Childhood* (Cambridge: Polity Press).

Jandl, M. (2004) 'The Relationship between Human Trafficking and the Asylum System in Austria', *Journal of Ethnic and Migration Studies* **30**(4): 799–807.

Javadian, R. (2007) 'Social Work Responses to Earthquake Disasters: a Social Work Intervention in Bam, Iran', *International Social Work Journal* **50**(3): 334–46.

Jessop, B. (1990) *State Theory: Putting Capitalism in its Place* (Cambridge: Polity Press).

Johns, R. (2003) *Using the Law in Social Work* (Exeter: Learning Matters).

Johnson, A. K. (2004) 'Increasing Internationalization in Social Work Programs: Healy's Continuum as a Strategic Planning Guide', *International Social Work Journal* **47**(1): 7–2.

Jones, A. (2001) 'Child Asylum Seekers and Refugees: Rights and Responsibilities', *Journal of Social Work* **1**(3): 253–71.

Jones, C. and Novak, T. (1999) *Poverty, Welfare and the Disciplinary State* (London: Routledge).

Jones, C. (1996) 'Anti-intellectualism and the Peculiarities of British Social Work Education', in N. Parton (ed.), *Social Theory, Social Change and Social Work* (London: Routledge).

Jones, C. (2002) 'Social Work and Society', in R. Adams, L. Dominelli and M. Payne (eds) (2002) *Social Work: Themes, Issues and Critical Debates*, 2nd edn (Basingstoke: Palgrave Macmillan).

Jones, S. (1991) 'We Are all Cousins under the Skin', *The Independent*, 12 December.

Jones, S. (1994) *The Language of Genes* (London, Flamingo).

Kabadaki, K. (1995) 'Exploration of Social Work Practice: Models for Rural Development of Uganda', *Journal of Social Development in Africa* **10**(1): 77–88.

Kasapoglu, A., Ecevit, Y. and Ecevit, M. (2004) 'Support Needs of the Survivors of the 1 August 1999 Earthquake in Turkey', *Social Indicators Research* **66**(3): 229–48.

Kaseke, E. (2005) 'Social Security and Older People: an African Perspective', *International Social Work Journal* **48**(1): 89–98.

Kasuma, M. (2007) 'The Space in-Between', *Qualitative Social Work Research* **6**(4): 489–93.

Katz, S. (1996) *Discipline in Old Age: The Formation of Gerontological Knowledge* (Charlottesville: University of Virginia).

Kearns, K. (2001) 'Social Democratic Perspectives on the Welfare State', in M. Lavalette and A. Pratt (eds), *Social Policy: A Conceptual and Theoretical Introduction*, 2nd edn (London: Sage).

Keller, A. S. et al. (2003) 'The Mental Health of Detained Asylum Seekers' (research letter), *The Lancet* **362**(9397): 1721–3.

Kelly, L. (1999) 'Violence against Women: a Policy of Neglect or a Neglect of Policy?', in S. Walby (ed), *New Agendas for Women* (New York: St Martin's Press).

Kelman, H. C. (1961) 'Process of Opinion Change', *Public Opinion Quarterly* **25**: 57–78.

Kempson, C. (1996) *Life on a Low Income* (York: Joseph Rowntree Foundation).

Kennedy-Lawford, P. and Murphy-Lawler, J. (2003) 'The Maternity Care Needs of Refugee and Asylum Seeking Women in Ireland', *Feminist Review* **73**: 39–53.

Kingdon, D. G. (2000) 'Schizophrenia and Mood (Affective) Disorder', in D. Bailey (ed), *At the Core of Mental Health Practice: Key Issues for Practitioners, Managers and Mental Health Trainers* (Brighton: Pavilion).

Kitzinger, J. (1994) 'Focus Groups: Method or Madness?', in M. Bolton (ed.), *Challenge and Innovation: Methodological Advances in Social Research on HIV/Aids* (London: Taylor and Francis).

Kitzinger, C. and Wilkinson, S. (2004) 'The Re-branding of Marriage: Why We Got Married Instead of Registering a Civil Partnership', *Feminism and Psychology* **14**(1): 127–50.

Kleinmann, K. (2002) *A European Welfare State? European Union Social Policy in Context* (Basingstoke: Palgrave Macmillan).

Kolb, D. A. (1982) *Experiential Learning as a Source of Learning and Development* (Englewood Cliff, NJ: Prentice Hall).

Laming, Lord (2003) 'The Victoria Climbie Inquiry: Report of an Inquiry. http://www.victoria-climbie-inquiry.org.uk/finreport/finreport/htm (accessed 22 October 2007).

Landman, T. (2006) 'Holding the Line: Human Rights Defenders in the Age of Terror', *British Journal of Politics and International Relations* **8**: 123–47.

Langan, M. (2002) 'The Legacy of Radical Social Work', in R. Adams, L. Dominelli and M. Payne (eds), *Social Work: Themes, Issues and Critical Debates*, 2nd edn (Basingstoke: Palgrave Macmillan).

Langan, M. (ed.) (1998) *Welfare: Needs, Rights and Risks* (Buckingham: Open University and Routledge).

Lash, S. (1994) 'Reflexivity and its Doubles: Structure, Aesthetics, Community', in U. Beck, A. Giddens and S. Lash (eds), *Reflexive Modernization: Politics, Tradition and Aesthetics in the Modern Social Order* (Cambridge: Polity Press).

Lavalette, M. and Pratt, A. (eds) (2001) *Social Policy: A Conceptual and Theoretical Introduction*, 2nd edn (London: Sage).

Lavalette, M. and Ferguson, I. (1999) 'Social Work, Postmodernism and Marxism', *European Journal of Social Work* **2**(1): 27–40.

Leonard, P. (1966) *Sociology in Social Work* (London: Routledge & Kegan Paul).

Lawson, R. (1995) 'The Challenge of "New" Poverty: Lessons from Europe and North America', in K. Funker and P. Cooper (eds), *Old and New Poverty: The Challenge for Reform* (London: Rivers Oram Press).

Leung, J. C. B. and Wong, Y. L. (2002) 'Community Based Service for the Frail Elderly in China', *International Social Work Journal* **45**(2): 217–28.

Lewis, G. (1998) *Forming Nation, Framing Welfare* (Buckingham: Open University in association with Routledge).

Lewis, G. (2003) 'Migrants', in P. Alcock, A. Erskin and M. May (eds), *The Students Companion to Social Policy* (Oxford: Blackwell).

Lewis, J. (1988) *Daughters Who Care: Daughters Caring for Mothers at Home* (London: Routledge).

Liebel, M. (2002) 'Child Labour and the Contribution of Working Children's Organisations in the Third World', *International Review of Education* **48**(3–4): 265–70.

Lind, A. (2007) 'Experience from Capacity-building for Social Workers in Iraq', *International Social Work Journal* **50**(3): 395–404.

Loewe, M. (2004), 'New Avenues to be Opened for Social Protection in the Arab World: The Case of Egypt', *International Journal of Social Welfare* **13**: 3–14.

Lucas, E. (2001) 'Social Development Strategies of a Non-governmental Grass-roots Women's Organisation in Nigeria', *International Journal of Social Welfare* **10**: 185–93.

Luhmann, N. (1995) *Social Systems* (Stanford.CA. Stanford University Press).

Lukes, S. (1974) *Power: A Radical View* (London: Macmillan).

Lymbury, M. (1998) 'Care Management and Professional Autonomy: the Impact of Community Care Legislation on Social Work with Older People', *British Journal of Social Work* **28**(6): 863–78.

MacDonald, C. (1995) *Assessment and Care Management: The Practitioner Speaks* (Stirling: Stirling University Press).

Macdonald, G. (1999) 'Social Work and Evaluation: A Methodological Dilemma?', in F. Williams, J. Popay and A. Oakley, *Welfare Research: A Critical Review* (London: UCL) Press.

Macdonald, K. M. (1995) *The Sociology of the Professions* (London: Sage).

Macnicol, J. (1987) 'In Pursuit of the Underclass', *Journal of Social Policy* **3**: 293–318.

MacKinnon, C. (1989) *Towards a Feminist Theory of the State* (Cambridge, MA: Harvard University).

McCarthy, M. (1993) 'Sexual Experiences of Women with Learning Difficulties in Long-stay Hospitals', *Sexuality and Disability* **11**: 277–86.

McCarthy, M. (1998) 'Whose Body is it Anyway? Pressures and Control for Women with Learning Difficulties', *Disability and Society* **13**: 557–74.

McDowell, L. and Pringle, R. (eds) (1996) *Defining Women: Social Institutions and Gender Divisions* (Cambridge: Polity Press and Open University Press).

McKie, L. (2005) *Families, Violence and Social Change* (Buckingham: Open University Press).

McMullen, C. (1991) 'Sexual Identity Issues Related to Homosexuality in Residential Treatment of Adolescents', *Residential Treatment of Children and Youth* **2**: 9–21.

McRobbie, A. (2006) 'Vulnerability, Violence and (Cosmopolitan) Ethics: Butler's Precarious Life', *British Journal of Sociology* **57**(1): 69–86.

Mafileo, T. (2004) 'Exploring Tongan Social Work: *Fakafekau'aki* (connecting) and *Fakatokilalo* (humility)', *Qualitative Social Work* **3**(3): 339–58.

Mager, D. N. and Sulek, R. (1997) 'Teaching about Homophobia at a Historically Black University', in Sears, J. T. and Williams, W. L, *Overcoming Homophobia: Strategies That Work* (New York: Columbia).

Mandanipour, A., Cars, G. and Allen, J. (eds) (1998) *Social Exclusion in European Cities* (London: Jessica Kingsley).

Mannheim, K. (1993) 'Competition as Cultural Phenomenon', in K. Wolff (ed), *From Karl Mannheim* (London: Transaction Books).

Manthorpe, J. (2002) 'Nearest and Dearest? The Neglect of Lesbians in Caring Relationships', *British Journal of Social Work* **33**: 753–68.

Marshall. T. H. (1950) *Citizenship and Social Class* (Cambridge: Cambridge University Press).

Martinez-Brawley, E. and Gualda, E. (2006) 'US/Spanish Comparisons on Temporary Immigrant Workers: Implications for Policy Development and Community Practice', *European Journal of Social Work* **9**(1): 59–84.

Marx, Karl (1970 [1867]) *Capital: A Critique of Political Economy*, vol. 1 (London: Lawrence and Wishart).

Marx, K. (1970) *The German Ideology* (London: Lawrence and Wishart).

Mason, A. and Palmer, A. (1996) *Queer Bashing: A National Survey of Hate Crimes against Lesbian and Gay Men* (London: Stonewall).

Massey, D. S. and Denton, N. A. (1993) *American Apartheid: Segregation and the Making of the Underclass* (Cambridge, MA: Harvard University Press).

Matsuda, N. (1993) 'Public Response to Racist Speech: Considering the Victim's Story', in M. Matsuda and C. R. Lawrence (eds), *Words that Wound: Critical Race Theory, Assaultive Speech, and the First Amendment* (Los Angeles, CA: Westview Press).

Mattinson, J. (1975) *The Reflection Process in Casework Supervision* (London: Institute of Marital Studies).

Melluci, A. (1980) 'The New Social Movements: a Theoretical Approach', *Social Science Information* **19**: 199–226.

Mendes, P. (2006) 'An Australian Perspective on Singaporean Welfare Policy', *Social Work and Society* **5**(1): 404–28.

Merton, R. K. (1946) 'The Focussed Interview', *American Journal of Sociology* **51**(6): 541–57.

Merton, R. K. (1968) *Social Theory and Social Structure* (New York: The Free Press).

Merton, R. K. (1972) 'Insiders and Outsiders: a Chapter in the Sociology of Knowledge', *American Journal of Sociology* **78**(1): 9–47.

Midgley, J. (1997) *Social Welfare in Global Context* (Thousand Oak, CA: Sage).

Miles, A. (1981) *The Mentally Ill in Contemporary Society* (Oxford: Martin Robertson).

Minh-Ha, T. (1989) *Woman, Native, Other: Writing Postcoloniality and Feminism* (Bloomington: Indiana University Press).

Minister for Disability Issues (2001) *New Zealand Disability Strategy* (Wellington: Office for Disability Issues).

Mishra, R. (1999) *Globalization and the Welfare State* (Cheltenham: Edward Elgar).

Mishra, R. (2005) 'Social Rights and Human Rights: Globalizing Social Protection', *International Social Work Journal* **48**(1): 9–20.

Modood, T., Berthoud, R. et al. (1997) *Ethnic Minorities in Britain: Diversity and Disadvantage* (London: Policy Studies Institute).

Morgan, D. (1985) *Focus Groups as Qualitative Research* (Newbury Park: Sage).

Morton. S. G. (1839) *An Essay on the Variety of Human Species* (Philadelphia: J. Dobson).

Mullaly, R. P. and Keating, E. F. (1991) 'Similarities, Differences and Dialectics of Radical Social Work', *Journal of Progressive Human Services* **2**(2): 49–78.

Mundy, B. (ed.) (1989) *The Crisis in Welfare: An International Perspective on Social Services and Social Work* (Hemel Hempstead: Harvester Wheatsheaf).

Munroe, E. (2001) 'Empowering Looked After Children', *Child and Family Social Work* 6: 129–37.

Murray, C. (1994) *The Underclass: The Crisis Deepens* (London: Institute of Economic Affairs).

Navarro, V. (1977) *Medicine under Capitalism* (London: Martin Robertson).

Navarro, V. (1978) *Class Struggle, the State and Medicine: An Historical and Contemporary Analysis of the Medical Sectors of Great Britain* (London: Martin Robertson).

Neal, S. and Ageyman, J. (2006) *The New Countryside? Ethnicity, Nation and Exclusion in Contemporary Rural Britain* (Bristol: Policy Press).

Nelson, J. I. (1995) *Post-Industrial Capitalism* (London: Sage).

Niner, P. (2004) 'Accommodating Nomadism? An Examination of Accommodation Options for Gypsies and Travellers in England', *Housing Studies* **192**: 141–59.

Nolan, B. and Whelan, C. T. (1996) *Resources, Deprivation and Poverty* (Oxford: Clarendon Press).

Noyoo, N. (2000) 'Human Rights and Social Work in a Transforming Society: South Africa', *International Social Work Journal* **47**(1): 359–69.

Nylund, D. (2002) *Treating Huckleberry Finn: A New Narrative Approach to Working with Kids Diagnosed with ADD/ADHD* (San Francisco, CA: Jossey- Bass).

Oakley, A. (1974) *Housewife* (London: Allen and Unwin).

OECD (2004) *OEDC in Figures* (Paris: OECD).

OEDC (2000) *Starting Strong* (Paris: OEDC).

Oliver, M. (1990) *The Politics of Disability* (London: Macmillan).

Oliver, M. (1996) *Understanding Disability: From Theory to Practice* (Basingstoke: Macmillan).

Orme, J., Dominelli, L. and Mullender, A. (2000) 'Working with Violent Men from a Feminist Social Work Perspective', *International Social Work Journal* **43**(1): 89–106.

Parker, J. and Bradley, G. (2004) *Social Work Practice: Assessment Care Planning Intervention and Review* (Exeter: Learning Matters).

Parry, N. and Parry, J. (1979) *The Rise of the Medical Profession* (London).

Parsons, T. (1937) *The Structure of Social Action* (New York: Free Press).

Parsons, T. (1962) 'The Law and Social Control', in M. E. William (ed), *The Law and Sociology: Exploratory Essays* (New York: Free Press).

Parsons, T. (1969) *Politics and Social Structure* (New York: Free Press).

Parton, N. (ed.) (1996) *Social Theory, Social Change and Social Work* (London: Routledge).

Parton, N. (2003) 'Rethinking Professional Practice: The Contributions of Social Constructionism and Feminist Ethics of Care', *British Journal of Social Work* **33**: 1–16.

Pateman, C. (1989) *The Disorder of Women* (Cambridge: Polity Press).

Patterson, O. (1982) *Slavery and Social Death: A Comparative Study* (Cambridge, MA: Harvard University Press).

Pawar, M. (2004) 'Community Informal Care and Welfare Systems in Asia-Pacific Countries: Phase I, Lessons from the Process and Evaluation of an International Project', *International Social Work Journal* **47**(10): 439–53.

Payne, M. (2002) 'Social Work Theories and Reflexive Practice', in R. Adams, L. Dominelli and M. Payne (eds), *Social Work: Themes, Issues and Critical Debates*, 2nd edn (Basingstoke: Palgrave Macmillan).

Payne, M. (2005) *Modern Social Work Theory*, 3rd edn (Basingstoke: Palgrave Macmillan).

Pearlman, H. H. (1973) *Social Casework: A Problem-Solving Process* (Chicago: University of Chicago Press).

Pellucid, A. (1980) 'The New Social Movements: A Theoretical Approach', *Social Science Information* **19**: 199–226.

Pharr, S. (1998) *Homophobia: A Weapon of Sexism* (Little Rock: Charndon).

Phillips, D. and Berman, Y. (2001) 'Social Quality and Community Citizenship', *European Journal of Social Work* **4**(1): 17–28.

Phillipson, C. (2007) 'The "Elected" and the "Excluded": Sociological Perspectives on the Experience of Place and Community in Old Age', *Ageing & Society* **27**: 321–42.

Phillipson, C. (1993) 'The Sociology of Retirement' in J. Bond, P. Coleman and S. Peace (eds), *Ageing and Society: An Introduction to Social Gerontology* (London: Sage).

Phillipson, C. (1998) *Reconstructing Old Age: New Agendas in Social Theory and Practice* (London: Sage).

Piaget, J. (1972[1927]) *Psychology and Epistemology.*, trans P. Wells (Harmondsworth: Penguin).

Pierson, C. (1991) *Beyond the Welfare State? The New Political Economy of Welfare* (Cambridge: Polity).

Pilgrim, D. and Rodgers, A. (1999) *Sociology of Mental Health and Illness* (Buckingham: Open University Press).

Pilkington, A. (2002) 'Cultural Representations and Changing Ethnic Identities in a Global Age', in M. Holborn, *Developments in Sociology*, vol. 18 (Ormskirk: Causeway Press).

Pincus, A. and Minahan, A. (1973) *Social Work Practice: Model and Method* (Itasca, IL: Peacock).

Postle, K. (2001) 'The Social Work Side is Disappearing: I Guess it Started with Us Being Called Managers', *Practice* **13**(1): 13–26.

Poulantzas, N. (1976) *Classes in Contemporary Capitalism* (London: Routledge & Kegan Paul).

Powell, J. and Biggs, S. (2004) 'Ageing Technologies of Self and Biomedicine: A Foucauldian Excursion', *International Journal of Sociology and Social Policy* **24**(6): 17–29.

Prandy, K. (2002) 'Ideal Types, Stereotypes and Classes', *British Journal of Sociology* **53**(4): 583–601.

Price, V. and Simpson, G. (2007) *Transforming Society: Social Work and Sociology* (Bristol: Policy Press).

Pringle, R. (1996) 'Women and Consumer Capitalism', in L. McDowell and R. Pringle (eds), *Defining Women: Social Institutions and Gender Divisions* (Cambridge: Polity with Blackwell Publishers and The Open University).

Prior, P. M. (2003) 'Removing Children from the Care of Adults with Diagnosed Mental Illness – a Clash of Human Rights?', *European Journal of Social Work* **6**(2): 179–90.

Punch, S. (2002) 'Research with Children: the Same or Different from Research with Adults?', *Childhood* **6**(3): 321–41.

Putnam, R. (2001) *Bowling Alone: The Collapse and Revival of American Community* (London: Touchstone).

Quinney, R. (1975) 'Crime Control in Capitalist Society: a Critical Philosophy of Legal Order', in I. Taylor, P. Walton and J. Young (eds), *Critical Criminology* (London: Routledge and Kegan Paul).

Qvortrup, J. (1990) 'A Voice for Children in Statistical and Social Counting: A Plea for Children's Rights to be Heard', in A. James and A. Prout (eds), *Constructing and Reconstructing Childhood* (Basingstoke: Falmer Press).

Race, D. (1999) *Social Role Valorization and the English Experience* (London: Wilding and Birch).

Race, D. (2003) *Leadership and Change in Human Services: Selected Readings from Wolf Wolfensberger* (London: Routledge).

Ramazanoglu, C. (1989) *Feminism and the Contradictions of Oppression* (London: Routledge).

Ray, L. (1993) *Re-thinking Critical Theory: Emancipation in the Age of Global Social Movements* (London: Sage).

Rees, J. (1998) *The Algebra of Revolution: The Dialectic and the Classic Marxist Tradition* (London: Routledge).

Richards, J. and Lambert, J. (1985) *The Sociology of Race* (Ormskirk: Causeway).

Ritzer, G. (2003) *The Blackwell Companion to Major Classical Theorists* (Oxford: Blackwell).

Roach-Anleu, S. L (2002) *Law and Social Change* (London: Sage).

Rodgers, A. and Pilgrim, D. (1996) *Mental Health Policy in Britain* (Basingstoke: Macmillan).

Roff, S. (2004) 'Nongovernmental Organisations: The Strengths Perspectives at Work', *International Social Work* **47**(2): 227–39.

Rojeck, C., Peacock, C. and Collins, S. (1988) *Social Work and Received Ideas* (London, Routledge).

Rose, H. (2000) 'Risk, Trust and Scepticism in the Age of the New Genetics', in B. Adams, U. Beck and J. Van Loon, *The Risk Society and Beyond: Critical Issues for Social Theory* (London: Sage).

Rose, N. and Miller, P. (1992) Political Power beyond the State: Problems of Government', *British Journal of Sociology* **43**: 173–205.

Rosen, V. (1993) 'Black Students in Higher Education', in M. Thorpe, R. Edwards and A. Hansen (eds), *Culture and Processes in Adult Learning: A Reader* (London: Routledge).

Runnymede Trust Commission on British Muslims (1997) *Islamaphobia a Challenge for Us All*. http://www.runnymedetrust.org/publications/17/74.html (accessed 12 February 2008).

Ryan, M. (2000) 'Gay Partners in Search of Green Cards', *National Journal*, 3 November: 804–5.

Sahibzada, M. (1999) 'The Politics of Rape in Pakistan: Victim or Criminal?' http://www.geocities.com/capitolHill/Parliament/3251/spring99/pakistan.html. 20081 (accessed 10 October 2007).

Sahibzada, M. (2007) 'An Easier Way to Rape Women', http://planksconsultant.org/blog/2007/09/an_easier_way_to_rape_women.html.

Said, E. (1997) *Covering Islam: How the Media and Experts Determine How We See the Rest of the World* (London: Vintage).

Said, E. (2003) *Orientalism: A New Edition* (London: Penguin).

Sanderson. I. (1992) *The Management of Quality in Local Government* (Harlow: Longman).

Sands, R. and Bourjolly, J. (2007) 'Cross-Cultural Barriers in Research Interviewing', *Qualitative Social Work Research* 6(3): 353–72.

Saraga, E. (1998) *Embodying the Social: Constructions of Difference* (Buckingham: Open University Press in association with Routledge).

Saunders, P. (1993) 'Citizenship in a Liberal Society', in B. S. Turner (ed.), *Citizenship and Social Theory* (London: Sage).

Savage, M. and Bennett, T. (2005) 'Editors Introduction: Cultural Capital and Social Inequality', *British Journal of Sociology* 56(1): 1–12.

Savage, M., Warde, A. and Devine, F. (2005) 'Capital, Assets and Resources: Some Critical Issues', *British Journal of Sociology* 56(1): 31–47.

Sayce, L. (1993) 'MIND's policy of user involvement', www.mimd.org.uk/information (accessed 12 October 2007).

Scharf, T., Phillipson, C., Smith, A.E. and Kingston, P. (2002) *Growing Older in Socially Deprived Areas* (London: Help the Aged).

Scheff, E. (1966) *Being Mentally Ill: A Sociological Theory* (Chicago: Aldine).

Schon, D. A. (1983) *The Reflective Practitioner: How Professionals Think in Action* (New York: Basic Books).

Scott, A. (2000) 'Risk Society or Angst Society? Two Views of Risk, Consciousness and Community', in B. Adam, U. Beck and J. Van Loon (eds), *Risk Society and Beyond* (London: Sage).

Scott, J. (1995) *Sociologial Theory: Contemporary Debates* (Aldershot: Edward Elgar).

Scott, J. (2004) *Social Theory: Central Issues in Sociology* (London: Sage).

Scourfield, J. (2001) 'Interviewing Interviewers and Knowing about Knowledge', in I. Shaw and N. Gould, *Qualitative Research in Social Work* (London: Sage).

Seers. J. T. (1991) *Growing Up Gay in the South* (New York: Haworth).

Segal, U. A. (2004) 'Child Welfare, Programs and Services: A Comparison of the USA and Japan', *International Journal of Social Work* 47(3): 370–80.

Shakespeare, T. (1993) 'Disabled People's Self Organisation: a New Social Movement?' *Disability, Handicap & Society* 8(3): 249–64.

Shardlow, S. (2002) 'Values, Ethics and Social Work', in R. Adams, L. Dominelli and M. Payne (eds), *Social Work: Themes, Issues and Critical Debates* (Basingstoke: Palgrave Macmillan).

Sharry, J. (2001) *Solution Focused Groupwork* (London: Sage).

Shaw, I. F. (1996) *Evaluating In Practice* (Aldershot: Arena).

Shaw, I. F. and Gould, N. (2001) *Qualitative Research in Social Work* (London: Sage).

Sheldon, B. and Chilvers, R. (2000) *Evidence-Based Social Care* (Lyme Regis: Russell House).

Sibeon, R. (1991) *Towards a New Sociology of Social Work* (Aldershot: Avebury).

Siegfried, N. (2000) 'Legislation and Legitimation in Oman: The Basic Law', *Islamic Law and Society* 7(2): 359–65.

Silavwe, G. W. (1995) 'The Need for New Social Work Perspectives in an African Setting: The Case of Social Casework in Zambia', *British Journal of Social Work*, 25: 71–84.

Simon, J. A. and Weiner, E. S. (eds) (1989) *The Oxford English Dictionary* (Oxford: Clarendon Press).

Simpkins, M. (1979) *Trapped within Welfare* (London: Macmillan).

Sinclair, H. (2003) 'Social Exclusion' in M. Holborn (ed.), *Developments in Sociology* (Ormskirk: Causeway Press).

Smith, D. (2000) 'The Limits of Positivism Revisited', paper from the ESCR seminar series 'Theorising Social Work Research', National Institute for Social Work website, http://www.nisw.org.uk/tswr/smith.html.

Smith, D. (2004) *Social Work and Evidenced-Based Practice* (London: Jessica Kingsley).

Smith, M. J. (1988) *Contemporary Communication Research Methods* (Belmont, CA: Wandsworth).

Social Care Institute for Excellence SCIE (2003) 'Practice Guide 1: Managing Practice', online June 2003, http://www.scie.org.uk/publications/practiceguides/bpgl/pgol. pdf (accessed 29 January 2008).

Social Exclusion Unit (SEU) Office of the Deputy Prime Minister (ODPM) (2002) *Creating Sustainable Communities,* online June 2002 http:www.cabinetoffice. gov.uk/social_exclusion_task_force_/publications_1997_to_2006/service (accessed 27 September 2007).

Solomos, J. (1986) 'Trends in the Political Analysis of Racism', *Political Studies* **xxxiv**(2): 313–24.

Solomos, J. (1993) 'Race and Racism', in J. Kruger (ed), *The Oxford Companion to the Politics of the World* (New York: Oxford University Press).

Spencer, H. (1889) *The Study of Sociology,*15th edn (London: Kegan Paul Trench).

Stanley, L. and Wise, S. (1993) *Breaking Out Again: Feminist Epistemology and Ontology* (London: Routledge).

State Statistics Bureau (1995) *China Statistical Year Book* (Beijing: State Statistical Publishers).

Steinitz, L. (2007) 'African Stars: Lessons Learned from Social Services in Africa', *Journal of HIV/AIDS & Social Services* 7–22.

Strydom, H. and Raath, H. (2005) 'The Psychosocial Needs of Adolescents Affected by HIV/AIDS: a South African Study', *International Journal of Social Work* **48**(5): 569–80.

Sullivan, M. (2003) 'The Social Democratic Perspective', in P. Alcock, A. Erskin and M. May (eds), *The Student's Companion to Social Policy* (Oxford: Blackwell).

Summerfield, D. (1999) 'A Critique of Seven Assumptions behind Psychological Trauma Programmes in War-affected Areas', *Social Science and Medicine* **48**: 1449–62.

Swain, P. A. and Cameron, N. (2007) 'Good Enough Parenting': Parental Disability and Child Protection',. *Disability & Society* **18**(2): 165–77.

Swanson, P. A. and Cameron, N. (2003) 'Good Enough Parenting: Parental Disability and Child Protection, *Disability & Society* **18**(2): 165–77.

Taylor, P. and Daly, C. (eds) (1995) *Gender, Dilemmas in Social Work: Issues Affecting Women in the Profession* (Toronto: Canadian Scholars Press).

Taylor-Gooby, P. and Dale, J. (1981) *Social Theory and Social Welfare* (London: Edward Arnold).

Templeman, S. B. (2004) 'Social work in the New Russia at the Start of the Millennium', *International Social Work Journal* **47**(5): 95–107.

Terry, J. (1997) 'The Seductive Power of Science in the Making of Deviant Subjects', in V. Rossario (ed), *Science and Homosexualities* (New York: Routledge).

Thomas, N. and O'Kane, C. (1998) 'The Ethics of Participatory Research with Children', *Children & Society* **12**: 336–48.

Thompson, N. (1993) *Anti-Discriminatory Practice* (Basingstoke: Macmillan).

Thompson, N. (1996) *People Skills* (Basingstoke: Macmillan).

Thyer, B. A. and Kazi, M. A. (eds) (2004) *International Perspectives on Evidence-Based Practice in Social Work* (Birmingham: Venture).

Touraine, A. (1977) *The Self Production of Society* (Chicago, IL: Chicago University Press).

Tourmaline, A. (1985) 'An Introduction to the Study of Social Movements', *Social Research* **52**: 749–87.

Townsend, P. (1997) 'Poverty and Policy: What can We Do about the Poor', *Sociology Review* September: 15–19.

Tregoubova, T. (2000) personal communication, cited in S. B. Templeman (2004) 'Social Work in the New Russia at the Start of the Millennium', *International Social Work* **47**(5): 95–107.

Triegaardt J. D. (2004) 'Social Policy Domains: Social Welfare and Social Security in South Africa', *International Social Work Journal* **43**(3): 325–36.

Trotter, C (1999) *Working with Involuntary Clients: A Guide to Practice* (London: Sage).

Tsang, N. M. (2000) 'Dialectics in Social Work', *International Social Work Journal* **43**(3): 421–34.

Turner, B.S. (1993) 'Outline of a Theory of Human Rights', *Sociology* **27**: 489–512.

UNECA (1999) '*The ECA and Africa (Accelerating a Continent's Development*', online May 1999; http://www.uneca.org/pulications/books/eca_and_africa/ton.htm (accessed 10 October 2007).

United Nations Economic and Social Council (UNESCO) (1995) *The World Summit for Social Development*, Copenhagen 1995 (Summary Report), Published 1997: 7–100, http://unescdoc.unesco.org/ulis/cgi-bin/ilis.pl (accessed 10 November 2007).

United Nations High Commission for Refugees (UNHCR) (2006) *Global Refugee Trends*, 9 June 2006); http://www.unhchr.ch/tbs/doc.nsf/385c2add1632f4a8c 1256a9004dc311/518e88bfb8 (accessed 5 November 2007).

US Department of Defense (2007) 'Measuring Stability and Security in Iraq', September 2007, Report to Congress in Accordance with the Department of Defense Appropriations Act 2007 (Section 9010, Public Law 109–289). http://www.defenselink.mil/pubs/pdfs/Signed_Version-070912.pdf (accessed 30 May 2008).

Vebrugge, L. M. and Chan, A. (2008) 'Giving Help in Return: Family Reciprocity by Older Singaporeans', *Ageing & Society* **28**: 5–34.

Villereal, G. (2007) 'Guatemala's Current and Future Globalization: Social Work's Continuing Education Role', *International Social Work* **50**(1): 41–57

Vincent, J. A. (2007) 'Science and Imagery in the War on Old Age', *Ageing & Society* **27**: 941–61.

Vogel, A. (2006) 'Who's Making Global Civil Society: Philanthropy and US Empire in World Society', *British Journal of Sociology* **57**(4): 636–65.

Wakefield, J. C. (1996) 'Does Social Work Need an Eco-systems Perspective? Part 1: Is the Perspective Clinically Useful?', *Social Services Review* **70**(1): 1–31.

Walker, A. and Wong, C.-K, (2004) 'The Ethnocentric Construction of the Welfare State', *International Journal of Health Services* **26**(1): 67–93.

Walker, P. (2007) 'Innovations in Social Welfare, Trust, Risk and Control within an Indigenous–Non-indigenous Social Service Partnership', *International Journal of Social Welfare* **16**: 281–90.

Wallerstein, I. (1974) *The Modern World System: Capitalism, Agriculture and the Origins of European World Economy in the Sixteenth Century* (New York: Academic Press).

Warburton, J. and Chambers, B. (2007) 'Older Indigenous Australians: their Integral Role in Culture and Community', *Australasian Journal on Ageing* **26**(1): 3–7.

Weeks, J. (2004) 'Same-sex Partnerships', *Feminism and Psychology* **14**(1): 158–64.

Weeks, J. (1995) *Invented Moralities: Sexual Values in an Age of Uncertainty* (Cambridge: Polity Press).

Weichman, D., Kendall, J. and Azarian, M. K. (2001) 'Islamic Law: Myths and Realities', electronic source http://irleand.iol.ie/afifi/Articles/law.htm (accessed 8 February 2008).

Weis, B. (1978) 'Interpretation of Islamic Law: Theory of the Ijtihad', *American Journal of Comparative Law* **26**: 199–212.

White, S. (2001) 'Auto-Ethnography ad Reflexive Inquiry: the Research Act as Self Surveillance', in I. Shaw and N. Gould (eds), *Qualitative Research in Social Work* (London: Sage).

White, V. and Harris, J. (1999) 'Social Europe, Social Citizenship, and Social Services', *European Journal of Social Work* **2**(1): 3–13.

Whitmore, E. (2001) 'People Listened to What We Had to Say: Reflections on Emancipatory Qualitative Evaluation', in I. Shaw and N. Gould (eds), *Qualitative Research in Social Work* (London: Sage).

Wilkinson, R. (1996) *Unhealthy Societies: The Afflictions of Inequality* (London: Routledge).

Williams, F. (1995) *Social Policy: A Critical Introduction*, 2nd edn (Cambridge: Polity Press).

Williams, F. (2003) 'Social Policy: Culture and Nationhood', in P. Alcock, A. Erskin and M. May (eds), *The Student's Companion to Social Policy* (Oxford: Blackwell).

Williams, L. and Nind, M. (1999) 'Insiders or Outsiders: Normalisation and Women with Learning Difficulties', *Disability & Society* **14**(5): 659–72.

Wilson, W. J. (1999) *The Bridge Across the Racial Divide* (Berkeley, CA: University of California Press).

Wilton, T. (2000) *Sexualities in Health and Social Care: A Textbook* (Buckingham: Open University Press).

Wise, S. (1995) 'Feminist Ethics in Practice', in D. Hugman and R. Smith (eds), *Ethical Issues in Social Work* (London: Routledge).

Witz, A. and Marshall, B. L. (2003) 'The Quality of Manhood: Gender and Embodiment in the Classical Tradition', *Sociological Review* **50**(3) 339–65.

Wolfensberger W. (1998) *A Brief Introduction to Social Role Valorization: A High Order Concept for Addressing the Plight of Socially Devalued People, and for Structuring Human Services* (Syracuse, NY: Syracuse University, Training Institute for Human Services Planning, Leadership and Change Agency).

Wolfensberger, W., Thomas, S. and Caruso, G. (1996) 'Some Universal Good Things in Life which the Implementation of Social Role Valorization can be Expected to Make More Accessible to Devalued People, SRV/VRS', *The International Social Role Valorization Journal* **2**(2): 12–14.

Wong, Y. L. (2004) 'A Unified Middle Class or Two Middle Classes? A Comparison of Career Strategies and Intergenerational Mobility Strategies between Teachers and Managers in Contemporary Hong Kong', *British Journal of Sociology* **55**(2): 167–86.

Wool, Z. H. (2007) 'Operationalizing Iraqi Freedom: Governmentality, Neo-liberalism and New Public Management in the War in Iraq', *International Journal of Sociology and Social Policy* **27**(11–12): 460–8.

World Bank (2000) *Press Conference World Development Report, 1999/2000*, 'Entering the Twenty-First Century', http://www.worldbank.org/wdr/pdf/transcript.pdf (accessed 10 October 2007).

World Bank/International Monetary Fund (2001) 'A Globalized Market: Opportunities and Risks for the Poor: Global Poverty Report 2001'.

World Health Organization (WHO) (2002) 'Missing Voices: Views of Older Persons on Elder Abuse', World Health Organization for the Prevention of Elder Abuse. WHO/NMH/VIP02.1. & WHO/NMH/NPH/02.2. http://www.who/int/violence_injuryprevention/violence.world_report/en/full_enpdf (accessed 28 January 2008)

Wright-Mills, C. (1959) *The Sociological Imagination* (Oxford: Oxford University Press).

Yaish, M. (2001) 'Class Structure in a Deeply Divided Society: Class and Ethnic Inequality in Israel, 1974–1991', *British Journal of Sociology* **52**(3): 409–39.

Yi, C. C. and Nauk, B. (2006) 'Gender, Marriage and Family Support in East Asian Families: Introduction', *Current Sociology* **54**(2): 155–63.

Yip, K. (2005) 'A Dynamic Asian Response to Globalization in Cross-Cultural Social Work', *International Social Work Journal* **48**(1): 593–607.

Young, I. (1980) 'Socialist Feminism and the Limits of Dual Systems Theory', *Socialist Review* **10**(2–3): 169–88.

Younghusband, E. (1967) *Readings in Social Work*, vol. 2: *New Developments in Casework* (London: Allen & Unwin).

Yu, W. K. (2007 'Pension Reforms in Urban China and Hong Kong', *Ageing & Society* **27**: 249–68.

Zuffery, C. and Kerr, L. (2005) 'Identifying Everyday Experiences of Homelessness: Some Implications for Social Work', *Australian Journal of Social Work* **57**(4): 343–53.

# Subject Index

# Author Index